"Martyn Lloyd-Jones was one of G⟨...⟩ twentieth century."

> **Mark Dever,** Pastor, Capitol Hi⟨...⟩
> President, 9Marks

"Lloyd-Jones's preaching was based on deep reading and scholarship, yet it was accessible to everyone—it stirred the affections and changed the heart."

> **Timothy Keller,** Founding Pastor, Redeemer Presbyterian Church, New York City; Chairman and Cofounder, Redeemer City to City

"I regarded Martyn Lloyd-Jones with admiration and affection during the years that we were both preaching in London, so I am delighted that his unique ministry is to be more widely available in the United States."

> **John Stott,** Late Rector Emeritus, All Souls Church, London

"Lloyd-Jones was a titan of Christian ministry, and it thrills me to see his influence accelerating today for the benefit of the church around the world."

> **R. C. Sproul,** Founder, Ligonier Ministries

"Without question the finest biblical expositor of the twentieth century. In fact, when the final chapter of church history is written, I believe he will stand as one of the greatest preachers of all time."

> **John MacArthur,** Pastor, Grace Community Church, Sun Valley, California; President, The Master's University and Seminary

"The preaching and subsequent writing of Lloyd-Jones have been and continue to be a huge source of inspiration in my own life and ministry."

> **Alistair Begg,** Senior Pastor, Parkside Church, Chagrin Falls, Ohio

"I loved to hear Lloyd-Jones for the sheer quality of his biblical expositions and his stance for evangelical Christianity."

> **I. Howard Marshall,** Professor Emeritus, University of Aberdeen, Scotland

A Merciful and Faithful High Priest

OTHER CROSSWAY BOOKS BY MARTYN LLOYD-JONES

Acts

The Assurance of Our Salvation

The Cross

Experiencing the New Birth

God the Father, God the Son

The Gospel in Genesis

Great Doctrines of the Bible

The Kingdom of God

Let Not Your Heart Be Troubled

Life in Christ

Living Water

Out of the Depths

Revival

Seeking the Face of God

Setting Our Affections upon Glory

True Happiness

Truth Unchanged, Unchanging

Walking with God Day by Day

Why Does God Allow War?

Studies in the Book of Acts

   Authentic Christianity

   Courageous Christianity

   Victorious Christianity

   Glorious Christianity

   Triumphant Christianity

   Compelling Christianity

A Merciful and Faithful High Priest

Studies in the Book of Hebrews

Martyn Lloyd-Jones

WHEATON, ILLINOIS

A Merciful and Faithful High Priest: Studies in the Book of Hebrews
Copyright © 2017 by Elizabeth Catherwood and Ann Beatt
Published by Crossway
          1300 Crescent Street
          Wheaton, Illinois 60187

Cover design: Crystal Courtney

First printing 2017

Reprinted with new cover 2020

Printed in the United States of America

Scripture quotations are from the *King James Version* of the Bible.

All emphases in Scripture quotations have been added by the author.

Trade paperback ISBN: 978-1-4335-6994-4
ePub ISBN: 978-1-4335-5805-4
PDF ISBN: 978-1-4335-5803-0
Mobipocket ISBN: 978-1-4335-5804-7

Library of Congress Cataloging-in-Publication Data
Names: Lloyd-Jones, David Martyn, author.
Title: A merciful and faithful high priest: studies in the Book of Hebrews / Martyn Lloyd-Jones.
Description: Wheaton, Illinois: Crossway, [2017] | Includes bibliographical references.
Identifiers: LCCN 2016058601 (print) | LCCN 2017014116 (ebook) | ISBN 9781433558030 (pdf) | ISBN 9781433558047 (mobi) | ISBN 9781433558054 (epub) | ISBN 9781433558023 (trade paperback) | ISBN 9781433558054 (ePub)
Subjects: LCSH: Bible. Hebrews–Meditations. | Bible. Hebrews–Sermons.
Classification: LCC BS2775.54 (ebook) | LCC BS2775.54 .L56 2017 (print) | DDC 227/.8706–dc23
LC record available at https://lccn.loc.gov/2016058601

Crossway is a publishing ministry of Good News Publishers.

VP		31	30	29	28	27	26	25	24	23	22	21
14	13	12	11	10	9	8	7	6	5	4	3	2

Contents

1

Salvation—The Greatest Need

HEBREWS 2:1–4

Therefore we ought to give the more earnest heed to the things which we have heard, lest at any time we should let them slip. For if the word spoken by angels was stedfast, and every transgression and disobedience received a just recompence of reward; How shall we escape, if we neglect so great salvation; which at the first began to be spoken by the Lord, and was confirmed unto us by them that heard him; God also bearing them witness, both with signs and wonders, and with divers [various] miracles, and gifts of the Holy Ghost, according to his own will?

These four verses typically illustrate the way in which the Bible everywhere addresses us and comes to us. There is a note of urgency, a note of solemnity, and a note of profound seriousness that is characteristically found throughout the Bible. You can read it for instance in the gospels; you will find it as you read through the book of the Acts of the Apostles with its records of the preaching of the apostles and the first Christian preachers, and you will find exactly the same note in all the various epistles that are gathered together in the New Testament. This is the idea: "Flee from the wrath to come" (Matt. 3:7; Luke 3:7).

John the Baptist, the first preacher in the New Testament, started on that note, warning the people, and our Lord and Savior Jesus Christ did exactly the same thing. "The kingdom of God is at hand: repent" (Mark 1:15), "He that hath ears to hear, let him hear" (Matt. 11:15; Mark 4:9; Luke 8:8)—those were his words; that was the spirit of his message. There is a note of desperate urgency, of profound seriousness, and even of solemnity. And as you go on to Acts you hear Peter on the day of Pentecost. This was the first sermon given, in a sense, under the auspices of the Christian church as we know her, and this is what he said: "Save yourselves from this untoward generation" (Acts 2:40). And that was his note as he continued to preach.

Turn to the preaching of the apostle Paul, and you will find the same thing. Take, for instance, his famous sermon at Athens. He told those people that "God . . . commandeth all men every where to repent: Because he hath appointed a day, in the which he will judge the world in righteousness by that man whom he hath ordained" (Acts 17:30–31), and all the way through his ministry you will find this self-same note. We see this in all the epistles, and the author of Hebrews puts it in a particularly powerful form in 2:1–4. People are urged and pleaded with and exhorted to pay attention to these things, to give earnest heed to them.

Now the author was addressing Christian people—all the epistles are written to Christians, to members of churches—and yet he urges them to give earnest heed to the things they have heard. Their problem was that they did believe the gospel, but they were living in a difficult world. They were suffering persecution, they were experiencing famine and all sorts of things, and some of them were beginning to waver. They had not lost their faith, but some of them were being shaken, and the author exhorts them not to slip away from the things they have heard and believed, not to be negligent of them. His message, I repeat, was primarily addressed to Hebrew Christians, but it is a fair deduction to say that if it was important for those believers to hold on to these things, how much more important is it for those who have not believed. If those who have believed are liable to forsake it, if that is a possibility, what is the predicament of those who have never believed? So everything that this man urges upon believers is even more crucial in the case of those who are not believers, those who have not become Christians.

The gospel of Jesus Christ, the message of the book of Hebrews, calls upon the world to give earnest heed to what it has to say. The world is not merely to give it a quick glance or read a casual article about it or have an occasional discussion about it or on special days or occasions listen to what the church has to say. Earnest heed means undivided attention. There is a very good illustration of this in the sixteenth chapter of the book of Acts where we read about the apostle Paul preaching the gospel for the first time in Europe. A woman named Lydia heard Paul's witness, "whose heart the Lord opened, [so] that she attended unto [heeded] the things which were spoken of [by] Paul" (Acts 16:14). She paid attention or considered or studied; she did not just sit and listen and then go away and forget it all. She paid earnest heed, realizing the vital importance of the gospel message.

Another way the author puts this exhortation is that we must be careful not to drift away from it. He probably had in mind a ship that is moored just outside a harbor. It is being carried away unawares by the tide, drifting past the harbor where it was intending to go, and that is a very sad and serious thing. It is possible, according to the Scriptures, for us to do that with the gospel of Jesus Christ, and that has happened to many men or women. Some have come face-to-face with the gospel; they have felt an interest in it; they have, as it were, been at the entry into the harbor. They simply had to go a little further, and they would have arrived in the port. But alas, for some reason or another, they have not committed themselves, they have not accepted it, and they have allowed themselves to drift past it. What a horrible thing it is to be in sight of the haven only to drift past! The author of Hebrews warns these people against that danger, and that is the warning of the gospel throughout the Scriptures. Our Lord spoke of this in a famous parable, the parable of the sower. He said a man can listen to the gospel—like seed that is being sown in the ground—but the birds come and take it away, and nothing happens—he is drifting past. I cannot imagine anything more terrible to a soul than that he should come face-to-face with the gospel of Christ and should even have felt something of its power but then drift past never to see it again. The author warns against that danger, and throughout his letter he again and again offers that warning.

The third way in which he puts it is, "How shall we escape, if we neglect so great salvation?" He says this because we are so occupied with other things that we do not pay attention to it. We know it is there, but we "neglect" it. Many people in this world know something about the gospel; they know in their heart of hearts it is right and true, and they propose someday to pay attention to it and deal with it and listen seriously to what it has to say. They know something about heaven and hell and God and sin; they are aware of certain propositions, certain statements of the truth, but they neglect it all. Men and women are absorbed so much in other things that the gospel does not receive their time or attention; they neglect the truth.

The Bible everywhere exhorts us to avoid those three fatal possibilities; it appeals to us to listen to the gospel and give it earnest heed, but the world is doing the exact opposite. The world does not see why it should listen to the gospel, though it pays great attention to many other things. I am thinking now not only of thoughtless people but also of thoughtful people. Many men and women are desperately and seriously concerned about the present state of the world. They know what has already happened, they see certain portents and indications with regard to what is likely to happen, and they are afraid of the future. Philosophers and thinkers and leaders of thought have grappled with all this. But when we come to them with the gospel they say, "I am not going to listen to that; it is irrelevant." The gospel does not seem to have anything to say to them, and they do not see why they should listen to it. Thus vast numbers of men and women in this perishing world are refusing to do the very thing that this author appeals to them to do.

Why should we listen to the gospel? Why should not the doors of every church be shut? Why should not the Christian church be abolished? How do we justify ourselves in this modern world in standing before mankind to make the unique claim that we have the only answer to man's problem? Why should anybody listen to this gospel? I want to show you that in these four verses this man gives us the three main general reasons for listening to it. The three reasons for listening to the gospel are also the three themes of the epistle to the Hebrews. So these four verses are in and of itself a kind of summary of the entire epistle.

What are those reasons? The first reason for listening to the gospel is the source of the gospel, or the authority of the gospel—the authority with which the message comes to us because of the source of the message. His second reason is the dangerous and alarming condition and position of all men and women who do not believe the gospel and who do not heed it. And his third and last reason is the nature or character of the gospel.

Before we consider these three reasons why everybody should give the gospel careful consideration, let us make perfectly certain that we are agreed as to what we are talking about. It is no use saying, "I must give earnest heed to it" unless we are agreed as to *what* it is. Before we come to these tremendous arguments for not neglecting the gospel or drifting away, we must be absolutely clear that we know what we are considering, and unfortunately this is not something that can be assumed today. We are sufficiently aware of the methods and the devices of Satan to know that when the Devil knows he has failed in his claim to keep a man altogether, he next encourages him to consider the gospel in a wrong way. Large numbers of people in the world have never given the gospel a thought, and they do not propose to do so. They say they have no use for it whatsoever; it is entirely outside their lives. The Devil keeps them under his control in that way.

Other people have a sense of failure or disappointment in life. They may have a sense of great loneliness in this world or perhaps are assaulted by some other trouble. But these people are beginning to think and to turn in the direction of God and the gospel of Jesus Christ and the church. At this point the Devil will do everything he can to persuade them that they are basing their thoughts on the right thing when their thoughts are actually based on something far removed from that; he will encourage in them a false interest in religion. This is always the danger in a time of crisis, when things are difficult and hard and troublesome in this world. It always happens at a time when men and women tend to become frantic and are prepared to clutch at anything that seems to give them hope and deliver them out of their troubles. Therefore I say it is something of which we have to be very careful at this present time, and, thank God, the New Testament itself warns us about this and teaches us and enables us to confront it. Many people in the world believe things about God and Christ and yet do not believe what the author of Hebrews calls "the things which we have heard" (2:1). Many people think they are true believers in God and in Christ, but we can tell very clearly from the pages of the New Testament that there is no value in their belief in God. This is one of the most dangerous things that can happen to a soul.

Other people are not entirely wrong about these matters, but they grab hold of certain aspects of the truth that particularly appeal to them and regard that as the whole truth. They tend to equate Christianity with a certain aspect or view of Christianity. They maintain certain presuppositions and certain ideas in their mind about the gospel; they extract a part of the gospel and say that is the whole.

Let me illustrate this with a few examples. Many people in the world are searching for happiness. For various reasons they have been made unhappy, and they have been trying the various things that offer to make men and women happy. Then they come to the Bible and to the church and to the gospel of Jesus Christ seeking happiness. As they listen to the gospel, they are concentrating on that one goal or desire, and they find certain verses in the Bible that seem to offer happiness; they clutch at them and listen to nothing else, and they feel happy, and often they fondly imagine they have therefore become Christians. But they are not Christians at all. What I mean is this: Many cults and agencies in the world offer people happiness. Christian Science, for example, claims to go by the Scriptures and calls itself Christian. But when you examine its beliefs and put them side by side with the gospel you find you are looking at two entirely different things, yet they call themselves Christians. You see, they have got hold of a theory, a philosophy, a form of psychology that certainly makes them feel happier, and because it uses certain phrases of the Bible they believe their experience is truly Christian.

Others do the same thing in a more or less completely psychological manner. A great deal of psychological treatment is going on in the world using Christian terms but not preaching the Christian gospel. A psychologist with his theory can come to the New Testament and pick out certain phrases that suit his patient and then give his own teaching, which is not the teaching of the New Testament though he uses Christian terminology. Men and women may then imagine they have thus become Christians. There is also so-called science of thought and similar things. It uses Christian terminology when it suits it, but it ignores fundamental postulates of the gospel that was preached to these Hebrew believers.

That is the kind of danger I am elaborating upon. A search for happiness can lead people to extract some things from the true Christian gospel but ignore the rest.

The same thing happens to many people who are seeking to lose their sense of worry. They have become anxious and burdened, and they may be on the verge of a nervous or a mental breakdown. All they want is to be delivered from that. So they come to the teaching that offers them deliverance. Such teaching uses certain Christian terms, and they accept what they hear. But the question is, have they become Christians? I remind you again that many agencies in the world can make us feel much happier and deliver us from worry and still leave us in a non-Christian position.

Or consider the large numbers of people who are seeking comfort and consolation. There are many broken hearts in this world. They feel they have lost everything that made life worth living, and they long for comfort, for happiness, for fellowship. That is why many of them go to separatists and various other agencies. Even the gospel of Christ can be presented as just something that comforts people and no more; some deal directly with that particular need and do not mention the other things.

Many people are interested in the question of guidance. Life is bewildering and perplexing today, and the great question that is confronting us all is, what am I to do, which of these two courses am I to follow, what am I to make of my life? The problem of guidance is a real problem to all of us in this life and world. The Bible has a great deal to say about guidance. So these people come to the Bible, and they pick out everything they can find about guidance, and they say, "This is the thing I want," and they think they have found the Christian way of living and of guidance. But when you listen to them or read their books you will often find that the whole gospel seems to them to be just a question of guidance; nothing else is mentioned at all. They say nothing about the sacrifice on the cross; it seems to be unnecessary. They see Christianity merely as a way of being guided in life.

Others are immensely interested in physical healing of the body. We all, as the result of sin in this world, are subject to illness and disease; sin has brought that in, and we all face it. There is perhaps nothing more universal in all of life than this longing and craving for healing and physical health. But danger comes in with this, as with everything else, when some people think the gospel is nothing but the way to produce healing. They talk about nothing else, and you are given the idea that the gospel of Jesus Christ is simply the way and the mechanism for being healed. That view too is psychology clothed with Christian terminology, masquerading as the gospel. But it is not the gospel of Jesus Christ.

Others say they want to be "in tune with the Infinite"; they want to feel they are at one with the heart of the universe, and they come to the Bible because it suggests it can do that for them, and they extract that out of it but nothing more. Indeed I would say that many in this world are genuinely concerned about believing in God; that is the greatest ambition in their lives. They say they want to know God, and many of them are practicing mysticism, and they grab onto whatever in the Bible encourages them in this mysticism. They are wearily trudging the mystic way in an attempt to find God, but they ignore some of the fundamental elements of the gospel of Jesus Christ. They sometimes refer to him as the greatest mystic of all, the greatest pioneer in the realm of religious thinking.

Finally there are those whose one great absorbing interest in life is how to live a good life. They are highly moral people, and they are seriously concerned about moral and ethical questions. They say they are not interested in the destiny of their souls after they go out of this world. What they are concerned about is how to live in this world, how to be worthy of the name of man, how to uplift the race, how to live a moral and ethical life. Of course, the Bible has a great deal to say about this, and they take out all they want and ignore the rest.

I have considered all this at length not only because I want to be practical but because I know myself, my own heart, my own tendency by nature to do the very thing I've been talking about. I know so many who are doing this and who get temporary satisfaction and then find they have nothing, and it is the things we have been discussing that are keeping them from the gospel of Christ. People who think they have found satisfaction are obviously not going to seek any longer. Those who feel they have arrived are no longer going to travel. I want to show you that all the things I have been mentioning in and of themselves make up the wrong approach. The gospel of Jesus Christ gives happiness, it delivers us from worry, it administers comfort, it gives guidance, it teaches that the body can be healed miraculously, it puts us into touch with the Infinite, it helps us to know God, and it enables us to live a godly, moral, ethical life. But it does all that *after it has done something else.* All blessings follow in the Christian life from something else that has gone before, and what I want to assert with all the dogmatism I can command is this: If you think you will have the Christian blessing without having this other thing first, you are deluding yourself, you are a dupe of Satan, the god of this world who has turned himself into an angel of light and is deceiving you. The blessings of the gospel follow belief in the gospel's central message.

"Therefore," says the author of Hebrews, "we ought to give the more earnest heed"—to what?—"to the things which we have heard" (2:1)—and not to anything else. The people to whom the epistle to the Hebrews was written were to give more earnest heed, they were to beware of slipping away, they were to beware of neglecting the specific things they had already heard. The gospel of Jesus Christ is perfectly clear; it is not something vague or nebulous or indefinite. The gospel is the particular message that was first of all preached by Christ himself and then preached by the apostles, and it has been preached throughout the running centuries. That is the specific message that we find in the Bible.

This must be preached as a whole. I have no right to take parts and ignore the rest. I either preach the gospel or I do not preach the gospel. The apostle Paul in bidding farewell to the elders of the church at Ephesus reminded them he had not failed to deliver unto them "all the counsel of God" (Acts 20:27), and any man who preaches without delivering the whole counsel of God is a false prophet. What the author of Hebrews means by "the things which we have heard" (2:1) is the whole gospel of Jesus Christ in its entirety—not only healing, not only ethics, not only comfort, but the whole message, the essence of this particular message that is found in the New Testament.

I say there is no question at all as to what this message is. The apostle Paul had to define it in his letter to the church at Corinth, and he said that what he preached to them was what all the other apostles were preaching. He says in essence, "I have no private message for you. I preach to you that which was delivered unto me, which is according to the Scripture and which is preached by my other brethren." There was no contradiction between these men; there was no uncertainty and no hesitation. Read the book of Acts and you will find this same central, essential message. And what is the message? In its essence it is the message of what is called *salvation*. "How shall we escape," says the author of Hebrews, "if we neglect so great salvation?" (2:3).

The first question, therefore, that we have to consider is how to be right with God for time and for eternity and how can that take place. You may have a broken, heavy heart. Some dear one was killed perhaps in the last war [World War II] or in the first war [World War I], or you have lost some dear one quite apart from war altogether, and your heart is bleeding. But that is not your first or even your greatest problem. Your most important problem is that you have a soul within you that is immortal, that you have to die, and that after your death you will face God in the judgment and your eternal destiny will be pronounced. I say therefore to you, your most urgent need is to consider your own condition before God.

You may have a body that is diseased, and you long for health. But even before the question of your physical health, you must consider the question of your soul, your spiritual health. That is where we go wrong. The Devil makes us put secondary things first, and as a result we never come to the first. Actually bereavement and sorrow have sometimes been the greatest blessing that have entered a man's life. There are people in this world who came to know God in Christ because someone very dear to them had died. While this dear one was alive they never thought about these things; they enjoyed one another, and they lived for one another, and God was neglected. They never gave God a thought. Many are living like that, and then a dear one is taken away by death, and the surviving loved ones' souls are at last awake, and eventually they find God in Christ. Bereavement and sorrow awakened their souls. Thomas Chalmers was one of the greatest preachers in Scotland in the nineteenth century. He was always a very able man and a great preacher; he had a scientific mind and used to preach marvelous scientific sermons. He had a great ministry in Scotland for ten years and then was stricken down by an illness that kept him in his sick chamber for nearly twelve months. It was then that he began to realize that he not only had never preached the gospel of Christ truly, but he had never truly believed it himself. He was talking about God and about Christ in his sermons, yes, but in his helpless condition he saw that he had never known Christ as his personal Savior. His illness was the means used by God to bring Thomas Chalmers to the light and to the full knowledge of the truth. So he thanked God for the illness that laid him aside, and afterward he went and preached the gospel in a new way and with a new power and was greatly used by God.

Nothing is more dangerous than to put secondary matters in the first position. We can test ourselves very easily about this. If you would like to know whether you have been deluded by Satan and whether you are holding on to something that is not really the gospel, although it uses Christian terminology, there is a simple way in which you can do so. Do you really know that you are a lost, hopeless, helpless, desperate sinner? You may have received guidance from the Holy Bible, extraordinary things may have happened to you, but if you have not seen yourself as a condemned sinner in the sight of God, you are not a Christian whatever else you may be.

Let me ask you another question. In your scheme of things is the Lord Jesus Christ absolutely central and essential? Would it be right to say that you have no system at all apart from him? I do not mean simply that he is a great teacher or that he lived a perfect life and set a great and glorious example. I mean, is he central in the sense that there is nothing without him? According to the things the Hebrews had heard, Christ was in that position. You may, I say again, have received wonderful guidance, extraordinary things may have happened to you, but many have experienced that kind of thing and yet do not claim to be Christians at all. I was reading the autobiography of a famous actor in this country [England] who never pretended to be a Christian. He said the turning point in his life was when he had a marvelous bit of guidance one afternoon. Strange things happen in this world. Shakespeare's Hamlet said truly, "There are more things in heaven and earth than are dreamt of in your philosophy." You may likewise have experienced wonderful healing for your physical body. You may have been crippled with rheumatoid arthritis, and now you can run and leap and walk. But if you want to know whether you are a true Christian and whether your healing was truly the result of knowing Jesus Christ, I ask you to face two questions: Have you seen yourself as a hopeless lost sinner in the sight of a holy God? Is the Lord Jesus Christ essential to you to deliver you from the wrath of God and to reconcile you to God?

Let me put it still more specifically in a third question. Is the death on the cross absolutely vital to you? Paul said to the Corinthians, "I determined not to know any thing among you, save Jesus Christ, and him crucified" (1 Cor. 2:2). If you would come within the scope of the things we have heard, the death of Christ on the cross will be to you central, vital, absolute. You say you realize that if he had not died on the cross you would have no hope of having your sins forgiven, no hope of seeing God, no hope of heaven; you know you would be destined for hell and eternal misery. These are the things that are central and vital and essential. These are the things that were preached in the book of Acts. Read the sermon that Peter preached on the day of Pentecost. Isn't this the truth he preached, isn't it what Paul preached, isn't it the argument of every one of the New Testament epistles—the blood of Christ, his death on the cross, to the Jews a stumbling block, to the Greeks foolishness? These men put this message in the forefront in spite of everything. Why? Because they had no gospel apart from it. Are you interested in these things?

I say again solemnly, before you begin to consider your happiness, before you begin to long to be delivered from worry, before you yearn for comfort for your broken heart, before you want guidance, before you seek healing for your body, before you want to get in tune with the Infinite, face the fact of your spiritual state. All of us we are in a passing, transient world. The Isaac Watts hymn "O God, Our Help in Ages Past" puts it like this: "Time, like an ever-rolling stream, bears all its sons away; they fly forgotten, as a dream dies at the opening day." You are at this moment a living soul going on inevitably to a final day, and as you do so, salvation is your first need, the need of knowing God, knowing he has forgiven you, knowing that he is your Father in the Lord Jesus Christ. Prepare for your latter end. Make certain that you are ready to die, that you are ready to meet God, that you know Jesus Christ, the Son of God who came into the world to reconcile you to God by dying for your sins and by rising again to justify you. I promise you if you get to know God like that, you can take your other problems one by one to him with confidence, and he will never say nay. But God forbid that anyone should find temporary satisfaction for lesser needs without having first of all satisfied the need of the soul for Jesus Christ and him crucified. Amen.

2

God's Only Way of Escape

HEBREWS 2:1–4

Therefore we ought to give the more earnest heed to the things which we have heard, lest at any time we should let them slip. For if the word spoken by angels was stedfast, and every transgression and disobedience received a just recompence of reward; How shall we escape, if we neglect so great salvation; which at the first began to be spoken by the Lord, and was confirmed unto us by them that heard him; God also bearing them witness, both with signs and wonders, and with divers [various] miracles, and gifts of the Holy Ghost, according to his own will?

We are living in an age when it is somewhat unusual for people to meet together to consider the gospel. It is not as common now as it was a hundred years ago for people to gather together on Sundays to hear the preaching of the Christian message. Many regard such a practice as an anachronism. They see very little point or purpose in it, and they regard those of us who do so as rather strange. What is our exact reason for doing so? We need to know this not only so we can have an answer to give to others who ask us why we do it, but also so we will know for our own good.

These days comparatively few persons go to church, but it is also possible for some to go for the wrong reason, because they have not considered why they do so. We must know exactly why we pay earnest heed to these things. The author of Hebrews was primarily addressing Christian people who were in danger of slipping past these things and becoming neglectful of them, but what he says to them is equally true of unbelievers. He makes this earnest, solemn appeal to them to give earnest heed and attention to these things, to be very careful that they do not allow life, as it were, to carry them in its current so that they drift past the haven and find themselves, at the end, lost. He warns them of the terrible possibility of neglecting these things, not perhaps willfully, but by being too preoccupied with other matters. Life is so full and so attractive and enticing, and there is so much to be done, that many people's agenda is so full that they do not think about these things. So this man warns us against all that, and he is not content only with warning us, he gives us reasons for doing so; he tells us why the gospel should be considered.

First of all he tells us, as we have seen, to make quite sure that what we are considering really is the gospel and not something else. We must give earnest heed to the things we have heard, the things that were preached at the beginning. Again the great reason why we should all listen to this gospel is the source from which it comes, the authority behind it. We saw that though it is only natural that we are anxious for our problems to be solved, before we begin to consider other things, even perfectly legitimate things, we must first face the problem that applies to the whole of mankind—our predicament and position as human beings. We must earnestly consider what the gospel really is and that it is a record of something that has happened in history. The gospel is a message from God; it asks us to face something that happened in this world historically concerning the person of the Lord Jesus Christ.

The next great reason given by the writer for our earnest attention is the dangerous, we could even say desperate, position and condition of all who do not believe the gospel. "How shall we escape, if we neglect so great salvation?" (2:3). It is a great characteristic of the Bible always to emphasize the danger of the position of all those who do not know God and who are not Christians. Many people think of the gospel of Jesus Christ primarily as a noble and wonderful view of life and a teaching concerning life. They think about it, therefore, as something that we can contemplate as we consider various philosophies and views of life. They realize that they ought to make some sort of contribution in this world; they want to live life in the best way possible. So they consider the gospel as a way of life in the same way as they consider other views and teachings, and thus they think it has to be taken up and applied to life and put into practice. That is their idea of the gospel, so they take it up and call themselves Christians. They have no idea of it as a message that addresses them directly. They have never been aware of any sense of urgency or of any great need in themselves. They have never felt there is anything about them that makes it necessary for the gospel to say to them, "Flee from the wrath to come" (see Matt. 3:7; Luke 3:7). They have never thought of the gospel like that. They think it is just a very noble and uplifting teaching with respect to life that any decent person will take up and put into practice.

The real trouble with people like that is that they have never really seen themselves and their lives as they are in this world. They have a view of life that has sometimes been described as a spectator view. They consider the disease of mankind objectively, from the outside, whereas in reality they themselves are the patients. They have never realized that something needs to be done about themselves because they only consider these other aspects, and that is why such people, when they read words like "How shall we escape" (2:3) really do not know what they mean. They say they know, of course, but they don't. Some people live a very profligate life; they see some need to escape from that, but they cannot see they are in any danger, and they do not understand this idea of escape. The real trouble with people like that is that they have never seen themselves in terms of their relationship to God.

Some have an active objection to this kind of teaching and preaching. They say, "This 'how shall we escape' idea is insulting and selfish." Or people say, "I have no use for the sort of gospel that emphasizes this; telling someone to be sure their soul is saved is so self-centered." The whole teaching seems to be repugnant to these people. They say, "You are proudly saying of yourself that you are not going to hell and that you are going to heaven. That is so terribly selfish and arrogant."

The thing is, those who have this objection to a personal salvation do not seem to have the same objection to the various things they look for so constantly and readily in life—food and drink and safeguarding the future. They do not regard any of that as being selfish and self-centered. Or if they were suddenly taken ill with a terrible pain in their side and they sent for the doctor because they thought the thing might kill them, they would be amazed if the doctor told them they had no right to be concerned about themselves—why didn't they ignore the pain, why all this concentration on self? According to these people, it is all right for someone to be concerned about the salvation of their body for a few years, but it is terribly selfish for them to be concerned about the eternal destiny of their immortal soul. How foolish we can be! Such people have never realized the truth about themselves. A person who is in a house that is on fire does not stop to philosophize about whether they will be saved; they just dive out of a window to save their lives. If men and women only realized their true predicament in regard to their eternal destiny, they would not speak in the way we have described.

Let's consider another objection. Some feel that this whole idea of warning and fear is insulting to the modern man and the modern mind. We boast today that the preaching of hell and of judgment and of punishment belongs to the past. We modern-day people are never happier than when we are contrasting ourselves with everybody who has gone before us. We are so advanced, we are so superior! Of course, we do not pay much attention to things like world wars or atomic bombs that blast people out of existence. We are better than those in previous centuries, we say; we must be because each century is bound to be better than the previous one. And one of the ways in which we express this extraordinary superiority of modern man is that we no longer preach hell and the wrath of God and the fear of judgment. We do not ask such a question as "How shall we escape?" (2:3); we have outgrown that sort of thing!

Let us be straight with one another. What does our [twentieth] century have to do with this question? What difference does scientific knowledge make? We are not discussing scientific things that can be seen and touched and handled; we are discussing unseen things in the realm of the soul and the spirit and God, a God who does not change, who is everlastingly the same, and about whom we know nothing apart from what we have in the Bible. It is fatuous for men and women to think that because they are modern-day people they cannot believe this sort of doctrine.

I am not interested in frightening or alarming anybody. There is no need to try to frighten people at a time like this; the facts are doing that themselves. Yet sometimes doctors sort of have to frighten people into having an operation or taking a vacation or undergoing certain treatment. They give them the facts, but they do not listen. The doctor has a deeper understanding of the seriousness of the situation, and he makes his point again, but the patient shakes his head. At last the doctor has to bring pressure in order to save them from the disease that he knows can be cured. The doctor has to frighten the patient not because he likes alarming the man but because he knows the facts and is concerned about the patient's good. I say again, in the presence of God, my Maker and Judge, that I have no more interest in frightening people than just that. This idea that our forefathers, some of the greatest saints and preachers the world has ever known, men such as Charles Haddon Spurgeon, Jonathan Edwards, and other giants of the past, enjoyed alarming people is an insult to their memory. Those men knew the truth, and it was their concern about souls that made them preach as they did. I fear that the condemnation that some of us who are preachers today will have to face is that we never held before the people what really is coming to meet them. We were so afraid of being called offensive, we were so afraid of being called out-of-date, we were so afraid of being condemned because we were preaching hellfire and trying to frighten people, that we did not present the truth. If I may use the language of the apostle Paul, "knowing therefore the terror of the Lord, we persuade men" (2 Cor. 5:11).

That brings me to the last reason we must consider: some feel that this teaching is entirely incompatible with the doctrine of the love of God. They say they cannot reconcile the idea of eternal punishment and the wrath of God with the love of God. They say the two things surely seem to be quite impossible, and their idea is that the love of God is somehow or another going to secure salvation for all. There are two groups at this point. Some believe that this salvation for all will be achieved the moment everybody dies. Their view is that it does not matter how people live in this world or whether they believe or not—the love of God will put them right, and they will go to heaven. Others are afraid to say that, so they say that ultimately everybody will have a second chance. The love of God makes that an absolute necessity, they believe, so when the impenitent and those outside of Christ die, they will have another chance, so that eventually all, by the love of God, will be saved.

What is the teaching of the Scriptures on this? Much time and energy could be saved in our discussion about these things if we only realized that the first question to settle is this one: On what am I basing my case? What is my authority for the view that I hold? If we are not agreed at this point, the whole discussion will be futile. It comes down to this: Either I believe the Bible or I believe human ideas. There is no other alternative. I am either going to take my view of life and eternity and everything else from God's Book or I am going to say, "What I believe is this" or "Professor So-and-so says this or that, and I base my whole position upon that." I want to remind you of what the Bible has to say about this particular subject. You do not have to mine it out of the depths; it is right there on the surface. I do not hesitate to go so far as to say that no message is found more prominently in the Bible from beginning to end than just this: "How shall we escape?" (2:3). The Bible is a book of warning. Let me remind you of the biblical teaching.

In a sense we are bound to start with the idea of man because this statement in Hebrews elicits two positions that men and women take with regard to the gospel and with regard to this question of escape. The first is the biblical view that tells us that man is a responsible being. This book tells us that man is a special creation of God and that God made man in his own image. He made him on his own pattern, if you like, and placed certain things that belong to himself into man, putting him quite apart from the rest of creation. He made men and women in such a way that he can address them, he can converse with them, an exchange can take place between them and God. Men and women are accountable to God, they live their lives under God, and they are meant for God. That is the biblical view of man.

Of course, this view is very different from the prevailing view today.

We frequently hear that man has somehow or another worked his way up from primitive slime. He is not a special creation, but just an animal that has developed a little more than the other animals. Man essentially is just an animal with no end and object, no ultimate purpose in view. He lives his brief life in this world and then dies exactly like the animals or the flowers die. In a sense because of his development he has a certain amount of responsibility, but that is only for the sake of society, only for the sake of life while he is in this world. When he dies that is the end. He is not accountable in an eternal sense; he will not have to stand at the end of time and render an account. There is nothing of that in the modern view.

But the biblical view is very different. Man, according to the Bible, is a great person, a great creature, if you like, and he is altogether different from the animals. This makes him superior; he is the lord of creation. You find this later on in the second chapter of Hebrews: "What is man, that thou art mindful of him? or the son of man that thou visitest him?" That is what the Bible says about man. He is not just a sort of developed beast that shuffles himself across the stage of life, then shuffles off it again. Not at all! He has a destiny. He has come from the hand of God, and he is going back to God.

Clearly this is very important, and I would ask you very solemnly, what is your view of yourself and of your life in this world? The Bible asks us to give earnest heed to that; it asks us to realize the truth about us. I am not concerned to show you which of these two views pays a compliment to man and which insults him. I am not concerned to show you the curious way in which modern man contradicts himself, boasting on one hand about his great superiority and turning himself almost into a god, and then on the other hand describing himself as a beast that comes and dies and that is the end. I am simply asking you to meditate seriously about the biblical view of you, which tells you that though you may not know it, you are a responsible, accountable being and that as you go through life in this world, your every action is known and is recorded, and you will have to give an explanation for all of it. You will have to face and answer the Supreme Being who is addressing you and who has spoken to you and has even sent his Son to speak to you. You will have to give your response to God.

Furthermore, the Bible not only tells us about man, it tells us about God. God has given us a revelation of himself in the Bible. We know nothing about the character and nature of God apart from what we find in his Book. What do you know about God, and from where have you derived your knowledge? What do you know about the love of God? What is your authority for all this? We know about God only through the revelation given in the Holy Scriptures. Look at it in the Old Testament. Look at what we are told about the nature and character of God way back at the beginning when he made man and began speaking to him. God revealed his holiness. God told man he had to live a life of subservience to him. God gave him commandments, and God told man that if he did not obey his commandments he would be punished and would undergo death and would be driven out of the garden. But in his folly man disobeyed God. So God showed that his words were not idle words. He *did* punish man. Death did come upon him and upon the whole human race; man was driven out of the garden. Thorns and briars came up, and the ground was cursed, and life became as we know it. That was not only God doing something to man—it was God revealing himself to man.

Then consider the story of the flood. God has revealed his character. He has shown us that man is responsible and accountable. He has pleaded with mankind to come back to him, but man has ignored him. God called a man named Noah who for 120 years preached a doctrine of righteousness and warned the people to escape God's wrath through God's repentance. But they would not listen, and they laughed at Noah. But God vindicated Noah's character and the truth by sending the flood. He did it again in the giving of the law, and in the law God reveals himself supremely. He tells us he is a holy and a jealous God: "Thou shalt have no other gods before me" (Ex. 20:3). God told the nation of Israel about the punishment that would follow if they repeatedly disobeyed.

But the Old Testament is not merely a revelation of what God has said—it is also a revelation of what God has done. Even a man like Moses, whom God especially favored, to whom God gave the Law, when he disobeyed was punished. The great leader that brought the people out of Egypt and through the Red Sea was not allowed to go into Canaan. Why? Because he rebelled against this holy God. Read the stories of other divinely favored men like David and others and you will find the same thing. Look at the terrible punishment that descended upon individuals, God's own people, but look also on the nation as a whole, the chosen race. They were God's own people, the people whom he made out of the one man Abraham, called to be a special possession for himself. What happened to them? They were carried away captive into Assyria and into Babylon. They were God's own chosen people, but that is what happened to them. Why? Because they had forgotten that God is holy and that his word is true. The nation of Israel is a standing memorial to the truth that God is holy and just and righteous and will punish iniquity and sin even in his own people.

"But, ah," says someone, "that is in the Old Testament, and I do not take much interest in the Old Testament. I am interested in the New Testament." Consider John the Baptist, the man who preached a baptism of repentance for the remission of sins. He warned the people to "flee from the wrath to come" (Matt. 3:7). His urgent message is, "Escape, escape," and coupled with that is his other great message: "Behold the Lamb of God, which taketh away the sin of the world" (John 1:29). Pointing to Christ, he urged the people to come to him; he even sent his own followers to Jesus Christ.

We must also consider the teaching of our Lord himself. First of all there is the message of repentance. Read the Gospels. You say you believe in the love of God alone. Do you know more about the love of God than the Lord Jesus Christ? Is he not the very incarnation of God's love? No one knew anything about it in the way that he did. And he preached repentance: "Jesus began to preach, and to say, Repent: for the kingdom of heaven is at hand" (Matt. 4:17). He also expounded the law, and he did away with the idea of the law as merely mechanical. The law is spiritual. For example, it is not just a matter of not committing adultery in a physical sense; if a man even looks lustfully at a woman he is committing adultery in his heart. That is how our Lord interprets the Law. He makes it infinitely more impossible than it was before. Read the Sermon on the Mount, and you will see this.

We all like John 3:16: "God so loved the world."—Ah, says man, that is what I believe: "God so loved the world, that he gave his only begotten Son . . . " Yes, but he gave him "that whosoever believeth in him should not perish, but have everlasting life." And our Lord goes on to say, "he that believeth not is condemned already, because he hath not believed in the name of the only begotten Son of God" (John 3:18). He says later on that "the wrath of God abideth on him" (John 3:36). How easy it is to argue from our own presuppositions, but if you believe the Book, if you believe that Jesus Christ is the Son of God, that is what he taught, and that is what you will believe.

Read too what he says about the final judgment when all mankind will appear before God, and all the nations of the earth will come, and there will be a division of the sheep and the goats. Have you ever read his words on the subject of hell? It was the Lord Jesus Christ who spoke about Dives and Lazarus. It was he who spoke about the eternal torment of the flames and the great gulf between the rich man in Hades and the other man in Abraham's bosom and about the impossibility of passing from one to the other. There is no talk about a second or third chance or about everybody being put right, but rather of "a great gulf fixed" (Luke 16:26). This is not my idea; it is not the thought of some philosopher. It is the Son of God who says these things.

Then listen to him as he talks about his coming again into this world on the clouds of heaven accompanied by the holy angels to reap and to judge. Above everything else listen to him as he tells you about his purpose in coming into this world and especially as he tells you about the manner of his death. "The Son of man came not to be ministered unto, but to minister, and to give his life a ransom for many" (Mark 10:45). As he was facing death upon the cross and his disciples were trying to save him from it, he said to them in essence, You do not understand. Do you not know that I could command twelve legions of angels and escape from this? But if I did that, I would not accomplish the task I have come to do. "As Moses lifted up the serpent in the wilderness, even so must the Son of man be lifted up" (John 3:14). He said, "This is the only way." But go on from there as the author of Hebrews urges you to do. He says in summary, "This is the gospel that was preached at the first by the Lord Jesus Christ himself. He taught the people about holiness and their own position, the judgment that was coming and the gulf that was fixed. That is his message." "The Son of man is come to seek and to save that which was lost" (Luke 19:10).

Then read the apostles, those who had listened to him and had been with him, and you will find they all talk about the coming judgment. Peter preached it on the day of Pentecost. Paul preached it in Athens. They all preached it everywhere—repentance, the exhortation to flee from divine wrath, the only way of escape. These men remind us that God accompanied their preaching with heavenly sanction. They said this power that had come upon them was given to them by the Holy Spirit. Ananias and Sapphira evidently did not believe this, and Peter said to them, "Thou hast not lied unto men, but unto God" (Acts 5:4), and they dropped dead. Signs and miracles and wonders attested the message, and the message of judgment is still true today. As you read the epistles, you will find this same solemn message everywhere, but nowhere perhaps more than in this epistle to the Hebrews. "It is a fearful thing to fall into the hands of the living God" (Heb. 10:31). We must "serve God acceptably with reverence and godly fear: For our God is a consuming fire" (Heb. 12:28–29). I am almost afraid to share these words, but they are part of Holy Scripture, and we must face them. You and I must answer to the living God in all his holiness and justice and righteousness and power, and he has revealed himself to us. Read the book of Revelation and you will see all this in a most extraordinary manner, this warning, this pronouncement of the final judgment that is coming.

But thank God that face-to-face with all that we have the glorious, loving revelation of God's way of salvation. God has sent his only begotten Son into the world to rescue us from wrath and judgment. We have all sinned; we have all forgotten God. We have all insulted him. We have put other things before him, and there is no greater insult to God than that. We are all in this predicament; we are condemned. What can we do? We can do nothing, but God has done everything. He sent his Son. The blood of bulls and goats and the ashes of a heifer sprinkling the unclean is not enough to save us, but thank God the blood of Christ is. "Having therefore, brethren, boldness to enter into the holiest by the blood of Jesus . . . " (Heb. 10:19). That is God's way, the only offering for sin. God sent his Son, and the Son has borne our sins, and they have been punished in him. Reject this and "there remaineth no more sacrifice for sins" (Heb. 10:26). If you turn your back on the blood of Christ, there is nothing left but certain future torment and agony, the fate of the unbeliever throughout eternity. My friends, it is as simple as this: you either believe what this Book says from cover to cover about this matter or you do not believe it. But this Book tells us this is the only way, and because he knew it, this writer says, "How shall we escape, if we neglect so great salvation?" (2:3). We cannot; it is impossible. May the Lord have mercy upon us and by his Spirit enable us all to see that he has provided the way for us to meet him; if we reject that way, there is no other. Amen.

3

The Authority of the Gospel

HEBREWS 2:1-4

Therefore we ought to give the more earnest heed to the things which we have heard, lest at any time we should let them slip. For if the word spoken by angels was stedfast, and every transgression and disobedience received a just recompence of reward; How shall we escape, if we neglect so great salvation; which at the first began to be spoken by the Lord, and was confirmed to us by them that heard him; God also bearing witness, both with signs and wonders, and with divers [various] miracles, and gifts of the Holy Ghost, according to his own will?

I am directing your attention to these four verses again so we may all know the true answer to crucial questions and because the author of Hebrews exhorts the people to whom he was writing, Hebrew Christians, to do this. He appeals to them to give earnest heed, careful, undivided attention to these things. He tells them to be very careful that they do not let these truths slip past them; they must avoid the terrible danger of having looked into the face of Christ without really getting to know him and being eternally saved by him. He warns them against the terrible danger of being so preoccupied with other matters that they neglect these things, of being so busy with the world and its legitimate affairs and cares and problems that they somehow just do not think about him. It is not that they purposely refuse to have anything to do with him. Many people go through this life and arrive on their deathbed without having met and known the Lord Jesus Christ, simply because they were so busy with other things that they neglected him altogether. Those are the dangers against which this author warns these Hebrew Christians to whom he was writing, and it stands as a warning to us and to all other people today.

The writer says, "We ought to give the more earnest heed to the things which we have heard" (2:1), and those are the only things to which he calls our attention. Often people, quite mistakenly, think that something is the gospel that is not the gospel at all. There is terrible danger in turning to certain aspects of the gospel only instead of to the whole gospel and in taking certain blessings of the gospel as the whole gospel of Christ. As we have already seen, the only thing we are exhorted to pay attention to is the gospel message itself and the whole of that message. This message concerns our Lord and Savior Jesus Christ and "so great salvation" (2:3) in him; that is what we must consider.

The question many people are asking today is, Why listen to that old gospel? What if someone approached you and said, "Why do you think it is a sensible thing to listen to the preaching of this old message?"

I have suggested that the author, in the space of four verses, gives us three answers to that question and at the same time introduces us to the three major themes of his epistle. There are three main reasons why we should "give the more earnest heed to the things which we have heard" (2:1), and this whole letter is simply an exposition of them. The first is the source and the authority of the message, the second is the precarious and dangerous position and condition of all who listen to the message, and the third and last reason is the greatness of the message and the wondrous blessings it has to give. These are the three major themes of this epistle, and they are also the main reasons why anybody should listen to the gospel. Not only should we listen to it—we should spend time thinking and meditating upon it; we should accept it and lay hold upon it and not drift past it.

Now I want to take up the first of these reasons: The source of the message, or the authority with which the message comes to us. I can imagine someone saying, "Why do you put that first?" Many are tempted to ask that question because they only want to know, *does it work?* That is commonly called the pragmatic test, and many people in the world are pragmatists. Their problem can take many forms. It may be purely physical, it may be mental, it may be a problem of the heart and the affections, it may be a problem of the spirit. It may be some disappointment, some great loss in life. As we know from experience, a thousand and one problems attack us from all directions; in some way or another we all find life difficult and eventually discover ourselves to be defeated, and we are looking for a solution. We seek an answer, and the world offers its own remedies. Consider all the books, advertisements, newspapers, and societies and you will find a multitude of agencies offering to meet us where we are and to deliver us from our particular need. Large numbers of people, face-to-face with all that, ask simply one question: Does the proposed answer work? That is their only test, and they regard us as being pedantic and difficult if we insist upon applying other tests.

But I repeat that the first test you must apply has to do with the source and the authority of the message. This must come first for several reasons. First of all, the purely pragmatic test is insufficient and wrong. We must have a standard in life. Truth surely must come first. Anybody who claims to be up-to-date in knowledge, and especially the man who claims to be purely scientific, must agree that the greatest possession men and women have is their brain, their understanding, their power to reason, their power to sift evidence, their power to discriminate, their power to select. And if that is their greatest and highest gift, it is clearly one that is to be used. Their mind is their greatest possession; it is the thing that differentiates them, after all, from the animals. That is what makes man man. The animals go by instinct, but men and women have this higher power, and it is a power, surely, they were meant to use and to put into operation. If you do not use your mind and your reason and your discrimination, you have no test in life, you have no standard, you are not able to evaluate, and you have no sense of judgment.

One thing that differentiates the gospel of Jesus Christ from so many of the ineffective remedies offered to mankind today is this: The gospel of Jesus Christ asks us to think. Nothing is so ignorant with regard to the gospel of Jesus Christ as to consider it as just some kind of emotionalism or sob stuff. I have no doubt there are times when the church of God does give that impression, that people just sit down and sing and sing until they are so intoxicated by their own singing that they cease to think. They become so emotionally charged that they are ready to listen to and accept anything. But that is not the gospel found in the New Testament. The gospel says, "Give the more earnest heed"—"Come now, and let us reason together" (2:1; Isa. 1:18). It claims to be truth, and truth is always something, primarily, that comes to the mind and asks us to think.

My second reason for rejecting a pragmatic attitude toward anything that offers us help in this world is the danger of considering our symptoms but ignoring the cause of our symptoms. There is a difference between disease and symptoms. Disease causes symptoms. Symptoms are not disease; they are manifestations of a disease. You and I, when we are ill, are often more interested in our symptoms than in our disease. We are well aware of our symptoms—shortness of breath, temperature, or whatever, and what we as patients always want is, of course, to be delivered from our symptoms. It is perfectly right and good to relieve a man of his symptoms, but on one condition only, and that is that he recognizes the disease that is causing the symptoms.

Think of a man writhing in agony with abdominal pain who wants only to be relieved of his pain. The doctor gives the man an injection, and the patient will be delivered from his pain. But if that doctor does that before he has discovered the cause of the pain, he may very well be behaving in a criminal way toward that man; indeed, he may be responsible for that man's death. Symptoms are provided by nature to call attention to the disease that is the cause of the symptoms, and if the doctor has discovered the cause, if he has diagnosed, say, appendicitis in this case, he realizes that the man must be operated upon if his life is to be saved. To give an injection to relieve the symptoms without knowing the cause of the disease would do the patient a terrible wrong.

There is nothing more dangerous than to have ease without solving your problem. Let me give you another obvious illustration. Why have many people turned to alcoholic beverages in order to avoid worry? They are so possessed with worry that all they want for the time being is to have a certain amount of release for their minds, and they know that if they drink alcohol, they will forget their worries, and for the time being they are happy. But the problem is still there. They are drugging themselves to enable them to forget for a while, but the problem and the disease remain. This is a terribly dangerous thing to do.

Furthermore, in this life and world we live in a world where, whether we realize it or not, we are surrounded by unseen spirits. The Bible talks about the *Holy* Spirit because it wants to differentiate him from the other spirits around and about us. It is not only human sinners that cause trouble; there is "the god of this world" (2 Cor. 4:4). Evil spirits have great power in this world. We have no better authority for this than the Son of God himself. In Matthew 24 we read that he said a day would come when evil powers would work lying wonders and miracles and things of that kind so cleverly as even almost to deceive the very elect themselves. Evil powers can counterfeit good actions. The Holy Spirit heals diseases and gives guidance and works wonders, but our Lord said other powers can do the same thing. That is why the New Testament exhorts us to "try the spirits" (1 John 4:1), to "prove all things" (1 Thess. 5:21). We must not just say, "Such and such has taken place; therefore it must be good." The Holy Spirit is at work, but other spirits are at work as well, and we must test and prove them and hold fast only to that which is good.

Let me say a final word about my reason for rejecting this view. In the last analysis what we should be concerned about is not what we feel, not merely our happiness, but our whole state before and relationship to God. What I should be really concerned about is not temporary relief or solving a particular problem. Before all that I must consider my condition face-to-face before God, especially when I die and stand before him in the judgment. Many things in this life and world can give us temporary relief. Many agencies really do help. Psychology can help; many of the cults help. They do help people feel better. But if you allow this relief to make you feel that all is well, if you say, "I am all right," and go on living without thinking about God and preparing to meet him, then the thing that is giving you temporary relief is a messenger from hell. It is standing between you and God and being ready to meet him.

That is what makes these things so alarming. Men and women are so content with temporary relief that they allow themselves to be soothed and comforted, ignoring eternal issues. My dear friends, you may be feeling happy because you have received some treatment. You may have lost your worry; you may feel well physically; you might think you're receiving remarkable guidance in your life. But what about death and eternity? These things that you have are not good if they stand between you and God. The thing that is giving you temporary satisfaction may be your greatest enemy. The gospel, in the first instance, calls upon us to listen to it, to pay heed to it, and to be careful of drifting away from it because of its source, because of its authority, because of the way in which it comes to us.

What does all this mean? Let me summarize it for you. The real reason, and in the last analysis the only reason, for listening to the gospel is that it is a message from God. The author of Hebrews points out in his letter, "God, who at sundry times and in divers [various] manners spake in time past unto the fathers by the prophets, Hath in these last days spoken unto us by his Son" (Heb. 1:1–2). God is still speaking to us. In the second chapter the author tells us again that God was bearing witness to the message. That is the whole case for the Bible from beginning to end. We do not meet in the church to consider some human idea or theory as to how we can all be healed and relieved and made happier in this world. There is nothing wrong with the study of psychology and so on, but this message starts on a different plane altogether. The Bible does not pretend to be a human book; it claims to be a divine Book. It claims from beginning to end that God is speaking in it, that in it God is giving us a message. It is not about man trying to discover God; in it God is revealing himself to man. It is not about mankind solving his problem; it is God outlining his solution for the problem.

So this message is unique, and that is the supreme reason why we should listen to it. We listen to what men have to say, and we see them all failing. We see the world in its terrible predicament. Is it not time for mankind to begin to listen to God? Consider the story of the children of Israel. They listened to other people and got into trouble; then they came back to God, and he spoke to them, and they found deliverance. How often that happened! I would not preach from the pulpit were it not for the fact that I am sure the message I am delivering is the message of God. I know nothing apart from God's Book. I have had theories and ideas about life and have tried to put them into practice, but they failed. The Bible is God's message, and that is the first great reason for listening to it.

The second reason is, it is not only God's message—it is God's message in a special way. The gospel of Jesus Christ is God's message to us through his Son (Heb. 1:1–3). As Christians we do not meet together to consider theories or ideas. We consider facts, history. All other proposed solutions that offer to help you with your problems and difficulties are theories and ideas that men claim will work, but the gospel is different. Why? Because it is based on historical facts. The gospel of Jesus Christ is not an idea or a theory; it is a record of things that have happened in this world and of the meaning of those things.

The gospel of Jesus Christ invites us in the first instance to consider definite facts. Forget your particular problem. No two of us are absolutely alike, and no two problems are identical. Some are looking for happiness; others want to get rid of worry; others are looking for physical restoration; others want guidance. Others are feeling utterly ashamed of themselves because they have fallen again to some sin and temptation; they want to be washed and cleansed, and they are looking for moral power. I want to suggest to you tenderly that you should forget all of that and listen to certain facts. We must face facts; we do not do anything to facts by refusing to consider them. Let us look as if for the first time at certain things that have happened in this world.

What is the message that we are to consider? It is that there has been one in this world whom the author of Hebrews refers to as "the Lord." "How shall we escape, if we neglect so great salvation; which at the first began to be spoken *by the Lord*, and was confirmed unto us by them that heard him" (2:3). God in times past spoke to mankind through men; he raised a prophet and gave him a message, then another, giving him also a message. Thus in various ways he revealed what he was going to do. He took hold of men like Abraham and Moses and spoke through them. But the Christian church is called that because something essentially different has happened. This Person of whom I am speaking, "the Lord," Jesus of Nazareth, spoke of this in a parable. He pictured his servants being sent one after another to his vineyard, but the workers in the vineyard ill-treated the servants. So the owner, "sent unto them his son, saying, They will reverence my son" (Matt. 21:37). The Lord spoke in such a way that the Pharisees and others who were listening at that moment knew he was speaking to them about himself.

That amazing New Testament story about an extraordinary thing that happened two thousand years ago tells how a young woman, a virgin, was visited by an angel one afternoon who told her that she was going to bear a child. She did not understand it and was confused. She said, "How can this be, seeing I know not a man?" (Luke 1:34) and the answer was given, "With God nothing shall be impossible" (Luke 1:37). The Holy Spirit was to come upon her. She was also told, "That holy thing that shall be born of thee shall be called the Son of God," and she believed it, and that amazing thing happened. She and the man to whom she was engaged went up to Bethlehem to be taxed because Joseph belonged to the house and lineage of David. The inn was full, and nobody would make room for a woman even in her condition— such is the selfishness of life. So she went among the animals in the stable, and there the child was born. Then another extraordinary thing happened. A number of shepherds came and told how they were in the fields keeping watch over their flocks by night, and angels appeared to them and told them they would find this baby in a manger. So they went and found things exactly as had been reported to them by the angels. Then wise men came from the east; they had been guided by a special star in the heavens.

Let me remind you again of a boy at the age of twelve baffling the doctors of the law in the temple. Let me remind you of a young man at the age of thirty who went out and began preaching in a way people had never heard before and caused even the Herodian soldiers to say, "Never man spake like this man" (John 7:46)—amazing teaching such as the world had never heard. He also began to work miracles. He could heal the lepers, cause the deaf to hear, even raise the dead. He commanded the billows and silenced raging storms. People saw him and lived with him and heard him, and all the time he was making great claims. He looked at a man and said, "Follow me," and the man rose up and followed him (Matt. 9:9). Read the four Gospels for yourselves. Then at the end he was arrested, and in apparent weakness, utterly defenseless, he was nailed to a cruel tree. There he seemed to be in terrible agony, and he died long before he would have died in the normal course of events. They took down his body and put it in a grave, but when they went to look at it on the morning of the third day it was not there. He had disappeared. Then he began to appear to his own disciples. He came among then when they were in a room with all the doors shut. He came and spoke with them and ate with them.

These are facts, and the gospel of Jesus Christ primarily asks you to listen to facts like that. It says that this Person was none other than God's only Son. It tells us that God sent his only begotten Son into this world. So I suggest that what you must face is not your aches and pains, not your unhappiness or misery, not the guidance you want to have, but this Person. If the Son of God has been in this world, that has something to do with you and me, and the Bible exhorts us not to give ourselves rest or peace until we know exactly what that means. Why has he come? What has he to do with me? What is the meaning of it all? I am speaking of facts, and the writer of Hebrews elaborates upon this. He says that God who has spoken to mankind has sent his only begotten Son, the One who was in the bosom of the Father from all eternity, the express image of his Person. God has sent him into the world and has spoken to us through him. That is why we must listen to this gospel.

The Son is not only superior to the prophets, he is superior to the angels. God has spoken to men and sent messages to the world through angels, but now, beyond the highest angel, he has spoken through his only begotten Son. Can we not see the importance of this? If Almighty God has sent his only Son into this world to speak to us, we must listen to him. The authority and the source of the message demands attention from every man and woman, and those who do not pay heed to God's address to them through his only Son must have taken leave of their senses. That is the message of the gospel; that is what those Jewish people had heard; that is what was preached to them. They heard that this Jesus of Nazareth was none other than the Son of God. The fact that Jesus is the Christ was proved not only by his birth or by the miracles that he worked or the teaching that he gave and the claims that he made for himself—it was especially proved by his rising from the dead ("declared to be the Son of God with power . . . by the resurrection from the dead," Rom. 1:4). That is what we must face.

I can imagine someone saying, "How do I know these facts are true? How can I be sure of them?" This writer answers that question when he tells us, "at the first [it] began to be spoken by the Lord, and was confirmed unto us by them that heard him; God also bearing them witness, both with signs and wonders, and with divers [various] miracles, and gifts of the Holy Ghost, according to his own will" (2:3–4). We know these things through the apostles, through the first messengers, through those men who were like ourselves, through whom the Christian church was founded and established, and from whom the message has come down the running centuries. We know these things because all these men who first preached them had witnessed them. They had spent three years with the Lord. Many of them had seen his miracles; they had seen the crucifixion, and they saw him after the resurrection. These men were witnesses, and they declared these things. *But why should I listen to them?* asks someone. If you examine their character, you will find they were all reliable witnesses. Even more, they were ready to be killed for testifying to these things that they loved. Cruel tyrants had them thrown to the lions in the arena, and they said, "You can do what you like with us. We cannot but speak of the things we have seen and heard."

But we are convinced not merely by their character and their readiness to suffer for their message—we have "signs and wonders, and . . . divers [various] miracles" (2:4), the gifts of the Holy Spirit that God provided in order to attest their message and in order to bear his own testimony to them. There would never have been a Christian church if these men had not spoken with power. Three thousand souls were converted on the day of Pentecost, and the church continued to spread. They worked wonders, they had extraordinary gifts that no one could explain, and these things established the church and set her going. God attested their message. When the clever rulers of Jerusalem looked at

Peter and James and John they said, "Are these the people who are causing this disturbance?" They were ordinary men, just fishermen, but then the rulers reminded themselves that these people "had been with Jesus" (Acts 4:13). That is it! They would have been dismissed, they would have gone into oblivion centuries ago, and we would never have heard of them, there would never have been a Christian church and a Christian message were it not for the signs that God gave them, manifestations of the Holy Spirit.

So our final reason for paying more earnest heed to these things is that it is a message from God, the blessed holy Trinity—God the Father, God the Son, and God the Holy Spirit. If you lack any other reason, here is *the* reason to pay heed: Almighty God is speaking to you. He is giving his message through the Son by the Holy Spirit. It is all in the Bible. So I ask you again to stand face-to-face with these things and never to give yourself a moment's rest or peace until you know exactly what they mean to you. You must face the fact that the Son of God left the courts of heaven and came into this world. Why did he do it? Why did he go to that death on the cross? He need not have gone. He said himself he could have avoided it. He could have commanded twelve legions of angels and escaped it, but he set his face steadfastly to go to Jerusalem. He insisted upon doing it. He said, "No man taketh [my life] from me, but I lay it down" (John 10:18). Why did he do that? Was it a mere display? Then what is the meaning of the resurrection, and why did he send the Holy Spirit? I beseech you once more to forget your nervous afflictions, forget your worries and your physical health needs, forget your need of guidance, forget everything. This is the only thing that matters.

Would you say that the Son of God has been in this world and has done the things that I have described but it has nothing to do with you, it has no relevance for you? Impossible! He came to die; he rose again. Why? Because it is the only way you and I can be saved, the only way we can be forgiven, the only way we can be reconciled to God, the only way we can escape hell and enjoy everlasting bliss. That is why we should give "the more earnest heed" to these things (2:1). Beware of being temporarily soothed and satisfied by things that tell you nothing about the Lord Jesus Christ and his coming and his dying and his rising again. They may make you happier, as pain-killing drugs or alcohol will, or anything that bludgeons the mind. But what matters is your sin problem that separates you from God, your soul, your relationship to God, your eternal destiny, and the gospel alone is the solution to that problem. Let us therefore beware lest we slip past these things, lest we neglect them. Let us give such earnest heed to them that we shall come to know for certain that the only begotten Son of God came into this world to die for each of us and for our sins and to reconcile us to God and to give us the blessings that he alone can give in time and in eternity. Amen.

4

Why Salvation Is Great

HEBREWS 2:1–4

Therefore we ought to give the more earnest heed to the things which we have heard, lest at any time we should let them slip. For if the word spoken by angels was stedfast, and every transgression and disobedience received a just recompence of reward; How shall we escape, if we neglect so great salvation; which at the first began to be spoken by the Lord, and was confirmed unto us by them that heard him; God also bearing them witness, both with signs and wonders, and with divers [various] miracles, and gifts of the Holy Ghost, according to his own will?

The author of the epistle to the Hebrews was addressing these words to Christian people, to Christian believers, but they were Christian believers who had come into a sad and sorry condition. Instead of rejoicing in their great salvation, they had become fearful and apprehensive as a result of persecution that they endured, and some of them were in such a state of fear that they were beginning to look back to their old Jewish religion and wondering if they had been a little foolish in turning their backs upon it and believing this new teaching, this new faith.

In order to deal with their discouragement and unhappiness this man wrote them this great letter. He suggests that their condition was mainly due to the fact that they were letting slip, or were slipping away from, the things they had heard, and he tells them that the cure for their spiritual depression, their uncertainty, their lack of assurance, was to give more earnest heed to the things they had heard and to make certain that they would never drift away from them like a ship drifting away from her moorings. But he is not content to tell them that. He warns them very seriously and very solemnly, saying, "if the word spoken by angels was stedfast"—that is a reference to the law given by God through angels to Moses and through him to the children of Israel, as we read in the Old Testament—if that was so, "and every transgression and disobedience received a just recompence of reward; How shall we escape, if we neglect so great salvation?" (2:2–3).

That is what I have to say to Christian people, to members of the Christian church, especially those who are in a like condition to these Hebrew Christians. I also address these words to believers who are not rejoicing in their salvation and to any who are not Christians. Why does the Christian church go on preaching? What is the justification for the continuance of the Christian church at the present time? Many people think that the church should shut her mouth, that her message is out-of-date. What can we say to such people? I want particularly to deal with the words, "How shall we escape, if we neglect so great salvation?" (2:3). Here is our message—"so great salvation." It is the message of the Bible we are concerned about, this "great salvation." Let us analyze this statement.

The first thing we notice is that the message of the Bible is a message of salvation, which means deliverance, setting free, giving health, curing some disease or sickness. It is spiritual health; it is salvation. The message of the Christian church is not merely exhortation to men and women to live a better life. That is not Christianity. Many agencies can do that and are doing that. The essential thing about the Christian message is that it is a message of good news ("gospel" means "good news," and it is good news about salvation, deliverance). I am emphasizing this because if you get your impression of what Christianity is from the newspapers, you might very well come to the conclusion that the

Christian message is nothing but a protest against hydrogen bombs, a protest against war, a protest against this, that, and the other thing. But that is not good news. There is no salvation in that. This message is the good news of *salvation*. That is the first thing we have to emphasize. It is the best and greatest and most wonderful good news that has ever come into this world. The author of Hebrews calls it "so great salvation" (2:3), and this is characteristic of all the New Testament writers. They always used that superlative when they wrote about this message. Paul does so in particular. He talks about "the exceeding riches of [God's] grace" (Eph. 2:7). He talks about "the unsearchable riches of Christ" (Eph. 3:8). He says, "Great is the mystery of godliness: God was manifest in the flesh" (1 Tim. 3:16).

But the adjective "great" as regards the greatness of salvation is not confined only to the Bible. Consider the great cathedrals of England and on the continent of Europe. What is the explanation for this magnificent architecture? Whatever you and I may think of cathedrals, we have to consider the men who built them; they tried to express in stone the greatness and the vastness and the magnificence of this great message of the Christian church concerning salvation. You see the same thing in art. Some of the greatest artists depict some doctrine or other concerning this great salvation (consider da Vinci's painting of *The Last Supper*). But some of the greatest masterpieces of eloquence and oratory have been delivered from Christian pulpits.

Let me give you a final illustration. I suppose everyone would agree that possibly the greatest musical composition ever composed was Handel's *Messiah* with its mighty, majestic choruses. Handel tells us himself that during the extraordinary short period when he was composing *Messiah*, he felt he had been lifted up to the heavens and had seen something of the glory of God and the mighty cross. The "Hallelujah Chorus" was Handel's way of giving expression to this "so great salvation." It is vast, immense, and free. Consider, too, the hymn-writer Isaac Watts's great hymn "When I Survey the Wondrous Cross." He does not just glance at the cross. Looking at the cross is like standing at the top of a tall mountain and viewing a great panorama stretching endlessly before you. Or consider the Charles Wesley hymn "O for a Thousand Tongues to Sing":

O for a thousand tongues to sing
My great Redeemer's praise,
The glories of my God and King,
The triumphs of His grace.

Is that the way in which you think of this message? Is that your characteristic conception of the Christian faith? Are you moved by its greatness, its vastness, its mightiness? Do you rejoice in it, and are you proud of it? Do you say with the apostle Paul, "I am not ashamed of the gospel of Christ" (Rom. 1:16)? The writer of the epistle to the Hebrews says in effect to these Christians, "Are you ashamed of this message? The trouble with you is you've never realized what a great salvation you have. If you had only realized the preeminence of Christ and the glories of the cross, you would never have looked back at your old Jewish religion." I wonder if those of us who claim to be Christians glory in the cross as we should. Do we exult in this mighty salvation that is ours? We may need to remind ourselves of it. We sometimes give the impression that our gospel is a small thing—the impression that to be a Christian means not to do certain things and to give up certain things. And yet we are believers in "so great salvation" (2:3), and our task in this evil hour in which we find ourselves is to show to men and women the greatness of what they are missing, the loss they are suffering.

Why has this man called this "so great salvation" (2:3)? Why is this salvation great? First, it is great in its authorship, great in its genesis, great in its conception. That is a good way of testing the greatness of anything. Who has produced it? Isn't that the test that we habitually employ, with respect to books, for instance? A man going into a public library may want to read a novel. How does he decide which book he wants? Does he look at the titles? If he is a wise man, he doesn't. He looks at the author names; he wants to read a book written by a great author. When I was a boy, I always went for a book by Sir Walter Scott, the greatest of all authors in my estimation. We go for the great authors. That is a sound policy, and it is a sound principle in every realm of life. Newspapers reported a sale at Sotherby's, and it was a great sensation because a certain painting was sold for 136,000 pounds. A few years before, the same painting had been sold by Sotherby's for less than 100 guineas—*the same picture*, yet now it sold for 136,000 pounds! Why? A well-known expert had looked at it and began to examine it, and he and other experts eventually agreed that this painting had been painted by the Spanish master painter El Greco. Although it was exactly the same painting, the moment they discovered that it had been painted by El Greco, the price soared to 136,000 pounds. What really determines the greatness of the painting is the greatness of the painter.

"So great salvation" (2:3). Why do we offer the world the message of the Bible? Why do we say that this message is great? This is not a human message. This is not a message that has been conceived in the mind of men. This is not a human theory or a human idea. I am not here to derogate from the greatness of any human teaching, but this message is essentially and fundamentally different. How so? "God, who at sundry times and in divers [various] manners spake in time past unto the fathers by the prophets, hath in these last days spoken unto us by his Son, whom he hath appointed heir of all things" (Heb. 1:1–2). Then in chapter 2, "If the word spoken by angels was stedfast, and every transgression received a just recompence of reward, How shall we escape, if we neglect so great salvation?" (2:3).

That is why the Christian church goes on. That is why we ask the world to listen to us. We are telling the world what God thinks, not what men think. Why is the world in such an ominous state? The answer to the problem is found in the Bible. God planned and fashioned this "great salvation." He planned it, and the Son volunteered and said, "Here am I, send me." He came, and the Holy Spirit has come into our lives as well. It is God's salvation. He is its author. This is one reason why we should glory in it. This is why we should ask everyone to listen. The world has gone mad. The world is unspiritual and full of trouble and tribulation. The need is to listen to God and to stop listening to one another. Listen to what God says. This salvation is great because of its authorship, because of its very composition.

Secondly, it is great because it delivers us from the great enemy. "How shall we escape, if we neglect so great salvation?" (2:3). Here is the second way of testing its value. Here is something that gives us health, which cures disease. The way to test its greatness is to realize what it saves us from. "How shall we escape, if we neglect so great salvation?" (2:3). What happens to us if we neglect it? Have you ever thought of that? Let me put it again in the form of a simple illustration. We read a lot in our newspapers about various drugs being used by doctors to cure diseases. We read about the Ministry of Health spending too much money on drugs. How do you estimate and test the greatness and value of a drug? Aspirin is a wonderful drug, a wonderful cure for aches and pains, but it is quite inexpensive. But think of so-called lethal drugs. Why are they so wonderful? These drugs do not merely cure headaches and aches and pains. These drugs cure diseases that until they were discovered were invariably fatal. We estimate the value or the greatness of a drug in terms of the seriousness of the disease that the drug can relieve or cure.

"How shall we escape, if we neglect so great salvation?" (2:3). "If the word spoken by angels" (2:2) is a reference to the Old Testament law, that is, the Mosaic Law. Notice what he says about it. He says it was a terrible law in itself. It condemned what he calls "transgression and disobedience"—the breaking of the Ten Commandments (2:2). God is a holy God. Anyone who breaks the law is to be punished. This is the law of God. "The soul that sinneth, it shall die" (Ezek. 18:4, 20). "Do you realize your position?" asks this man. "Do you realize that you ought to believe in this gospel, this so great salvation? Do you realize what it saves you from?" I think we are touching here the very thing that keeps the masses of the people outside the Christian church. Why don't they come to church? Why don't they believe the gospel? Why don't they come to Christ? There is only one answer. They have never seen any need of him. They have never realized the terrible condition in which they are. They are like a man with a cancer growth who says, "I am all right." He has a growth in him that can kill him, but he is unaware of it. We are to remind men and women that they are under the wrath of God. The apostle Paul gloried in the gospel. "I am not ashamed of the gospel of Christ: for it is the power of God unto salvation to everyone that believeth; to the Jew first, and also to the Greek" (Rom. 1:16). "The just shall live by faith" (Rom. 1:17). The wrath of God from heaven falls upon all ungodliness of men. "I am proud of the gospel," says the great apostle, "and I am willing to preach it for this reason: All men have sinned and come short of the glory of God. It is because I know that there is none righteous, no, not one. It is because I know that all mankind fell in Adam and that there is only one thing that can save them—this gospel, this righteousness from God by faith in Jesus Christ." That is why you and I should ask all men and women to listen to the gospel.

The world has forgotten the fact of death. It has forgotten the fact of the coming judgment. "It is appointed unto men once to die, but after this the judgment" (Heb. 9:27). This is the thing that Dr. Thomas Chalmers discovered. He had forgotten two great matters: The smallness of life and the greatness of eternity. The moment he saw that, his whole life was changed, and he became a preacher in evangelistic circles. Death is not the end. Each one of us has to die, and after death we will stand in the presence of God. That is the message of the Bible from beginning to end. The question that you have to consider is this: How are you going to stand before God and give an account of your life? What will you say to God when he tells you that he gave you a soul, when he tells you that "the chief end of man is to glorify God and to enjoy him forever"? He will ask you "Did you do that? Did you live to glorify me? Did you live to enjoy me? Did you keep the Ten Commandments?" What will you say? "The soul that sinneth, it shall die," and the condemnation that is meted out by the Lord for failing to live to the glory of God and to keep his commandments is eternal banishment from his presence in the suffering of hell. All your righteousness will be as filthy rags in the sight of God. What can you do? You can do nothing. How shall you escape? There is only one way to avoid the wrath of God, and that is to believe in the Son of God "who was delivered for our offences, and was raised again for our justification" (Rom. 4:25). It is to believe that "The LORD hath laid on him the iniquity of us all" (Isa. 53:6). It is to believe that God "hath made him to be sin for us, who knew no sin; that we might be made the righteousness of God in him" (2 Cor. 5:21). It is to believe that the Son of God "his own self bare our sins in his own body on the tree, that we, being dead to sins, should live unto righteousness, by whose stripes ye were healed" (1 Pet. 2:24). "How shall we escape?" (2:3). This is why he calls it "so great salvation" (2:3). Here is the only message that can deliver a man from the judgment of God, from the misery and the terror of eternal punishment away from the presence of Almighty God. What a salvation! It reconciles us to God and delivers us from the awful possibility of spending eternity in a state of perdition and loss. It is clearly great if you consider what it saves us from.

But also, positively, consider what it saves you to, what it saves you for. "Wherefore in all things it behoved him to be made like unto his brethren, that he might be a merciful and faithful high priest in things pertaining to God, to make reconciliation for the sins of the people" (Heb. 2:17). These are some of the things that the gospel does for us. Our first need is forgiveness. We need to be reconciled to God. We are alienated from God and have rebelled against him. We are under his wrath and damnation. We are guilty and need to be forgiven. "How then can man be justified with God?" (Job 25:4). How can a man be right with God? How can we get rid of our sins? That is the question, and here is the answer. In Christ Jesus we are reconciled to God. "God was in Christ, reconciling the world unto himself, not imputing their trespasses unto them" (2 Cor. 5:19). "God sent not his son into the world to condemn the world; but that the world through him might be saved" (John 3:17). This is what he does. The Lamb of God has taken away the sins of the world. We are forgiven. We are reconciled to God. What a salvation! Nothing else in the world can give us that. You can have the knowledge of Oxford, Cambridge, St. Andrews University, Aberdeen, Edinburgh, and Glasgow, and it will never give you a knowledge of sins forgiven. But if you believe in Christ, you have it. You know that he died for you and for your sins. You are reconciled to God.

There is even more! If you believe on the Lord Jesus Christ as your sin-bearer, as the Lamb of God who takes away your sin, you are not only reconciled to God, you are adopted into his family. Notice how he puts it: "It became him, for whom are all things, and by whom are all things, in bringing many sons unto glory, to make the captain of their salvation perfect through sufferings" (Heb. 2:10). He goes on, "for both he that sanctifieth [that is, the Lord Jesus Christ] and they who are sanctified [that is, those who believe in him] are all of one" (Heb. 2:11). One what? One nature. One with him. " . . . for which cause he is not ashamed to call them brethren" (Heb. 2:11). You are not just forgiven and then left standing in the street. You are brought into the house, into the family, and become a brother of the Lord Jesus Christ. Jesus Christ says, "I will declare thy name unto my brethren, in the midst of the church will I sing praise unto thee. And again, I will put my trust in him. And again, Behold I and the children which God hath given me" (Heb. 2:12–13). We are not left outside in our rags. We are adopted into the family of God. We are sons of God, his children.

Then the author of Hebrews goes on,

> Forasmuch then as the children are partakers of flesh and blood, he also himself likewise took part of the same; that through death he might destroy him that had the power of death, that is, the devil; and deliver them who through fear of death were all their lifetime subject to bondage. For verily he took not on him the nature of angels; but he took on him the seed of Abraham. (Heb. 2:14–16)

Sins forgiven; reconciled unto God; adopted into the family of God and becoming a child of God. But we still have to live in this world, and we need strength.

> Wherefore in all things it behoved him to be made like unto his brethren, that he might be a merciful and faithful high priest in things pertaining to God, to make reconciliation for the sins of the people. For in that he himself hath suffered being tempted, he is able to succour them that are tempted. (Heb. 2:17–18)

When you are tempted you will be able to say:

> I need Thee every hour;
> Stay Thou nearby;
> Temptations lose their power
> When Thou art nigh.
>
> Annie S. Hawks, "I Need Thee Every Hour"

He is with you. He has been through it all—"in all points tempted like as we are, yet without sin" (Heb. 4:15). What a salvation!

Where does this lead us?

For unto the angels hath he not put in subjection the world to come, whereof we speak. But one in a certain place testified, saying, What is man, that thou art mindful of him? or the son of man that thou visitest him? Thou madest him a little lower than the angels; thou crownest him with glory and honour, and didst set him over the work of thy hands: Thou hast put all things in subjection under his feet. (Heb. 2:5–8)

God has not prepared the world to come for angels. For whom then? For us: "Are they [the angels] not all ministering spirits, sent forth to minister for them who shall be heirs of salvation?" (Heb. 1:14).

In this modern world there is nothing quite so wonderful as this "so great salvation" (2:3). What is comparable to the knowledge of sins forgiven? What is more wonderful than to be able to put your head on the pillow knowing that if you die during the night it doesn't matter, knowing that you have already passed from judgment to life and that you will go to heaven and wake up there as a child of God? Oh, how wonderful is the companionship of Christ. But there is something still more wonderful—the world to come. This world is a doomed world. It is a sinful world, and the New Testament does not offer to make it better. In fact it tells us that it will get worse and worse. But it does offer us "new heavens and a new earth, wherein dwelleth righteousness" (2 Pet. 3:13). It tells us that Christ, the Son of God, is coming back to this world to render judgment. The elements will melt with fervent heat, and all will be made new. Who will live in the new heavens and new earth? You and I if we are Christians—"For unto the angels hath he not put in subjection the world to come"—"Are they not all ministering spirits, sent forth to minister for them who shall be heirs of salvation?" (Heb. 1:14). "Heirs of salvation"—yes, we are that. "If children, then heirs; heirs of God, and joint-heirs with Christ" (Rom. 8:17). "For we know that the whole creation groaneth and travaileth in pain together until now, and not only they, but ourselves also, which have the first-fruits of the Spirit, even we ourselves groan within ourselves, waiting . . . the manifestation of the sons of God" (Rom. 8:22–23, 19). Perhaps an atomic bomb will destroy this world, but that does not trouble the Christian. His treasure is not in this world. His treasure is not his bank account or his profession. He lives for another world. He sets his heart upon the glory that is to come, "the world to come, whereof we speak" (Heb. 2:5). That is what is offered by this "so great salvation" (2:3). We are being prepared for a glory that is indescribable. Listen to our Lord: "Let not your heart be troubled: ye believe in God, believe also in me. In my Father's house are many mansions: if it were not so, I would have told you. I go to prepare a place for you. And if I go and prepare a place for you, I will come again, and receive you unto myself; that where I am, there ye may be also" (John 14:1–3). That is the world to come offered by this "so great salvation" (2:3). Do you believe it? Are you rejoicing in it?

Thirdly and finally, the greatness of this "great salvation" (2:3) is the greatness of the way in which it is being prepared for us. Everybody today is interested in drama. Many excuse not being in church on Sunday nights because they don't want to miss their favorite television shows. "Such great drama, it was glorious." The greatest drama of all time, the greatest drama in all eternity, is found in this Hebrews 2. "We see Jesus," Jesus of Nazareth, the carpenter, "who was made a little lower than the angels" (Heb. 2:9). Jesus looked like an ordinary man. He hadn't been to the schools. He wasn't a trained Pharisee. Who is he? "God . . . hath in these last days spoken unto us by his Son, whom he hath appointed heir of all things; by whom also he made the worlds; who being the brightness of his glory, and the express image of his person, and upholding all things by the word of his power . . . " (Heb. 1:1–3). Jesus was made a little lower than the angels, but he made the angels. That is what we are told in the first chapter of Hebrews. " . . . being made so much better than the angels, as he hath by inheritance obtained a more excellent name than they" (Heb. 1:4). Everything was made through him, and nothing was made without him. He upholds everything by the word of his power. Otherwise everything would collapse.

But that little babe lying in the manger at Bethlehem—who is he? None other than the Son of God veiled in flesh. "Hail the incarnate Deity," says the Charles Wesley hymn. " . . . who, being in the form of God, thought it not robbery to be equal with God: but made himself of no reputation, and took upon him the form of a servant, and was made in the likeness of men" (Phil. 2:6–7). The everlasting Son of God in all the glory of his perfectness became a helpless babe, a carpenter, a worker with his hands.

> Forasmuch then as the children are partakers of flesh and blood, he also himself likewise took part of the same; that through death he might destroy him that had the power of death, that is, the devil; and deliver them who through fear of death were all their lifetime subject to bondage. For verily he took not on him the nature of angels; but he took on him the seed of Abraham. (Heb. 2:14–16)

He did this for you and for me. He left the courts of heaven and came in the likeness of sinful men. Even more, he was tempted in all points just as we are. The Son of God humbled himself for us.

But it does not stop at that. "We see Jesus, who was made a little lower than the angels for the suffering of death, crowned with glory and honour; that he by the grace of God should taste death for every man" (Heb. 2:9). He is the Creator, the sustainer, the Lord of life, but he dies in shame and ignominy. Why did he do it? Why was he condemned to death? Had he sinned? No. Nobody could convict him of anything. Even the Devil could find nothing. Jesus was like a lamb led to the slaughter, silent. Why? So that you and I might be saved, so that you and I might escape the damnation of hell. He left the courts of heaven for no other purpose. "The Son of Man is come to seek and to save that which was lost" (Luke 19:10). "The Son of man came not to be ministered unto, but to minister, and to give his life a ransom for many" (Mark 10:45). That is why he came from the highest courts of heaven to the cross of deepest woe. He did it so that you and I might escape the eternal damnation of hell. We are rescued, redeemed, ransomed, delivered, and reconciled, being made children of God and heirs of the glory of the world to come.

He died on the cross, but thank God it didn't stop there. He rose again. "We see Jesus, who was made a little lower than the angels for the suffering of death, *crowned with glory and honour*" (Heb. 2:9). As the author of Hebrews puts it in the first chapter, "When he had by himself purged our sins, [he] sat down on the right hand of the Majesty on high" (Heb. 1:3), and he tells us later on in that first chapter that Jesus is waiting until his enemies are made his footstool, waiting until all the elect are gathered in, waiting until every soul for which he shed his precious blood has actually been brought into the kingdom of God. Furthermore, he will come again and destroy his enemies and set up his everlasting kingdom. Then all who believe in him will be with him. They will see him as he is, and they will be like him, and they will reign with him and judge the world with him, and they will enjoy eternal glory in his glorious presence.

This "great salvation" (2:3) was prepared for us. Jesus, "the brightness of [God's] glory, and the express image of his person," was "made a little lower than the angels" to go to the death of the cross and rose again, and he did it all without complaint (Heb. 1:3; 2:7). He did it in spite of the fact that we are his enemies, his critics, his deniers. He loves us in spite of all that. "The Son of God . . . loved me, and gave himself for me" (Gal. 2:20). "So great salvation" (2:3). In the words of Isaac Watts:

> Join all the glorious names
> Of wisdom, love, and power,
> That ever mortals knew,
> That angels ever bore:
> All are too mean to speak His worth,
> Too poor to set my Savior forth.

Or to quote another Charles Wesley hymn:

> O for a thousand tongues to sing
> My great Redeemer's praise,
> The glories of My God and King,
> The triumphs of His grace.

As another wonderful hymn says:

> Crown him with many crowns,
> The Lamb upon his throne.
> Hark! How the heavenly anthem drowns
> All music but its own.

> Awake, my soul, and sing,
> Of him who died for thee,

And crown him as thy matchless King
Through all eternity.

Do you crown him? Do you believe in him? Are you rejoicing in this "so great salvation" (2:3)? Are you praising the name of your Savior? Do you want the whole world to know him? Have you seen the greatness of the glory, the immensity and wonder of Christ's salvation? Look at him again. Look at him being born; look at him living and dying for you. Yield yourself to him.

May God open all our eyes by his Holy Spirit to see the greatness of this "so great salvation" (2:3). Amen.

5

The Purpose of His Coming

Therefore we ought to give the more earnest heed to the things which we have heard, lest at any time we should let them slip. For if the word spoken by angels was stedfast, and every transgression and disobedience received a just recompence of reward; How shall we escape, if we neglect so great salvation, which at the first began to be spoken by the Lord, and was confirmed to us by them that heard him; God also bearing them witness, both with signs and wonders, and with divers [various] miracles, and gifts of the Holy Ghost, according to his own will?

We have already considered what makes this "great salvation" great (2:3). The first reason the author of Hebrews gives is the source of the message. It is a message that comes from God the Father through the Son by the Holy Spirit. It is a message that has a unique sanction and special authority. His second solemn reason why this "great salvation" is great is that there is no escape if we neglect this message; it is a warning to us to "flee from the wrath to come" (Matt. 3:7). It is a message of judgment, the message found throughout the Bible that the righteous God, the Judge of the whole earth, will judge the world at the end. Neglect this, says the writer, and nothing remains for us but the certainty of terrible wrath and suffering and punishment.

Now we come to his third great reason, which he puts in these words: "How shall we escape, if we neglect so great salvation?" (2:3). The very greatness of the salvation that is offered should in itself be an inducement to us all to pay careful, earnest heed to it and never to neglect it. Hebrews 2:5 to the end of the chapter is a commentary on this theme of "so great salvation" (v. 3). The greatness of salvation is here opened up before us and displayed to our wondering gaze, and what a commentary and what a statement this is!

The author of Hebrews has been making a great claim for the Lord Jesus Christ. He has already claimed that Jesus Christ is altogether superior to the prophets—"God, who at sundry times and in divers [various] manners spake in time past unto the fathers by the prophets, Hath in these last days spoken unto us by his Son" (Heb. 1:1–2). Then in that first chapter he takes up the theme of the superiority of the Son to the angels; he says that while these angels are wonderful and mighty in their strength and power, they are not equal to the Son. He shows the preeminence and superiority of this Person, the Son of God, over all the great and holy angels.

But immediately he seems to suggest that this may raise a problem in the minds of some people and especially in the minds of these Hebrew Christians. "If," they would argue, "you say that Jesus of Nazareth is the only begotten Son of God, the brightness and express image of his person and so on, if he is altogether superior to the holy elect angels, how do you explain his lowly birth? How do you explain his apparent weakness? How do you explain the fact that he suffered and how do you explain the fact that he went to that cruel death on the cross and there in apparent utter weakness and defeat died? If he is superior to the angels, how do you explain all that?"

The author of Hebrews has to reconcile the life and death of Christ with the claim of his preeminence over the angels, and in doing so he explains to us the greatness of this wonderful salvation that is recorded in the New Testament.

Why did the Son of God ever come into this world? Why did he ever do what he did in this world? Why did he die upon that cross? These are very good questions, and we should be perfectly clear in our minds as to the answers. It is not enough simply to say that we believe vaguely that Jesus was the Son of God and that he came into this world. He came and he did what he did, he suffered and endured for one reason only, and that was to make possible this "great salvation" (2:3).

First I want to look at this in a general sense. This phrase, "so great salvation," has fascinated God's people from the very beginning (2:3). Approaching it is like approaching a magnificent structure full of treasures and wealth. You do not rush into such a building. Having heard something about it you approach it with a sense of wonder. You look at its exterior, and you are even amazed at the things you see on the outside. Then you enter into the porch, and you tarry there too. There are things to be seen even as you approach such a site that are worthy of your careful consideration. If it is like that with an earthly building or any earthly spectacle, it is infinitely more so when you come to look at and consider this "so great salvation" that God has told us about in his Word (2:3).

Let us consider first of all the greatness of salvation in terms of its purpose. What is the object of this "great salvation" (2:3)? The fifth verse of Hebrews 2 says, "For unto the angels hath he not put into subjection the world to come, whereof we speak." "What is this salvation you are talking about?" asks someone. "What is the message of your Christian gospel?" It tells us about the wonderful world to come. Some say this does not only mean something in the future. I am not disposed to argue with them. I think it means everything that has come in Christ, but I think it is mainly in the future, for "we see not yet all things put under him." There is a world to come, and this is the very essence of Christian salvation.

I fear sometimes that I have robbed myself for years, and many people are doing the same thing, of some of the most wonderful things of all about this gospel because we tend to think of it so much in terms of personal experience and of subjective states and conditions. But before the gospel comes to give us anything like that, it tells us that something is going to take place in the whole world. It refers to cosmic things before it mentions individual aspects. So once more I would invite you not to think only about yourself and your personal needs—thank God you can do that, we are entitled to do so, indeed he encourages us to do that, and he meets us at that point of need—but God forbid that we should ever narrow it down merely to that.

The world is as it is today because of sin, because of man's disobedience. Because of the fall of man the world is full of unhappiness and suffering. There is disease in it, death, fighting, discord, chaos. So the first thing we come to in the matter of this "great salvation" (2:3) is to realize that God has done something about this sin-wrecked world, and he is going to produce another world, a world to come. In this world we are experiencing the results of man's folly, the results of man's sin and disobedience. The problem, if one may so put it, confronting God was how to come into this world that he himself had made and that he pronounced good and that was perfect but that has been marred by sin. How could God restore the world to what he meant it to be and indeed make it even more wonderful?

That is what salvation is about. As we come into this deliverance we are lifted out of preoccupation with ourselves and our inward moods and states; at once we begin to look at ourselves as citizens of heaven belonging to eternity. God is going to produce a new world. We are told that God has a great plan, a great program. A world will come that is full of glory, full of wonder. It will be a world in which there will be no sin, no sorrow, and no suffering; there will be no illness or disease. There will be no quarreling and fighting. Even the animals that now are opposed to one another will lie down together. A little child will be able to lead animals that are normally violent, ravenous beasts.

That is the picture given to us in the Bible, in the Old Testament as well as in the New Testament. Prophets, through whom God spoke before Christ came into the world, wrote about this world. They saw something of the wonderful state of affairs that is going to come to pass. Our Lord himself in his teaching not infrequently dealt with this. He said that when he came back everything would be made new. He always talked about the kingdom he was going to establish and the wonderful things that will happen in that kingdom. Isaac and Abraham will sit down in this kingdom, and others will come and enjoy themselves in its wonderful glory.

We also find this referred to constantly in the New Testament epistles. Peter often preached about it. After the day of Pentecost in Jerusalem he told about "the times of refreshing" (Acts 3:19) that would come from the presence of the Lord and the ushering in of the kingdom itself in all its glory and wonder. The apostle Paul constantly looked forward to it. He told the Philippians that when Christ comes he will not only deliver us from sin in the matter of our spirit, but "our vile body" will be changed and "fashioned like unto his glorious body" (Phil. 3:21). We see this too in the book of Revelation. The City of God coming down out of heaven with all its splendor and wonder and glory—that is the imagery that is employed there to describe the world to come. The object of salvation is to produce and bring in that world where everything will be so different from the world as we now know it. Peter says there will be "new heavens and a new earth, wherein dwelleth righteousness" (2 Pet. 3:13), and he exhorts Christian people to look forward to it and to hasten its coming.

When that great day comes, when that new world is ushered in, one of the wonders will be that man will dominate it and control it. David, in the eighth Psalm, said,

> What is man, that thou art mindful of him? and the son of man, that thou visitest him? For thou hast made him a little lower than the angels, and hast crowned him with glory and honour. Thou madest him to have dominion over the works of thy hands; thou hast put all things under his feet. (Ps. 8:4–5)

That is a prophecy of that wonderful new and glorious world that is to come and in which man will be the lord of creation; he will sit in judgment over the world. Man will be thus exalted, and Jesus Christ came into this world in order to bring all that to pass.

That, I repeat, is the essential first statement of the Christian gospel. It is not primarily something that has just been designed to do certain things for you and me. It does do them, but before that and beyond it is this tremendous idea, this glorious vista: the Lord Jesus Christ came into this world to redeem and rescue this world, to deliver it from sin and all its effects, to make it perfect and glorious and to hand it back to God. That is the idea.

As we begin to look at this, we see that the author chooses his words very carefully when he talks about "so great salvation" (2:3). It is a cosmic scheme. In writing to the Ephesians, Paul says that it is God's purpose that all things in Christ should be united and reconciled everywhere, in heaven and on earth, and that Christ came into the world in order to establish such a kingdom (Eph. 1:10). He came in order to build and perfect it and eventually to complete and finish it. The City of God will be absolutely perfect and without a blemish.

The history of man started with paradise. Then sin came in and ruined it. But God brought restoration, regeneration, that the world might again be as it should be—"the world to come, whereof we speak" (Heb. 2:5). Read the book of Revelation, especially chapters 21 and 22, and you will begin to see what all this means.

Secondly, we will consider the subjects of salvation, and this is something for which we should thank God. Listen to the author of Hebrews again: "For unto the angels hath he not put in subjection the world to come, whereof we speak" (Heb. 2:5). If not the angels who then? Man. It would be wonderful if God made that perfect world that is to come for angels to enjoy, but he has done it for man, and that is why he brings in the eighth Psalm at this point. It is man who is going to enjoy that new world, and here the author of Hebrews tells us that man has been made a little lower than the angels. That means not so much that we are lower than the angels in ability and power and things like that, but rather that the angels are not subject to suffering or death, but mortal man, as the result of sin and the fall, is. We have been made lower than the angels for a little while. He later says of Jesus Christ, "We see Jesus, who was made a little lower than the angels" (Heb. 2:9). Again he means lower than the angels for a period of time.

This is the most wonderful thing of all. This "great salvation" (2:3), this feast of glory, this feast of the world to come, is being prepared for you and for me, for man. The psalmist under the influence of the Holy Spirit saw this prophetically, and it is not surprising that he cried out as he did so, saying, "What is man, that thou art mindful of him? and the son of man, that thou visitest him?" (Ps. 8:4). We have all defied God, we have sinned against him, we have debased ourselves and defiled God's image upon us. We have made ourselves in many respects lower than the beasts of the field. We have spat, as it were, into the face of God. We have brought upon ourselves suffering, pain, confusion, animosity, war, and all the horrors of life and death itself because of our disobedience and foolishness. But the amazing thing, says this man—what a great salvation this is!—is that "the world to come, whereof we speak" (Heb. 2:5) is being prepared for us—not for the holy angels who never left their first estate, not for those bright angelic spirits who do the bidding of God, but for us. As he said in the first chapter, describing the angels, "Are they not all ministering spirits, sent forth to minister for them who shall be heirs of salvation?" (Heb. 1:14) Who are these heirs? You and me—all who believe in Jesus Christ. The great, mighty, obedient angels are our servants. God uses them to bless us, but we are the people whom God has chosen for this signal honor of salvation, for this unimaginable event.

Does this sound like a fairy tale? If it does, you are not a Christian, you do not believe the gospel. The essence of the Christian gospel is that those who believe on the Lord Jesus Christ, though they may have been as vile as hell itself as the result of sin, though they may have disobeyed God and turned their backs upon him for years, though they may have been beasts and worse, if they believe on the Lord Jesus Christ and are in him, they are going to dwell with him in his glorious kingdom. They are going to walk upon the face of this earth when it has been renewed and renovated, when that burning fire will come that will dissolve the elements with a burning heat, when all sin and evil and dross will have been done away with and the whole world is perfect and righteous. They will walk in the light and the brightness of his face. They will be companions of the Son of God; they will see God and enjoy him. They will be ministered to by the holy angels that at this moment surround the throne of God and spend their time singing and crying, "Holy, holy, holy, is the LORD of hosts" (Isa. 6:3).

That is the Christian gospel. It is a message of man being given a glimpse of himself in the glorified state. If we belong to Christ, we will live in that indescribable glory and will spend eternity in his holy presence. Are you surprised that the author of Hebrews calls it "so great salvation" (2:3)?

Whose plan is this? Listen to Hebrews 1:10: "And, Thou, Lord, in the beginning hast laid the foundation of the earth; and the heavens are the works of thine hands." To whom does he refer? The answer is, of course, that it is none other than God himself. It is God's plan, and the writer tells us about God, "for whom are all things, and by whom are all things" (Heb. 2:10). There is almost something ridiculous about a little man like myself attempting to handle such infinities and immensities, for what I am feebly trying to tell you is that the great and almighty and glorious God himself has planned this glory for you and for me, this God "for whom are all things" (Heb. 2:10). Everything that exists is for him, and everything that exists is by him. He is almighty, the Absolute, the Eternal. He is self-existent. He created us. He dwelt in eternity self-sufficient in all his holiness. Yet he decided to make the world and to make us, but that is not the most wonderful thing. I can understand, in a sense, God's greatness and his power and his might and his creative ability. But the thing that staggers me is that you and I, pigmies as we are, in our blindness and ignorance, have defied such a Being who has given us birth and has given us all our faculties, that we rebelled against him and brought ruin upon ourselves, and yet though we have been so foolish and so guilty, he who could blast us and our world into nothingness in a flash has not done so. This great self-existent God who does not need us has nevertheless planned a way of salvation. "It became him, for whom are all things, and by whom are all things, in bringing many sons unto glory, to make the captain of their salvation perfect through sufferings." " . . . so great salvation" (Heb. 2:10, 3)! Its author is the holy God against whom we have sinned.

If you have never been amazed at the fact that this eternal, holy, absolute Being who is described in the tenth verse should ever have done anything about you and about this world in its sin and shame and violence, then again I am tempted to say you are not a Christian. What made him do it? The answer is found in the ninth verse: "But we see Jesus, who was made a little lower than the angels for the suffering of death, crowned with glory and honour; that he by the grace of God should taste death for every man" (Heb. 2:9). As Philip Dodderidge cried:

> Grace! 'tis a charming sound,
> Harmonious to the ear.

Were it not for the grace of God, you and I and our whole world and all its citizens who ever have been and ever will be would be consigned to perdition and hell and eternal punishment. Oh, the undeserved kindness of God! " . . . that he by the grace of God should taste death for every man" (Heb. 2:9). Grace is favor, kindness, mercy, and compassion to people who do not deserve it but who deserve the exact opposite, people who deserve wrath and punishment. But God deals with them in love and mercy and compassion because he is a God of grace. Charles Wesley contemplated these things:

> O for a thousand tongues to sing
> My great Redeemer's praise,
> The glories of my God and King,
> The triumphs of His grace.

Why did the Son of God come down to earth? He came to die for us, and this was the grace of God, this amazing love that saw us as we are and did not blast us but instead made a way of deliverance and salvation.

How has God done this? Through his only begotten Son: "For it became him, for whom are all things, and by whom are all things, in bringing many sons unto glory, to make the captain of their salvation perfect through sufferings" (Heb. 2:10). That is the essence of the plan of salvation. Jesus Christ is the captain, the author, the leader of our salvation. In other words, this holy God, "for whom are all things, and by whom are all things" (Heb. 2:10), unutterably holy and perfect, looked down upon the world that he had made and that sin had ruined, saw our shame, misery, mortality, suffering, death, and confusion, and said, "I must do something about it." So he sent his only Son. The Son became man and was made flesh, entering our condition so he could draw us out of it. He put on our nature, and we received his righteousness. He is "the firstborn among many brethren" (Rom. 8:29). "Behold I and the children which God hath given me" (Heb. 2:13). He calls us his brethren, and he is not ashamed to do so. He is the second Man, the last Adam, and he is preparing all this.

That is the way in which we should think of the purpose of the coming of the Son of God into this world. We do well to reflect on the

Lord Jesus Christ coming out of heaven and being born as a baby in Bethlehem and on everything he did and said and all that he endured. Why did he do all that? To start the new humanity, new citizens that will dwell in the world that is to come. That world will be glorious and wonderful, and only those who belong to him will dwell there. No others can be there. He has not stretched out his hand to angels but to the seed of Abraham, to you and me, and he himself will lead us into the realm of glory that we will share with him throughout the countless ages of eternity.

Do you understand the greatness of this salvation? Do you realize that it is true of you? Have you believed in Christ? Do you long for that kingdom of glory? Do you realize this is the whole purpose of salvation? This is what is taking place in history, and it will go on until the end. "Not yet," says the author of Hebrews, but it is coming. The resurrection of Jesus is the guarantee of it, and all who believe on him will rise with him and share with him in his glory and splendor. Consider this, take earnest heed, do not slip away from this, do not find yourself in hell when salvation is offered to you. Do not miss the glory that awaits the children of God; do not neglect it. Do not allow anything, however legitimate, to come between you and God. Do not give yourself rest until you know that you belong to Christ and that you are part of his plan and that you are waiting for glory. Believe on the Lord Jesus Christ, and the glory shall be yours. Amen.

6

His Death for Us

HEBREWS 2:8b–9b

For in that he put all in subjection under him, he left nothing that is not put under him. But now we see not yet all things put under him. But we see Jesus, who was made a little lower than the angels for the suffering of death, crowned with glory and honour; that he by the grace of God should taste death for every man.

People often ask, why do you listen to a consideration of that old gospel? In the first four verses of Hebrews 2 we are given the answer to that question, and it must be carefully considered. In fact we must avoid at all costs slipping away from it or neglecting it because of the authority with which it comes and because of the source of the message—none other than God himself. God the Father sent the Son and spoke through him and made known what he has done through the Son by the Holy Spirit through the church. We pay attention to authority, and there no greater authority than this. This is a message from God himself to our distracted world and to us as individuals in our weakness and shame and helplessness.

The second great reason he gave for considering this message was, "How shall we escape, if we neglect so great salvation?" (Heb. 2:3).

Whether we like it or not, we are all living in this world under judgment, and we will all have to give an account of what we have done with our souls in this life. This is the great message of Scripture from beginning to end. God has made man in such a way that he holds him responsible. Man is not an animal; man is not a machine. He was made in the image of God, and so he has great dignity and is a responsible being. God holds man responsible for the way he has lived in this world and what he has made of his life. How shall we escape, therefore, if we neglect the only way to be reconciled to God and to escape the awful consequences of sinning against him and misusing our life in this world?

The third great reason he gives for considering this gospel is the greatness of the gospel: "How shall we escape, if we neglect so great salvation?" (Heb. 2:3). To use a favorite word of the hymn-writer Isaac Watts, we should "survey" this great salvation, and it is not something to be surveyed in a hurried glance or glimpse. It is something to be looked at, to be gazed upon. No greater purpose is conceivable than the purpose of God for men and women in Jesus Christ, which is to raise them from the degradation and the downfall of sin to the glory that he is preparing for them. The gospel speaks of a world to come, a world out of which sin and evil will have been entirely banished. That will be a life of glory in the new heaven and the new earth, wherein dwells righteousness. According to this plan and purpose, all who are in Christ are going to reign in that world; they will share in glory with Jesus Christ. He is going to judge the world; he is going to be raised up to an amazing position of glory. That is God's plan; that is Christian salvation. Salvation is the forgiveness of sins in and through his Son who is appointed the captain, the author, the initiator, the originator of this great divine purpose.

Remember the tenth verse that says, "It became him, for whom are all things, and by whom are all things, in bringing many sons unto glory, to make the captain of their salvation perfect through sufferings" (Heb. 2:10). Everything that we find outlined here had to happen because it is the only thing that is consistent with the being and character of God. Some ask, why didn't God save man without sending his Son to the cross and its shame? The answer is, "It became him" (Heb. 2:10) to suffer for us. It is the only thing that is consistent with God as the moral governor of the universe; it is the only thing that does justice to God as one who is just and righteous and holy. He cannot look upon sin because he is of such a pure countenance. Jesus's death was the only way to save sinners and also do justice to the perfection of God. Man not only needs forgiveness of sin, he needs to keep the law completely. He needs someone who will enable him to conquer Satan. He needs a new nature. He needs a High Priest who can sympathize and understand and help him. He needs someone to present him to God at the end. All that is provided in Christ, and it would not have been provided unless God had chosen this way of the Son's incarnation and suffering and death upon the cross and burial and resurrection. What a perfect salvation this is; what a perfect Savior. This is the only thing that does justice to God's love.

Consider with me the greatness of this salvation as seen from the aspect of the greatness of the cost of this "so great salvation" (Heb. 2:3). We are all very interested in the price of things; it is one of the most common standards that we ever use. That may be an evidence of sin in us. Many of us only value a thing if it costs a lot. Often people do not know the intrinsic value and worth of something, but if they know it is worth such and such they begin to take a fresh interest in it. We tend to evaluate not according to something's worth but its price. Regarding salvation let us consider the price that has been paid. God purposed to take hold of certain people and lift them from this degradation of sin into eternal glory. But we do not really see the greatness and the wonder of it all unless we understand something of what it cost, the price that was paid in order to make it possible. This is dealt with in this amazing second chapter of Hebrews, and in a sense this is the theme of all of the epistles; in fact, it is the theme of the whole Bible. What is the meaning of some of those statements at the beginning of the Old Testament about Adam and Eve being clothed with the skins of animals? What was the difference between the offering of Cain and the offering of Abel? Why do men have temples, why did they offer sacrifices, why did they have tabernacles and all the regalia with respect to it, why is so much said about the different types of offerings, and why must the offerings be consecrated with blood? Go on to the prophecies in different forms and with different emphases, and you will find the same message. Go through the Old Testament, and you will find it is all pointing forward to something and to someone. It all points forward to Jesus Christ and to him crucified.

What is the New Testament all about? Why is so much space, relatively speaking, given to the facts connected with our Lord's death? Read the Acts of the Apostles, and notice the emphasis in the preaching of Peter and Paul and the others, and you will find in the forefront that the Christ must suffer and die and that Jesus is the Christ. There is no attempt to camouflage that. The view is not that his death on Calvary is something to be ashamed of, and therefore we must put forward his life and teaching and example. The Scriptures deliberately put the cross in the front, and as you read the New Testament epistles you will find that everywhere. It is the essential doctrine upon which everything turns and without which you cannot understand the argument of the gospel. It is the great theme of the Bible, but it is also the great theme of our hymnbooks. Some of the most comforting and blessed hymns point to this.

A true preaching of the gospel must always be centered upon Jesus Christ and him crucified. The author of Hebrews says we ought to give "earnest heed" (Heb. 2:1), not to the way in which we receive miraculous guidance or a kind of happiness that comes flooding into our life or healing in a physical sense, but primarily to the things that we have heard, to the gospel. Those people to whom this man refers were not preaching a philosophy, they were not teaching people how to be happy. They were heralds of the gospel; they went about talking about Jesus who claimed he was the Son of God and who was nailed to a tree, was buried, and rose again. That was the inference they drew and the doctrine they deduced. That was why Paul was determined at Corinth not to know anything among them save Jesus Christ and him crucified.

People who do not pay attention to that, people to whom that is not absolutely central and crucial and vital, have never really seen what this "great salvation" (Heb. 2:3) is. They do not understand it, and they know nothing of the painful cost it took to make that salvation possible. Whether we like it or not, the touchstone of our Christian profession is the cross. Here is the test by which we can test ourselves as to whether we are Christians or not: Is the death of Jesus Christ, the Son of God, upon the cross absolutely central and vital and essential to us? I want to suggest to you that if it is not, we had better examine our foundations again. I want to put it in this way to you: Is it possible that he paid the price and yet that is irrelevant to you? The greatness of the cost is the proof of the centrality of the cross. There was no other way of salvation for us. The cross, Jesus's death for us, is absolutely essential, and I say again that we are not really Christians unless the cross is vital and central to us, the foundation of our whole position.

Notice too that the New Testament bases many other arguments upon this. The great New Testament appeal for holiness in a sense is based upon it. The apostle Peter in writing his first epistle puts it this way: "Pass the time of your sojourning here in fear" (1 Pet. 1:17). This is written to Christian people: "Pass the time of our sojourning here in fear." Why? Because you must remember that "ye were not redeemed with corruptible things, as silver and gold, from your vain conversation received by tradition from your fathers; but with the precious blood of Christ, as of a lamb without blemish and without spot" (1 Pet. 1:18–19). When a man realizes the awful price that has been paid for his redemption he will want to be holy; the failure to be holy is due to our failure to understand the price that has been paid. That is the New Testament way of putting the argument. Jesus Christ gave himself for us, says Paul to Titus, not merely so that we might have our sins forgiven—he gave himself for us that he might separate unto himself "a peculiar people, zealous of good works" (Titus 2:14).

Many other arguments point in the same direction, and the great comforts and consolations that are so often given to us in the Scriptures are based entirely upon what our Lord endured and suffered while he was in this world. There are more than sufficient reasons to look at this great matter, and if you read some of the biographies of the saints who have gone before us, the driving motive of their lives has been the realization of the cost that was paid for our redemption. Consider the young man Count Zinzendorf, the leader of the Moravians who meant so much to John Wesley and others. The turning point in his life was when he looked at a great picture of the crucified Christ with its message, "I have done this for thee, what hast thou done for me?" That has been the thing that has made men and women forsake home and comfort and traverse the oceans and endure agony and suffering. They have thought about what he has done for them and for their redemption. The failure in the lives of most Christians is simply due to the fact that they have not realized this truth. I am simply reminding you of the facts that are so plainly put before us in the New Testament and indeed also in the Old Testament and of which we are given such an amazing reminder in this second chapter of the epistle to the Hebrews.

What is this price that has been paid, what is the cost of this great salvation? Let us consider Jesus and why he had to endure what he endured, the price of this great redemption. We must start with his coming into the world, his incarnation. We read in Hebrews 2 that both "he that sanctifieth and they that are sanctified are all of one" (Heb. 2:10), and "Forasmuch then as the children are partakers of flesh and blood, he also himself likewise took part of the same; that through death he might destroy him that had the power of death, that is, the devil" (Heb. 2:14). Have you ever contemplated that? Jesus Christ, the Son of God, came from the realms of glory. He is God of very God, coequal with the Father. Do you realize what coming to earth meant to him? Do you realize what it meant to him to start upon this path that was going to end with the cross and the grave? The apostle Paul gives us an insight into this by saying, "[He] made himself of no reputation," he who "thought it not robbery to be equal with God" (Phil. 2:6–7). He had the right of exalted Deity, but he did not hold on to that. He humbled himself and came to earth and took upon himself the form of a servant. "[He] was made," as the author of Hebrews puts it, for a little while "lower than the angels" (2:9). In other words, he chose to limit himself and to come within the limits of human flesh and so to be subject to suffering and mortality. God cannot die—in order to die he had to become man. We are trying to look at something that is quite inconceivable; our minds are overwhelmed with the very thought of it. But that is the essence of the New Testament message. That helpless baby lying in the manger is none other than the eternal Son of God. He has deliberately come down to this level within these limits, he is making himself subject to suffering and mortality and death, and he did it all so that you and I could be redeemed. If he had done nothing further the price paid would have been beyond measure and utterly incomprehensible, but the story doesn't end at that point.

Having come as a baby he now humbled himself further. He submitted himself to his parents and to their teaching. Can you imagine what that was like for the One who created the whole world? Can you conceive what it must have meant for the One who was with God and was God from all eternity, by whom all things consist, to share the life of ordinary people, doing manual work as a carpenter, perhaps knowing what it was to have insufficient food and so on? He knew what it was to be tired and weary, what it was to experience the frailty of the flesh. He to whom belonged the whole world and the cosmos was subject to such limitations. But this process of humbling and humiliation didn't stop there. He was also subject to temptation: "in that he himself hath suffered being tempted, he is able to succour them that are tempted" (Heb. 2:18). Scripture tells us that God tempts no man and cannot himself be tempted (James 1:13). But amazingly, Jesus Christ, very God of very God, so humbled himself that he became subject to temptation. We can read in the Gospels about his temptation in the wilderness, but that wasn't the only time he was tempted. What must it have cost him who is God above all the angels, the eternal Son of God, to now be subject to the attack of Satan. Read the Gospels and keep your eye on that, and remember as you do so that he subjected himself to all that so that you and I might have a faithful and merciful and sympathetic High Priest, so that we might know One who could redeem us and prepare us for the glory that yet awaits us.

The author of Hebrews also describes the "contradiction of sinners against himself" (Heb. 12:3). Think of the Lord of Glory, the Lord of Creation, suffering as he did at the hands of the Pharisees and scribes as they questioned him and tried to trap him in his talk, how they jeered at him and mocked him and laid their traps for him. Consider how they threw stones at him, how they detested him and sought how they might destroy him. Even his own chosen disciples did not understand him. His mother and his brothers at one time felt he was insane. Can you imagine what all this meant to this One who had come from the realms of glory and who is God himself? That is a part of the cost he has paid for our redemption. Then look at him standing by the grave of his friend Lazarus, and listen to him as he groans in his spirit. "Jesus wept" (John 11:35). I sometimes think those two words are the most tremendous words in the whole of Scripture. The only begotten from the bosom of the Father groaned, trembling in agony and weeping. This is not human weakness; it is suffering so that you and I might be redeemed and become heirs of glory. Look at him likewise weeping over Jerusalem and again groaning, but also come with me to a garden called Gethsemane just before the end of his life on earth, where a solitary figure is praying. Three of his chosen disciples had gone with him into the garden. He asked them to watch and pray while he went to fight a battle, and while they were asleep he sweat drops of blood, an expression of the agony through which he was passing. You know the agony that makes you sweat a cold sweat, but can you imagine a suffering that makes you sweat blood? What was happening to Jesus was not a fear of death; he was not shrinking from physical pain. He knew what was going to happen on the cross and that he would be made an offering for sin. He saw that coming, and he asked that it might be avoided. The anticipation of what was going to happen on the cross caused him to sweat great drops of blood.

If everybody realized that the Son of God sweat drops of blood for their salvation, there would be no need to appeal to anybody to decide for Christ, no need to bring pressure upon people, to tell stories and play upon their emotions. Realizing that he had to go through all that before we could be saved from the wrath of God would be enough. These things have happened, these things are history, these things have taken place. The night he was betrayed by Peter was part of his suffering. One of the most pathetic statements not only in the Bible but in the whole of literature is "The Lord turned, and looked upon Peter" at the moment of Peter's third denial (Luke 22:61). The Son of God had come from heaven in order to save Peter. He had endured so much so that Peter might be redeemed. Peter had been with Jesus and had seen the miracles. He had been with him on the Mount of Transfiguration; he had been with him in the garden. Peter had said he would follow Jesus everywhere whatever the rest might do, but at the crucial moment he denied him with oaths and curses. Can you imagine what that meant to Jesus? "The Lord turned, and looked upon Peter" (Luke 22:61).

The one whom he had come to save denied him; the one for whom he was going to die said he did not know him. That is part of the price he paid for us.

But go on with the story—the mocking and the jeering, the scourging of his holy back. The Creator of the world, the One in whom was no sin, stood as a felon, condemned, with a crown of thorns upon his holy head with all the accompanying agony of it all. But all this was but a prelude to his death on the cross. That death on the cross was no accident; it was the most deliberate thing he ever did. We are told elsewhere that he set his face steadfastly to go to Jerusalem. They tried to dissuade him, but he insisted on going. He said he could command twelve legions of angels to protect him, but he had come to die. We see Jesus "made a little lower than the angels"—why?—"for the suffering of death" (Heb. 2:9). Why did the Son of God come into this world? What is the meaning of the incarnation? The answer is he came to die; that was his goal. Read the Gospel of John and keep your eye on the expression "the hour"—"the hour cometh," "his hour was come," and so on. Everything leads to the cross, to his death. The phrase "the suffering of death" (2:9) is a significant phrase. What does it mean? First, it means the shame of it all. "Cursed is every one that hangeth [dies] on a tree" (Gal. 3:13). It was the death of a felon; it was the most shameful death that anybody could die. He was nailed upon the cross with all the shame and degradation attached to it. Oh, the ignominy of such a death, a felon's death. He suffered that. There is a physical aspect to this. He experienced and suffered a terrible thirst, and the agony of it is beyond description. But I want to emphasize that he tasted death or died for every one; he was "made a little lower than the angels for the suffering of death" (2:9).

Here we come to the climax of this matter. This means, if we may borrow the language of the apostle Paul in the fifth chapter of Second Corinthians, that he was indeed made "sin for us, who knew no sin" (2 Cor. 5:21). It means, if we use the language of Isaiah, that God has placed upon him "the iniquity of us all" (Isa. 53:6). He is innocent, he has kept the law, he has honored his earthly father and mother, he has never been disobedient. Yet God takes your disobedience and mine and your guilt and mine and puts it all on him. God makes him to be sin—not a sinner, but sin. So what this all really means is this: on that cross he was exposed to the full weight of God's holy wrath against sin. God, looking upon him there, sees all our sin, and all the holy wrath of the Almighty against sin was there poured upon Jesus Christ. That is what it all means and nothing less. He tasted death for every man, suffering death. None of us will have to die like that because the weight of it all came upon him. No one knows what it is to suffer death as the Son of God did. What it meant for him was this: he who was coequal and coeternal with God and in the bosom of the Father for all eternity, he who had never been separated from God, he whose supreme delight had forever been to have fellowship with God, came to a terrible moment when he could not see the face of God. He felt forsaken and cried out, "My God, my God, why hast thou forsaken me?" (Matt. 27:46). That was the thing he was speaking about back in the garden of Gethsemane, where he prayed in essence, "Is this the only way? If it be possible let this cup pass from me." He asked this three times. But that was the only way whereby man could be forgiven, and he submitted himself to it. "Nevertheless not as I will, but as thou wilt" (Matt. 26:39).

Our sin was put upon him, and he felt forsaken. Do you know what killed him? Crucifixion was a slow mode of death, and they were amazed to find he was dead already. But it wasn't only his being suspended on that tree that caused his death; it was the unspeakable agony of being forsaken by his Father that killed him. That broke his heart even in a literal sense. I agree with those who say on medical grounds that his heart had literally physically ruptured, and when the spear was put in, clots of blood and water formed. But his spiritual suffering was even more intense. The agony of losing the face of God, of being made a sacrifice for sin, the banishment, the wrath, the awfulness all came upon him and broke his heart, and he died. We can never measure that agony. He did all that so that you and I could be forgiven, so that you and I might be heirs of this "great salvation" and enter into his glory.

Then they took down his dead body and buried it in a grave. Just imagine—the eternal Son of God was buried in a grave, and a stone was placed over it, and he entered into the place he had mentioned to the dying thief as Paradise, among the dead. What a cost he has paid.

If that does not make us see the greatness of this "so great salvation" (Heb. 2:3), I don't know what can. The Word was made flesh. He, said John the Baptist, is the Lamb of God that takes away the sins of the whole world (John 1:36). Or listen to the amazing way in which Peter put it in his sermon in Jerusalem: "Ye denied the Holy One and the Just, and desired a murderer to be granted unto you" (Acts 3:14). He was telling them, "You preferred a murderer to the Son of God, and you killed the Prince of Life." We see the same thing in this chapter and in the twelfth chapter of Hebrews. We killed the author and finisher of our faith, the author of life, and that is the measure of his suffering and his agony for us. He humbled himself and "became obedient unto death, even the death of the cross" (Phil. 2:8).

It is not surprising that he commanded his disciples and followers just before he died to meet together from time to time to eat pieces of broken bread and to drink wine in remembrance of him. He wanted to make sure that the church would never forget what he had come to do and the price he has paid in order to accomplish our salvation. You are redeemed from "your vain conversation received by tradition from your fathers," not with gold or silver or such metals, but "with the precious blood of Christ, as of a lamb without blemish and without spot" (1 Pet. 1:18–19). "God so loved the world, that he gave" (John 3:16). Do you know that the Son of God endured and suffered all this so that you might become a son of God and an heir of the glory that awaits all who believe in him? Do you realize that he so loved you that he suffered all that in your stead so that your sins might be forgiven and so that you might have a new birth and a new life, so that he might lead you by the hand through this world and at the end present you faultless before the presence of God with exceeding joy? Amen.

7

Two Views, Two Destinies

HEBREWS 2:8b–9a

For in that he put all in subjection under him, he left nothing
that is not put under him. But now we see not yet all things
put under him. But we see Jesus, who was made a little lower
than the angels for the suffering of death, crowned with
glory and honour.

It is the custom of most of us to use the beginning of a new year as
an occasion to take stock of our life and to consider the situation in
which we find ourselves. As we do so, we must consider two obvious
questions. Why are things as they are? What are our prospects? That
is, are there any hopes of improvement, what are things going to be
like in the future? The successful businessman does that. He looks at
his books, whether the business is solvent or insolvent, and so on. We
all look at our life as it is and as it presently confronts us. Then having
done that, we look to the future.

I would suggest there are only two possible views with regard to
those two questions. There is the non-Christian view of life, and there
is the Christian view of life. The non-Christian views divide themselves
up politically, socially, economically, nationally, racially, and in all sorts
of other ways, but they are all non-Christian. Take the view that you

get, for instance, in the popular press and in books and on the radio, the attitude of the average man who is not a Christian. I think that most serious thinkers today agree that things are not as they would like them to be. They cannot look on the present condition of life in this world and feel satisfied and happy. I do not know that anybody in the world feels satisfied with things as they are. We read in the newspapers about people who seem to have more money than sense and who go from one party to another. I cannot imagine, if they think about it at all, that they can really be happy about life as it is in this world. Men and women are full of foreboding; they no longer say glibly that God's in his heaven and all's right with the world. All who are looking at life seriously are profoundly concerned about the present state of the individual and of society and of the whole world.

There are many causes for this—the world situation, the uncertainty of life, all we have endured and suffered in the modern age, and so on. Interestingly, many of the serious thinkers and philosophers who are not Christian at all are some of the most pessimistic. *The Decline of the West* by Oswald Spengler was a desperate book written long before the Second World War, and the author seemed to see it coming. Men like this who are watching the trend of history and are watching things happening among the nations find the situation alarming. Also some of the greatest pessimists are some of the leading scientists; men who know the most about atomic power are some of the most frightened. They say that unless something happens to bring man to his senses he will probably blow up his world and destroy his own civilization. Listen too to what sociologists have to say about increasing crime, lawlessness, murders, and robberies. People are seriously disturbed about the selfishness that is being shown, the drinking, the gambling, the immorality and vice. Life in general is not as ethical and moral and safe as it was fifty years ago. Others are gravely concerned about possible world famine, about the overwhelming increase in the population of the world year by year and the gradual diminishing of food supplies. The whole world may be heading up to some terrible calamity. The non-Christian thinker who seriously looks at life today is filled with a profound feeling of disquiet and dissatisfaction; he is concerned and alarmed and full of foreboding.

Now at this point he seems to be a little contradictory because he still tries to cheer himself up, refusing to be a complete pessimist. He finds it impossible to admit to himself that the situation is really hopeless and that nothing can be done. So we see attempted optimism at the beginning of every year. The newspapers try frantically to give us some relief and to give us something to hold on to. But year by year they are becoming less and less confident. You cannot go on saying things are bound to become better if they do not become better. It is useless to say today that man is evolving and is becoming better and better when we have had the most horrible wars that civilization has ever known. These facts are staring men in the face; the things to which we have pinned our faith for many years have failed. Many were confident that political action, education, and people getting to know one another would solve the problem and banish war, and then we would all be happy together and enjoy an unparalleled period of prosperity.

But that has not come about. As they look to the future and search for a word of hope and comfort, they have nothing to say except what they have been saying for so long, but they are doubtful and hesitant as they say it. Take, for example, a typical modern thinker who has been given great prominence in the press and on the radio, Bertram Russell and his book *New Hope for a Changing World*. What new hope does he offer us? He says all our troubles are due to the fact that we do not think, that we do not employ reason. Here is a man who knows his philosophy, and his remedy is to exhort us to think. That is what Aristotle and Plato and Socrates told mankind three or four centuries before Jesus Christ was ever born into this world. For a hundred years we have been telling ourselves that all we have to do is to think, to fix our problems with reason. We just have to provide primary and secondary schools and multiply our universities, and once we are told what to do we will all rise up and do it. But we have had two world wars, and we have an appalling increase in immorality and vice, and all this despite man's greater opportunity of thinking than ever before. Never have we been trained so much for thinking as in recent years, but I say there is no new hope in that. Surely man ought to have learned at least that to tell men to think is not enough. Every medical doctor knows that to take alcohol in excess is bad and to persistently indulge in it is to ruin the constitution. Does that now mean that every doctor is a teetotaler? No. The trouble is not a lack of reasoning or thought. What is the trouble? Here we come to the failure of every non-Christian view.

The non-Christian view always lets us down because it fails to realize three fundamental things that are true of man and his life in this world. The first is that man's troubles are entirely in himself and in his own nature. It is not what happens to us, it is what we are. We must not blame God for wars, for example. Who produced them, where do they come from? James 4:1 answers that question: "Even [out] of your lusts that war in your members." Man produces wars. But, says someone, the average man does not want war; politicians, malign persons, are manipulating the forces of state. My dear friends, they are only humans like ourselves. When Hitler invaded Poland, some said, "What a foul thing to do. Why did he do it?" The leader of the German nation looked at other nations and said, "I want them; therefore I will take them." Many were horrified, but they did not seem to be horrified when they did exactly the same thing in their personal life with regard to another man's wife. There is no difference. What men do collectively is as bad as what one person does individually, and men and nations do these things because their natures are evil and perverted and foul. Non-Christian thinkers fail to realize why they can never expect things to be better—fallen human nature. "This is the condemnation," says Christ, "that light is come into the world, and men loved darkness rather than light, because their deeds were evil" (John 3:19). It is not enough to tell men what is right—we have to get them to love it. But they prefer the darkness. They love the darkness rather than the light. To think otherwise is the first fallacy.

The second fallacy in the non-Christian view is that it forgets about the Devil. But surely, says someone, you don't believe in the Devil in this enlightened age. I look at the world, and I ask what is manipulating men and women and making them behave as they do, and the Bible has given us the answer all along—the Devil. The Bible described him as "the god of this world" (2 Cor. 4:4), "the prince of the power of the air, the spirit that now worketh in the children of disobedience" (Eph. 2:2). Whether you know it or not, this world in which you and I live is inhabited by unseen, foul, malign, devilish spirits who have but one interest and one objective, and that is to make this world a shambles and to wreck humanity and the whole course of history. Evil forces and powers are working upon us and are intent upon our destruction. The non-Christian view ridicules that, and that is why it simply cannot understand why the world is as it is in spite of educational endeavors. Its believers asks why things go wrong, and they do not realize it is because of this evil potentate.

The third thing they always forget is that man, because of his sin and his rebellion against God, is under the wrath of God, and because he is under the wrath of God, "There is no peace, saith the LORD, unto the wicked" (Isa. 48:22). They forget that entirely, but it is stated in the Bible from beginning to end. Man, says the Bible, as long as he is not in right relationship to God will never be happy. He can acquire great knowledge, he can amass the wealth of the universe, he can do a thousand and one things, but he will never be happy if he is not right with God. He is under the wrath of God; he incurs the displeasure of God; he is under the curse of God.

The man who is not a Christian does not realize that his world is in a state of misery and that there is no hope whatsoever with regard to the future apart from God. He does not understand the cause of his trouble. He is wrong in his explanation, and therefore he is wrong in his cure. He has been attempting the same solution for many years, and he is hopelessly wrong. That is the non-Christian view.

The Christian view is stated perfectly in this text, and the author starts in the same way as the other view does. As they look at the present world the Christian and the non-Christian views are very much the same. The Christian says, "But now we see not yet all things put under him" (2:8). Let us be quite clear about this. The Christian says exactly the same thing about the world at this moment as the non-Christian. The only difference is that the Christian says it much more clearly than the unbeliever. He has a deeper analysis. The Christian view of life is much more realistic and honest and courageous than the non-Christian one. The non-Christian, though he admits the facts, also tries to cover them up. He tries to say that things are getting better, that there is some good in him after all. The Christian does not do that; he looks at things exactly as they are. He strips off the camou-flage; he is honest. I have said before that if I had no other reason for believing the Bible to be the Word of God, this would be enough for me. This is the only Book that knows all about me and tells me the stark, absolute truth about myself. Newspapers flatter us, other people flatter us, but here is a Book that tells us the entire truth about our-selves. This is what it tells us: the human heart is desperately wicked and deceitful (Jer. 17:9); within us there is an abundance of evil things (Matt. 12:34); we are creatures who have ugly, foul, jealous, envious thoughts; we hate one another by nature. That is what the Bible tells us about ourselves, and it is the truth. It also tells us worse things are coming. It does not paint rosy pictures of a gradual improvement in the world; it tells us there will be wars and rumors of wars to the end (Matt 24:6) and that the world at the end will be very much the same as it was before the flood. At that time they were eating and drinking until the flood came and carried them away; even so, says Christ, shall it be at the end (Matt 24:38).

So the first statement of the gospel is, "Now we see not yet all things put under him" (2:8). Things are bad, says the Christian and the non-Christian. Far from being the lord of creation and ruling over all things, man is in a state of turmoil and is being manipulated by a power outside himself; he is ruled rather than ruling. "Now we see not yet all things put under him." Some might object, "What a pessimistic view of the present world. Is that all you have to say?" No, it is not. Our text continues with a word that you will find nowhere else in the world. It is a little word with three letters: "Now we see not yet all things put under him. But . . . " (2:8–9). The whole gospel of Christ is in that one word "but." That is the essential difference between the non-Christian and the Christian views. The non-Christian has no "but" that he can put in his picture of the present because he knows he has nothing to offer except what he has offered in the past; he has no hope. But the Christian starts with this word "but": "But we see Jesus . . . crowned with glory and honour" (2:9). Some people say Christianity is just a doctrine that tells us we must all love one another and if we do that well, we will banish wars. That all sounds so nice and theoretical, but that is not the Christian message.

If I look at the world as it is tonight I am profoundly pessimistic; it is dark, and there is no hope of any improvement. What does the gospel invite us to do? It asks us to stop looking at that black picture and look at Jesus. "We see Jesus . . . crowned with glory and honour" (v. 9). What does that mean? What do I see as I look at him? It asks me to look at the baby who was born in Bethlehem and placed in a manger. It asks me to look at the one whom nobody could convict of sin. It asks me to look at this amazing Person who could work miracles, this One who said about himself, "I and my Father are one" (John 10:30), the One who asked people to leave their jobs and follow him and they did so, the One who to the amazement of everybody after three years of preaching was arrested in apparent weakness. His hands and his feet were nailed to a cross, and he died, and his body was buried in a grave. They rolled a stone over it, and everybody said that was the end of all that he said about himself. But they went to the grave on the morning of the third day and looked for him, but he was not there; the grave was empty. He had risen, and he began to show himself to his disciples, and he met with them and told them certain things about himself. Then he ascended into heaven and sent down the Holy Spirit upon his followers, and they began to preach, and the Christian church came into being.

These are the facts; that is the story. That is not human philosophy or human teaching and ideas. It tells us from the outset that the Son of God has entered this world. He has come into it to deal with the problems and the failures and the subjection of man to the Devil and his cohorts. It tells us he lived a perfect life, he gave perfect obedience to God's law, he failed in nothing. It tells us that single-handedly he met temptation and conquered Satan completely. Furthermore, it tells us that he conquered death and the grave, and the resurrection proves he is the Son of God. God has highly exalted him and crowned him with glory and honor. Jesus, who was in this world, is at this very moment seated at the right hand of God with a crown upon his head. Here is One who took human nature upon himself, and as man he has solved the problems that mankind had failed to solve. The result is that God has now handed over to Jesus Christ this world and its future because of what Jesus did when he was here on earth. Because of his life, death, and resurrection, God has handed this world over to him. It is in his keeping, and he can do as he likes with it.

This is the message of the New Testament gospel, and it affects you and me in this world. This world and its kingdoms belong to Satan, the Devil. But Christ is establishing a new kingdom, a new people. He is calling men and women out of this present evil world and putting them into his new kingdom. He has been doing that for nearly two thousand years. He sent the Holy Spirit so that might happen, and as the centuries have passed, men and women one by one have seen this truth and have entered into his kingdom. He is continuing this until the day comes when he will have completed and perfected it, and then he will come back into this world. He will then destroy Satan and all evil and everything that is sinful, he will introduce a new age, there will be a new heaven and a new earth, and not only will he dwell and reign in it, but all who belong to him will share it with him, the many sons that he is bringing to glory. The world to come that he is preparing for them will be shared by them; they will enjoy living in it, and it will be their eternal destiny. And as Paul tells us in the fifteenth chapter of 1 Corinthians, after redeeming and rescuing the world, and having perfected it, he will then hand it back to his Father.

That is the Christian gospel. It is not just a message to you and me to be morally good or a little bit better than we were last year. It includes that, but it is so much more—it is about Jesus and his program. We are dealing with facts. He has been in this world, and he has done the things we have mentioned. He came, and he will come again. People did not believe he was coming the first time. They laughed at the prophets who predicted it, and when he came they crucified him because they did not believe him. Men say they do not believe in the second coming, but they are putting themselves in the same category as those who disbelieved in his first coming. He is coming again, and he is going to destroy everything that is opposed to God in this world. But those who belong to him will be in glory with him. What does that mean to us personally? Christ first of all reconciles us to God. The world is as it is because man is under the wrath of God, and until the wrath and curse of God are removed from us, we cannot be happy. Christ has become the curse for us by dying on the cross. The wrath of

God was put upon him as he bore our sins, and now God forgives us. Man needs a new nature; his life is as it is because of his evil nature, and man cannot live in a state of glory as long as he has his old nature. He needs a new one, and Christ gives it to him, he has identified himself with human nature in order to identify human nature with himself, and he is "the firstborn among many brethren" (Rom. 8:29), the leader in a new humanity. We cannot overcome Satan and evil and hell, but he has overcome them all. He conquered Satan, and he enables all who look to him to do exactly and precisely the same thing, and when he comes back, he will finally cast Satan into the lake of fire where he will remain for all eternity (Rev. 20:10).

The author of Hebrews could face life as it was in the world in those days, which was as bad as it is now, and he could say, "we see not yet all things put under him. But we see Jesus . . . crowned with glory and honour" (2:8–9). If you read this epistle all the way through you will see that these people were being helped. The author tells us to keep our eyes on Jesus, the author and finisher of our faith, and that is what makes the difference. Do you see Jesus like that as you look at your world? Do you see Jesus crowned with glory and honor? Do you believe all that I have been saying about him? Do you see that the world is condemned and lost and without any hope apart from him? Do you see that the world is sinful and evil and that you yourself have an evil and sinful nature that you can never get rid of on your own? Do you know that you are a sinner? Do you hate the world and therefore do you hate the evil nature that is in you? Do you long to be delivered from it? Do you see everything as hopeless apart from Jesus? Do you see him as the One who has conquered it all and who says that all who look to him and trust him and give themselves to him can likewise be enabled to conquer and be delivered and are going to share with him the glory that is coming? Do you see Jesus like that?

What determines your eternal fate and future and mine is whether we see Jesus crowned with glory and honor or whether we do not, and what makes this such an urgent matter is that whether we like it or not a day is coming when we will all see Jesus, and what we are told about those who haven't seen him as he is now, crowned with glory and honor, is:

> And the kings of the earth, and the great men, and the rich men, and the chief captains, and the mighty men, and every bondman, and every free man, hid themselves in the dens and in the rocks of the mountains; and said to the mountains and rocks, Fall on us, and hide us from the face of him that sitteth on the throne, and from the wrath of the Lamb: for the great day of his wrath is come; and who shall be able to stand? (Rev. 6:15–17)

I preach this gospel because I know the day is certainly coming when every eye will see him; no one can escape it. That is the message of the gospel. We will all see him, and the most terrible thing in the world is the wrath of the One who was slain as a Lamb for the sins of mankind.

Do you see Jesus now crowned with glory and honor? Do you really believe that Jesus of Nazareth was the only begotten Son of God and that he took on himself human nature and was born out of the womb of Mary as a helpless baby and put in a manger? Do you believe he suffered all the things you read of in the Gospels for you and your sin? Do you see that if he had not done that you would have gone on to an eternity of misery and suffering, but that if you believe on him he is going to share his glory with you in the kingdom that he will bring in? Do you see him now crowned with glory and honor until all his enemies will be made his footstool when he comes back again and receives you unto himself and takes you with him to enjoy the indescribable bliss, the surpassing glory that is going to come in the age that lies ahead? I urge you about this because what I will have to answer for at the day of judgment is, did you tell them about Jesus, not, did you give them good advice, did you entertain them, did you make them feel a little happier? What the Lord will ask me on that day is, did you tell them about Jesus, the One who came from heaven to earth in order to deliver and rescue them, did you show them Jesus crowned with glory and honor, risen from the dead, now seated at the Father's right hand? May we all be found to be faithful in him. Amen.

8

Not Ashamed of His Brethren

But we see Jesus, who was made a little lower than the angels for the suffering of death, crowned with glory and honour; that he by the grace of God should taste death for every man.

There is no such teaching in the Bible as the universal fatherhood of God and the universal brotherhood of man. We are all flesh and blood, but the whole point of Christianity is that there is a division, a separation of sheep and goats, those on the right hand and those on the left, those who are Christians and those who are not Christians, those who are being sanctified and those who are not being sanctified.

There is nothing more important than this. Perhaps you are in trouble, and you have looked everywhere but cannot find the answers you need. You say, "I wonder whether the Christian church has anything to say to me." You must understand this: Jesus Christ is the answer, and he is your brother, and he has everything you need. But is he this to you?

The Scriptures are very clear about this; they always make a distinction. Our Lord himself did this. On one occasion he was teaching a great crowd surrounding him, and they told him in essence, "You must stop; your mother and your brothers are outside waiting for you"

(Matt. 12:47). This was his answer: "Behold my mother and my brethren! For whosoever shall do the will of my Father which is in heaven, the same is my brother, and sister, and mother" (Matt. 12:49–50). Jesus doesn't call everybody his brothers, but "whosoever shall do the will of my Father which is in heaven" (Matt. 12:50). The greatest fallacy of all is to tell the world as it is, unchanged, that Christ is its brother; that is not true.

Listen to our Lord again in that apocalyptic statement in Matthew 25:40 when he talks about the final judgment as the King upon his throne (Jesus himself) separates the nations on the right hand and on the left, the sheep and the goats: "And the King shall answer and say unto them, Verily I say unto you, Inasmuch as ye have done it unto one of the least of these my brethren, ye have done it unto me." There it is again. These particular people were his brethren, and anything done for them is done for him. Or consider the words he used after his resurrection: "Jesus saith unto her [to Mary who was holding on to him in her amazement at his resurrection], Touch me not; for I am not yet ascended to my Father: but go to my brethren [the disciples, his followers], and say unto them, I ascend unto my Father, and your Father; and to my God, and your God" (John 20:17). Notice again this same conjunction of terms. He says, "go to my brethren" and "I ascend to my Father, and your Father; and to my God, and your God" (John 20:17). He is one with us, and yet he is eternally different.

So the message of the gospel applies only to these special people whom he calls "brethren." You have to be in a certain position before he calls you his brother; certain things must be true of you before you can apply and appropriate to yourself these wonderful promises. The answer to our every need, the solution to all our problems, is to realize that he is not ashamed to call us his brothers and sisters as we believe in him (Heb. 2:11).

Let us see what is involved in this statement that he is not ashamed to call us brothers and sisters. What had to happen to him to make this true? Here again we stand before the greatest of all mysteries. The apostle Paul looks at it in writing to Timothy and says, "Great is the mystery of godliness: God was manifest in the flesh" (1 Tim. 3:16). Who is this one?

God . . . hath in the last days spoken unto us by his Son, whom he hath appointed heir of all things, by whom also he made the worlds; who being the brightness of his glory, and the express image of his person, and upholding all things by the word of his power, when he had by himself purged our sins, sat down on the right hand of the Majesty on high. (Heb. 1:1–3)

That is who he is. He is "the Word [that] was with God . . . without him was not any thing made that was made" (John 1:1, 3). He is God, the eternal Son.

Language is inadequate to describe this. Our minds and imaginations boggle, and we cannot grasp it all. But this is the truth, and we must believe it. This glorious person—the perfect expression of the Godhead, God's only begotten Son—in order to come into the position of not being ashamed to call us brothers and sisters has submitted himself to certain things. What are they? This is a theme of the whole Bible, and we could discuss it for hours. I am merely reminding you of the essentials of the faith. That personal problem of yours, if only you realized that this Person is interested in you, will be solved. I am not trying to deal with your specific personal problem. I am just pointing you to Jesus. He has every answer. You must be right about him and your relationship with him.

So what has happened? Jesus Christ is "the brightness of [God's] glory, and the express image of his person, and upholding all things by the word of his power" (Heb. 1:3). Everything has been made through him. He is the appointed heir of everything, the whole cosmos. But he became "a little lower than the angels" (2:9). Remember, he had made the angels. The angels are created beings, created spirits. There was a time when there were no angels. But there was never a time when there was not a Son. The angels were made by him, and he is infinitely superior to them and greater than them. "But we see Jesus, who was made a little lower than the angels" (2:9). Have you ever heard anything as thrilling as that? He who made them was made a little lower than them. It was all done in order that he might not be ashamed to call you his brothers and sisters. He "thought it not robbery to be equal with God" (Phil. 2:6). He was in the form of God, and he was equal with God, coequal with the Father and the Holy Spirit. But he made himself of no reputation. He laid aside something of that glory and submitted to being made a little lower than the angels.

But he went even lower than that, for the angels are greater than we are. They are "ministering spirits" (Heb. 1:14), but they have great ability and great power. He not only made himself a little lower than the angels; he made himself like us. He was made "in the likeness of sinful flesh" (Rom. 8:3). "Forasmuch then as the children are partakers of flesh and blood, he also himself likewise took part of the same" (Heb. 2:14). If you and I only realized what this means, what it meant to him and why he did it all and what results his love brings, we would be filled with such rejoicing that we could not contain it, and all our difficulties and problems would be dealt with.

"The Word was made flesh, and dwelt among us" (John 1:14). He submitted himself to living life as a man in this world. He was still God, but the marvel of it all is that while he was on earth he lived as if he were but a man. That is why he had to pray—he even prayed all night at times. He did not use the attributes of deity that were still his. He did not empty himself of his Godhead—that would be impossible. But he "made himself of no reputation" (Phil. 2:7). That means that he lived as if he were only a man and so was subject to our infirmities—weariness and tiredness and so on.

Not only that, he came under the law. The apostle Paul puts it like this: "God sent forth his Son, made of a woman, made under the law" (Gal. 4:4). He who is the Lawgiver, he who is from everlasting to everlasting, was subject to the law, accepting all the demands of the law as a man. Furthermore, he took upon him "the form of a servant" (Phil. 2:7). He was not born in a king's palace but in a stable. He knew extreme poverty, hunger, and thirst. He shared life with ordinary men and women. This blessed person submitted himself to all that.

Before he could become one who was not ashamed to call us brothers and sisters, all this had to happen to him. He had to become man in order to be able to say this, and that is the whole argument of Hebrews 2. Before he could regard us as brothers and sisters he had to become flesh and blood, and he has done so. Why are we so blind to all this? Why do we meditate so little about it? Why are we so obsessed with ourselves and our subjective moods and states and conditions?

The world needs to know that "God was manifest in the flesh" (1 Tim. 3:16).

What did this lead him to do? It led him to share our life. He knows what it is to be a helpless baby. He knows what it is to be a little boy. He knows what it is to be taught the law of the Old Testament. He knows what it is to work with his hands as a man, as a carpenter. He knows what it is to share the ordinary life of men and women. Gossip and jealousies and rivalries and envies were all happening round and about him. He was in the same world that you and I are in, and he knows all about it! He shared it to the uttermost; he truly became a man.

Not only that, but as we are told later in Hebrews 2, he became subject to temptation. Do you realize what that must have meant to him? "God cannot be tempted with evil, neither tempteth he any man" (James 1:13). He is above it all and outside it all. Yet here is the Second Person in the blessed Trinity who has become a man and made flesh and is made subject to temptation. At one time he was tempted for forty days and forty nights in the wilderness as the Devil personally tempted him and attacked him. "Wherefore in all things it behoved him to be made like unto his brethren, that he might be a merciful and faithful high priest in things pertaining to God, to make reconciliation for the sins of the people. For in that he himself hath suffered being tempted, he is able to succour them that are tempted" (Heb. 2:17–18). This happened to him because he is not ashamed to call us brothers and sisters. He took all this upon himself voluntarily in order that he might help us, that he might be a faithful high priest for us, that he might help his brethren. He submitted to temptation, to the bombardment of hell and all its evil in the person of the Devil himself, for us.

He knew what it was to suffer. "For it became him, for whom are all things, and by whom are all things, in bringing many sons unto glory, to make the captain of their salvation perfect through sufferings" (2:10). There is no suffering that you and I can ever know that he has not known before us. Indeed he went even further, identifying himself with our sin. When he asked John the Baptist to baptize him. John said, "I have need to be baptized of thee, and comest thou to me?" Jesus answered, "Thus it becometh us to fulfill all righteousness" (Matt.

3:14–15). Why was he baptized? He was putting himself alongside his brethren. He came from heaven in order to help them, and he identified himself with them. He was standing with them as if he were a sinner. He was putting himself in their position and taking on the burden. But it did not end even there. "But we see Jesus, who was made a little lower than the angels for the suffering of death, crowned with glory and honour; that he by the grace of God should taste death for every man" (2:9). This is the meaning of it all; this is why he came. He came from heaven so that he might taste death for his brethren. He did it all in order that he might go through the sufferings of death for those whom he is not ashamed to call his brothers and sisters.

He did all that for us. He did it all that we might be sanctified, set apart for him. "Both he that sanctifieth and they who are [being] sanctified are all of one" (Heb. 2:11). Vessels were sanctified in the temple; the Holy Mount on which God gave the law to Moses is called the Holy Mount because it was set apart for that object. The meaning of the word "sanctified," except in certain cases where the context makes a different meaning clear—is to be set apart for God, being put into a new relationship with God. It means separation from all that is evil and common and being dedicated, offered, put into the service of God.

Our Lord, "the brightness of [God's] glory, and the express image of his person" (Heb. 1:3), suffered death and then rose again and returned to heaven. Why? That you and I might be sanctified. This includes the whole of salvation—justification, sanctification, glorification. It means the whole process of taking us, sinful sons of men, and separating us unto God, making us his people. Jesus made himself a little lower than the angels and is not ashamed to call us his brothers and sisters. He came that he might, first of all, take away everything that stands between us and God. We are unhappy, we are miserable, we lack blessings because we do not know God and cannot pray to him. We need to be reconciled to God, and Jesus came to take away the sin that separates us from God. That is why Jesus suffered death; that is why he went to the cross; that is why he tasted death for us who believe in him, his own people, his "brethren."

Having done that, he makes us children of God. He is not ashamed to call us his brothers and sisters, and that means that we are in a like status and position to his own. He is the Son of God, and he makes us sons of God. He is not ashamed to call us his brothers and sisters, which means that we are the children of God in Jesus Christ, that along with him we are heirs of the glory that is coming.

We read in the second verse of the first chapter of Hebrews, "[God] hath in these last days spoken unto us by his Son, whom he hath appointed heir of all things," and we see in Hebrews 2 that "he is not ashamed to call [us] brethren" (2:11). Do you grasp what this means? It is a good thing to be on good terms with one who is an heir, is it not? Why? Because he will share all that he inherits with you. But here is one who is not ashamed to call us brethren and is the heir of all things! Do you feel poor and empty and weak and forlorn, that you have nothing and that you are nobody? Here is my answer to you: If you are a Christian, if you are in this process of being sanctified, the Lord Jesus Christ is not ashamed to call you his brother or sister, and he is the heir of all things. "All things are yours." Why? Because "ye are Christ's; and Christ is God's" (1 Cor. 3:21, 23).

All this means that he is very concerned about us. He says, "I will declare thy [the Father's] name unto my brethren, in the midst of the church will I sing praise unto thee. And again, I will put my trust in him. And again, Behold I and the children which God hath given me" (Heb. 2:12–13). He says to the angels in essence, "These are my brethren. They belong to me; they are my special people." We are the special object of his concern. We never need to feel lonely, forsaken, or forlorn. He has gone through all I have been trying to describe to you in order to become one who says that you are his brother or sister. He is not ashamed to be called our brother, to call us brothers and sisters.

Think too of his sympathy for us. "Wherefore in all things it behoved him to be made like unto his brethren, that he might be a merciful and faithful high priest in things pertaining to God, to make reconciliation for the sins of the people. For in that he himself hath suffered being tempted, he is able to succour them that are tempted" (Heb. 2:17–18). You might say, "He could have no idea of what I am going through. I have been so attacked by the Devil that I wonder whether I am a child of God or not." My dear friend, he knows all about it. Whatever has happened to you doesn't compare with what happened to him. He experienced sin at its worst. He saw the malignity, the bitterness, and the hatred of mankind steeped in sin; he knows all about it.

> In every pang that rends the heart
> The Man of Sorrows had a part;
> He sympathizes with our grief,
> And to the sufferer sends relief.

Michael Bruce, "Where High the Heavenly Temple Stands," 1764

Or you might say, "He was here on earth once, but now he is back in glory and knows nothing about life on earth." He does!

> Our fellow sufferer yet retains
> A fellow feeling of our pains;
> And still remembers in the skies
> His tears, his agonies and cries.

"Where High the Heavenly Temple Stands"

"We have not an high priest which cannot be touched with the feeling of our infirmities" (Heb. 4:15). He was tempted in all points just as we are, yet was without sin. Praise God for the sympathy of the blessed Savior for his brothers and sisters. But consider also the help he is able to give us: "grace to help in time of need" (Heb. 4:16). He has been through it all. He knows what it all means. The marks of the wounds are still in his hands and feet. He is the Lamb slain still, though he is also the Lion of the tribe of Judah.

Remember too that he has conquered the Devil. The author of Hebrews reminds us of this. Jesus has already destroyed "him that had the power of death, that is, the devil" (Heb. 2:14). He defeated the Devil when he tempted Jesus, and he defeated the Devil by dying and rising again. Now he is at the right hand of God, ever living to make intercession for us. He is there at this moment doing exactly that, and he will always be there. The writer argues this at great length in Hebrews 7. He says in summary: "This is the wonderful thing about Jesus. Those earthly priests that you want to go back to will die, and you will have to have a new man. They come and go, but this One is everlasting and has an eternal priesthood." "Wherefore he is able also to save them to the uttermost that come unto God by him, seeing he ever liveth to make intercession for them" (Heb. 7:25).The glory of it all is this: Jesus Christ is seated at the right hand of God's glory at this very minute, and he points at you and at me and as our great intercessor and advocate tells his Father and the hosts of heaven, "These are my brethren." "He ever liveth to make intercession for them" (Heb. 7:25). He presents your feeble prayers and mine to the Father, adding the incense of his own glory to them.

Furthermore he will go on doing this until you and I have been taken through all of our trials and troubles, even death itself, and he will "present [us] faultless before the presence of [God's] glory with exceeding joy" (Jude 24). What a comfort! "He is not ashamed to call them brethren" (Heb. 2:11). How different he is from us, and thank God he is. Thank God that Jesus is the eternal Son of God! God and those of us whom he is sanctifying are "all of one" and yet so different. Many of us tend to become ashamed of our relatives and our families. A man begins to succeed in life, but he is ashamed of his poor father or his mother's accent and pretends he doesn't belong to them. But God's Son, "by whom also he made the worlds . . . whom he hath appointed heir of all things . . . who being the brightness of his glory, and the express image of his person, and upholding all things by the word of his power, when he had by himself purged our sins, sat down on the right hand of the Majesty on high" (Heb. 1:2–3). He is seated at God's right hand, and the hosts of heaven are praising him, singing the praises of the Father and of the Son. And he still is not ashamed to call us his brothers and sisters. Realize this truth; act on it. Go into his presence and through him to God by the Spirit. Enter into your inheritance, "looking unto Jesus the author and finisher of our faith" (Heb. 12:2), and so become filled with joy, being more than conquerors. Amen.

9

So Great Salvation

HEBREWS 2:10

> For it became him, for whom are all things, and by whom
> are all things, in bringing many sons unto glory, to make the
> captain of their salvation perfect through sufferings.

I want to call your attention once more to the theme found in the first
four verses of the second chapter of Hebrews. In this study we will
particularly expound the phrase "so great salvation" (Heb. 2:3). "How
shall we escape," says the writer, "if we neglect so great salvation?"
(Heb. 2:3). The author is warning the Hebrew Christians not to allow
themselves to slip away from the gospel through neglect or indolence.
He exhorts them to give it their earnest heed, and he gives reasons for
saying that. He reminds them that the gospel is from God. He tells us
that we should pay earnest heed to it because it is from God the Father
through the Son by the Holy Spirit and attested by the Spirit.

He tells us that we must listen to the gospel and be careful not to
neglect it because of the terrible possible consequences of so doing.
"How shall we escape, if we neglect . . . " (Heb. 2:3). Fortunately he
does not stop on that negative note but goes on to urge us to listen to
it because it is "so great salvation" (Heb. 2:3). So before we begin to
concentrate on our personal needs, which are legitimate, we must look

at this great gospel that is unfolded to us in the New Testament. If you are looking for happiness, the best way is to look at the gospel first—not to be seeking happiness itself, but to seek the truth of the gospel. If you have what the gospel offers, you will have happiness, and almost every other blessing that you can think of will come with it.

The greatness of the gospel consists in its purpose, which is able to take hold of men and women like ourselves and transform us and the world in which we live. The program of God in salvation is not simply to do certain things to us while we are here in this world and to deliver us from hell. The whole universe will be purged of sin; the whole cosmos will be redeemed. There is a world to come that is indescribable in its glory and wonder, and the astounding thing of which this man reminds us is that you and I are the heirs of this great prospect and wonderful salvation. God is leading us into this, and our minds almost stagger as we reflect on it. Everything in this world that is evil and sinful will be purged, and there will be "new heavens and a new earth, wherein dwelleth righteousness" (2 Pet. 3:13), and in that world men and women will reign with Christ.

The Lord of the universe, the Creator of everything, is doing all this for us because of his grace, not because we deserve it (we know we do not). He does it entirely because of his heart of compassion and mercy, and he is doing it all through and by means of his own Son, the Lord Jesus Christ. Jesus is the captain of our salvation, or, if you prefer it, the author of our salvation. He is the One to whom God has committed this program. So the whole purpose of the coming of the Son of God into this world, the whole meaning and explanation of the advent, is to work out this program of rescuing sinful people and turning them into sons of God. It is they who will share glory with God and will reign in the renovated universe. What a program, what a prospect, what a great salvation this is!

A question occurs to some at this point. The claim that is made here is that Jesus of Nazareth is none other than the only begotten Son of God, superior altogether not only to Moses and the prophets, but also to the angels who kept their first estate, the elect angels themselves. He is the Son; that cannot be said of any of the angels. The question is: How can we reconcile the Jesus we see depicted here (Jesus as a man, lower than the angels) and the exalted Son of God? Or to put it another way, if God wanted to save mankind and the world, why did he do it in this particular manner? Could not an almighty God, who is also a God of love, have saved and delivered mankind without doing it in this particular way?

Or we could put it like this: Why did the Son of God have to come to earth so this program could be carried out? Why was it necessary that the eternal Son should be born as a helpless baby in Bethlehem? Why should the Son of God, in order to carry out this program, be humiliated as he was? "But we see Jesus, who was made a little lower than the angels for the suffering of death, crowned with glory and honour; that he by the grace of God should taste death for every man" (Heb. 2:9). Why did the Son of God have to enter into the limitations of humanity? Why did he have to become a little lower than the angels? Why did he have to suffer temptation and the contradiction of sinners against himself? Why did he ever have to suffer at all? And supremely, why did he have to go to that cruel, ignominious, painful death upon the cross on Calvary? Why the incarnation, why that life, why that death, why did all that have to happen? Perhaps that problem confronted those Hebrew Christians in an acute form because of their ideas of the Messiah, but it also troubles a large number of people today.

In a sense I feel that this second chapter of the epistle to the Hebrews is an extended answer to these questions. These people were stumbling: If you make this exalted claim for Jesus, then why did he have to become a man? We will in a sense be dealing again with the theme of "so great salvation" (Heb. 2:3). In answering the question of why the incarnation, why the suffering, why the death on the cross, we will be given another glimpse of that theme.

The answer to these questions can be found in a phrase in the tenth verse: "For it became him, for whom are all things, and by whom are all things, in bringing many sons unto glory, to make the captain of their salvation perfect through sufferings" (Heb. 2:10). The "him" referred to is none other than God himself. It became God, if you like, from whom are all things and by whom are all things, in doing this, in carrying out this plan, to make the author, the leader, the captain of our salvation perfect through suffering. This phrase "it became him" is a vital one. Here is what it means: This was worthy of God, or this was consistent with God, or this was congruous with God's character and nature as God. That is the key to the solution, the key to the answer to the question that was in the minds of these Hebrew Christians and possibly in the minds of many others.

This answer is the key to nearly all the questions man has ever asked about Christian salvation. It is the key that is always given by the Bible itself as the solution to all our ultimate problems and difficulties and questionings. If you want to understand the Christian faith, if you want to resolve the many problems that come to the natural mind, the one thing you must do is to start with the being and character of God himself. Because we fail to do that, many of us are oftentimes in difficulty. There are many questions concerning Christian salvation. Why are some saved and some not? Why are some elected and some not? How do we reconcile eternal punishment with the character of God? These are the questions people ask, but most of their difficulties are due to the fact that they invariably start at the wrong end. They take up these questions as if they were problems of philosophy, as if they were human problems, human questions. Instead of starting with the problem, start with the being of God. Contemplate him as best you can in the light of the Scriptures. Try to understand something of his being, his glory, and his personality, and put your question in that context. Remember we are not dealing with human problems; they are problems of understanding God's ways. When I realize that I am trying to understand the ways of such a Being, I immediately begin to do what was said of Moses at the burning bush and what was repeated to Joshua on another occasion—I take my shoes off because I begin to realize that the ground on which I am standing is holy ground (see Ex. 3:1–5; Josh. 5:15). If we approach these questions with reverence and godly fear, half our difficulties vanish. Our very attitude is sometimes our greatest difficulty. So the answer of the author of Hebrews is: "it became him" (Heb. 2:10). He takes us immediately to the character of God.

But he helps us by dividing that statement into its component parts. What does he mean by saying "It became [God]" (2:10) to do things like this? For one thing it means that the fact that God has done it in this way must mean that it is right in and of itself. I start with that quite deliberately because it is my way of saying that as I try to study the Word of God more and more and to live in it and dwell upon it, I come increasingly to the conclusion that perhaps the best definition of faith in the last analysis is to express it like this: Faith means that I am content not to understand certain things, and I am content with what has been revealed to me. Man by nature rebels against God and wants to understand everything. He says, "Why does God do this? If God is God, why does he allow and permit that?" The very way in which people put that question shows that their whole attitude toward God is wrong, and as long as they are in that attitude they will never understand anything. Whether we like it or not, the ultimate sin is pride of intellect. Paul does not hesitate to tell the Corinthians in his first letter to them that the gospel of Jesus Christ and God's way of salvation are what they are and take the form that they take in order to humble man's pride of intellect and in order that the wise of this world may be made foolish.

That means there are certain questions that you and I should not even ask. Not only must we not ask them in the wrong way, we should not ask them at all. While in this life and world we are not going to understand everything about God, and I promise you that as long as you live there will be things in God's wisdom and God's providence that you simply will not understand. If you and I could understand the whole of God's way we would be equal to God, but we are not. God has revealed certain things to us that, thank God, are enough, and faith is content with what has been revealed. As we face certain questions, the Bible exhorts us to take our stand by the side of Abraham and say, "Shall not the Judge of all the earth do right?" (Gen. 18:25). He cannot do anything else, and if God in his sovereign wisdom and will has decreed that this is the way of salvation, I say that you and I must say, "It is enough. Though I do not understand it fully, I humble myself before it. I bow my knees and thank God for it, knowing that whatever God does is right, whether I understand it or not."

That is the first explanation of the phrase, "It became him" (2:10). But we can go further. We can say with reverence that if there had been any other way whereby the sinful sons of men could become the sons and daughters of God and the heirs of future glory, if there was another way whereby God could take hold of us and turn us into his children without the incarnation and the suffering and the death of his Son, God would have used another way. Do you think it is conceivable that this almighty person of whom we read in the Bible would have allowed his only begotten, beloved Son to come into this world, to endure the indignity of being misunderstood by men and being spat upon by them, that God would have ever allowed his Son to sweat blood in the garden of Gethsemane and still more go to that cruel cross if there was another way? There was no other way.

But we can go even further, and this brings us to some positive exposition. The Scripture takes us further. "For it became him, for whom are all things, and by whom are all things, in bringing many sons unto glory, to make the captain of their salvation perfect through sufferings" (2:10). That was the only way that was compatible with the character of God. We must be careful here to avoid the danger, as we think of God, of isolating certain aspects or certain attributes of his character and being instead of looking at the whole. We are all guilty of that at times. When we are considering these great and mighty questions, we sometimes talk about the love of God and nothing else. We wonder how the love of God can be reconciled with other things; hence our troubles. But the way of salvation that is outlined in the New Testament is a way of salvation that shows us every aspect of God, his nature and character and being, and it is for that reason called "so great salvation" (Heb. 2:3). Salvation shows us something of the full-orbed and complete character of God.

I will try to show you this in terms of this second chapter of Hebrews, for it is all there. The first thing it does is this. The way of salvation in Jesus Christ shows us the character of God as the supreme governor of the universe. "For it became him," said the writer, "for whom are all things, and by whom are all things. . . . " (2:10). God is not only maker and Creator and sustainer of everything that is, he is the supreme governor of the universe in every respect. Everything is balanced, as it were, by him; nothing happens apart from him. He keeps it all going. God is to be obeyed and worshiped and glorified. The whole meaning and purpose of creation is to manifest the glory of God, and that is especially the great purpose of mankind, "Man's chief end" as the Westminster Catechism puts it, "is to glorify God, and to enjoy him forever." The heavens declare his glory; everything is meant to glorify God, the great governor of the cosmos.

That means that God is to be obeyed utterly and absolutely and that everything and all are to live for him, to minister to his glory, and anything that detracts from that must be denounced and reprobated. Sin disobeys God and his government and thus strikes at the core of glorifying and understanding God. The Devil said to Adam and Eve in the garden: "Hath God said?" or "Who is God to say this to you?" (Gen. 3:1). Man accepted that suggestion and has repeated it. We have all done it. Why does God allow this, why did God do that? That dishonors God and therefore must be denounced, and a way of salvation that does not denounce sin is unworthy of God.

To put it in another way, when God comes to save men, he must assert himself as the great governor of the universe, and that means exposing and denouncing sin and getting rid of it. The way of salvation revealed in the New Testament, the way of the cross, does that. Nothing reveals sin in all its utter horror as much as the life and death of the Lord Jesus Christ. Would you like to know what sin is? Then compare yourself with Jesus Christ. He not only preached, he practiced. He not only preached the Sermon on the Mount, he lived it. There was never a stain or blemish in him. Look at him and then look at yourself, and you will see your sin.

But look especially at the cross. Sin is so terrible, so awful, so profound that the cross was necessary in order to deal with it. God, by working out his plan of salvation in the way that he has, asserts his moral governance of the universe and his supremacy over all by exposing that which sets itself up against him and then getting rid of it. "It became him" (2:10). It would not have been God's way of salvation if sin had not been denounced and exposed and punished. Of course we do not think of it like that, do we? The way of salvation that you and I would have thought of would have been like this: God in his love said, "Everything is all right. I forgive you." But what would we know about sin if that was the way of salvation? How would we know the real character of sin, how would we know about this thing that has come to the world through Satan and his hosts and made such havoc of life? We would be ignorant of it. The way of salvation is consistent with God's character.

This way of salvation is consistent not only with the greatness of God but also with his justice and his righteousness. This is also propounded by Paul in the third chapter in the epistle to the Romans: How can God be just and at the same time the justifier of the ungodly person who believes in Christ? You cannot begin to understand this problem until you face that question. God is not only love—God is just, holy, unchanging. According to Paul, the great problem for God himself was how to forgive man and yet be just. Of course, there was only one way to do it, and that was for God to send his Son into the world to suffer death on the cross. God has given his law, and his law is the expression of God's being and character, and it must be honored. His justice and righteousness insist upon it. God has said he will punish sin, and having spoken, God does not go back on his word, he must carry it out; otherwise he is no longer just and righteous and holy. Beyond that, light and darkness cannot be mixed, and that which is sinful and unholy cannot dwell with the holy. God's holy nature demands this.

So there is the question, and I say once more that a forgiveness of sins that is inconsistent with the justice and righteousness and holiness of God is not worthy of God. But the salvation that is outlined in the New Testament shows us God's law and order, God's penalty exacted, the punishment of sin. And yet, because that punishment was levied upon another who was sinless and pure and holy, you and I can be forgiven. In this way God is just and the justifier of the ungodly who believe on the Lord Jesus Christ.

This great salvation proves to us and manifests to us the greatness of God. It establishes the law of God. As Paul puts it at the end of Romans 3, "Do we then make void the law through faith? God forbid: yea, we establish the law" (Rom. 3:31). Anything that does not establish the law is not worthy of God because it is his law.

Furthermore, this wonderful, "so great salvation" (Heb. 2:3) shows us the perfection of everything that God does. When God came to redeem and save man, because he is God, he had a plan as big as himself.

He did not merely want to forgive us. God's purpose was not only that we should be restored to the condition in which he made us at the beginning when he placed Adam in the garden of Eden, but that we should become his full-grown children. But before you and I can become children of God in an intimate relationship with him and before we can enter the glory that he is preparing for us and become lords of the universe, reigning even over the angels, certain things must be done. They are mentioned in Hebrews 2. The first is: God's law must be kept and must be honored. God has given his law to man, and he has said that unless man keeps that law he will not be accepted by God. Unless you and I somehow keep God's law and honor it, we are condemned.

The next thing that is necessary is that Satan, our adversary and enemy, must be conquered, the one who, because of evil, stands between us and God. He is ever tempting and attacking us, and he must be dealt with.

The next thing that is necessary is that our failure to keep God's law must somehow be dealt with fully. We need to be reconciled to God; our debt to God's law needs to be paid and settled. Along with this, death must be conquered, this sting with its open jaws that swallows up mankind. How can we escape death and eternal separation from God?

We are unworthy to come into his presence; we need a high priest to represent us, someone to plead on our behalf. Also before we can become children of God, we need One who can impart a new nature to us. We have no confidence in the presence of God until we know we have been reconciled to him, and before we can have that confidence, we must know that God is our Father and we are his children. But how can we do that? I know by nature I am an enemy of God; my nature is unworthy, and it has to be purified. How can I know God as Father and become his child?

I also need someone to help me face life and its temptations, someone who can sympathize with me, someone who can succour me in my need and helplessness. Indeed I need someone who can keep and hold me in his powerful hand and ultimately present me faultless in the presence of God in heaven. Those are the needs of mankind. Why was it necessary for Christ to become a man? Why was it necessary for him to be made a little lower than the angels? Why was he tempted? Why did he suffer as he did, why did he go to the cross? Couldn't God save man without this happening? I need all the things mentioned above, and Christ, by coming and by dying and by enduring all that he did, has accomplished all that. He became a man, and as man he fulfilled the law for me. Christian salvation means that God, as Paul puts it in the third chapter of Romans (we find it throughout the Scriptures as well), puts to my account Christ's righteousness. Christ has kept the law, and God says to us in summary, "I put you in Christ, and I put his righteousness on you, and therefore you are covered by it." To quote the hymn-writer Augustus Toplady:

> The terrors of Law and of God,
> With me can have nothing to do;
> My Saviour's obedience and blood
> Hide all my transgression from view.
>
> "A Debtor to Mercy Alone"

Jesus Christ died for our sins, and God has imputed his righteousness to us. Christ has kept God's law. The way of salvation would not be consistent with God's character if his law were not honored. Christ had to become man and share our life of humanity in order to redeem us. That is why he was, to quote Paul's letter to the Galatians, "made of a woman, made under the law, to redeem them that were under the law" (Gal. 4:4–5).

He has also met Satan for us and conquered him. Every time Satan came and tempted him, Jesus Christ defeated him and routed him. We know someone who can conquer Satan for us and enables us to conquer him. The Son could not have done that unless he had become man. Our debt must be paid, and on the cross Jesus paid it. He has borne the punishment for your sins and mine. Our debt has been canceled, the law has been honored, and we have been reconciled to God. Our failure to keep the law is the debt that we owe to God. We are debtors to the holy law, and we cannot pay what we owe, but Christ has paid it for us. If he had not come as man he could not have died, and you and I would still be in debt.

He has also conquered death. He burst asunder the bands of death and rose triumphant over the grave. Death could not hold him; he has gone through it and has emerged victorious on the other side. We know One who represents us before God, our great High Priest. He has entered into the heavens, and there he intercedes on our behalf. By his Holy Spirit he has made us children of God. "As many as received him, to them gave he power [authority] to become the sons of God" (John 1:12). We have been born of his Spirit, becoming partakers of his divine nature (2 Pet.1:4). He has taught us to say, "Abba Father" (Rom. 8:15). God is no longer a distant God. In Christ he becomes our Father, and while we are still here on earth he helps us face life. He has been tempted as we are, and "in that he himself hath suffered being tempted, he is able to succour them that are tempted" (Heb. 2:18). That is the very thing we need! He understands us because he has been here. He could not have sympathized with us unless he had become a man, but having come and having been tempted in all points, he is able to sympathize and to bear with our frailties and our ignorance. He is so mighty that when we surrender to him he can hold us in his powerful hand, lead us, and make us strong—in fact more than conquerors. The weakling who kept falling into a particular sin and could never conquer it has been made more than a conqueror by Jesus Christ and can laugh at temptation as he is strengthened by Christ.

Furthermore "he ever liveth to make intercession for [us]," and because he exists forever, "he is able to save them to the uttermost that come unto God by him" (Heb. 7:25). He is not One who is with us today and then leaves us. He is eternal, and he is "the same yesterday, and to day and for ever" (Heb. 13:8). He will take us through the remainder of the journey and at the end "present [us] faultless before the presence of his glory with exceeding joy" (Jude 24). What a Savior—what a salvation! This is indeed "so great salvation" (Heb. 2:3). It is not simply winking at my sin, not simply saying, "In my love I will forgive you whether you believe or not." God by his grace has chosen to qualify us as children of his Son, and he is going to lead us on to future glory. This "so great salvation" (Heb. 2:3) could only be carried out by his Son coming to earth as he did and living and dying for us and rising again.

This "so great salvation" (Heb. 2:3) not only shows the greatness of God, not only the justice of God, not only the perfection of God's plan and God's ways, but supremely it shows the love of God. Until we believe in all that Jesus has done for us, our idea of the love of God is a flabby sentiment that is not worthy of the name love. Herein is love, in this was manifested the love of God: God sent his only begotten Son into this world of sin and shame, and he endured all that we have discussed so that you and I might live, so that you and I might be forgiven. The real measure of the love of God is the distance from the eternity of glory to the depth of Calvary, and until you have measured it like that, don't talk about the love of God—you do not know anything about it. This "so great salvation" (Heb. 2:3) reveals, I say, the whole character of God because it is God's way of salvation. He sent his Son to die for us so we could be saved.

Hallelujah, what a Savior! Do you know him? Have you seen him like this? He came and did all that for you. Look to him, believe on him, surrender to him, give yourself to him, live by him, live for him, trust yourself entirely to him. Amen.

10

The Brethren

HEBREWS 2:11

For both he that sanctifieth and they who are sanctified are all of one: for which cause he is not ashamed to call them brethren.

This great epistle to the Hebrews, one of the longest epistles in the New Testament, is an epistle of comfort. It was written because certain conditions had arisen among the Hebrew Christians. They were in trouble, unhappy, and perplexed. There were many reasons for that. They were being persecuted, misunderstood, maligned, threatened—even with death itself. Not only that, some of them had a certain sense of disappointment within them. They had believed the gospel; they had heard preaching concerning the Lord Jesus Christ and his victory, and especially his triumphant final coming. But their life was hard. They said, "We prayed to God, but look what is happening to us. Is there any value in prayer?" The years passed, Jesus did not return, and it looked to them at times as if the main result of their believing the Christian faith was trouble coming upon them. And this trouble came from the Jews, their own countrymen, people among whom they had been born and bred. Because of all this the author wrote this letter to them to comfort and encourage them.

The interesting thing one notices at once about this epistle is that though it is a comparatively long epistle, and though on the surface the author has quite a variety of problems to deal with, he really has only one thing to say, he has only one message. He touches upon particular applications, but, unlike what we are so tempted to do, he does not take up their problems one by one and give a detailed answer. Indeed the New Testament itself never does that. The New Testament always, as in this great epistle, points immediately to the one solution of every problem—the preeminence of our Lord and Savior Jesus Christ—and that is the great theme here.

These people are in trouble, and they are in this condition for one reason only, he says, and that is their failure to realize the truth concerning our Lord and Savior Jesus Christ. So he sets out the truth concerning him. He does this in chapter after chapter beginning in the very first two verses: "God, who at sundry times and in divers [various] manners spake in time past unto the fathers by the prophets, hath in these last days spoken unto us by his Son" (Heb. 1:1–2). He throws down the gauntlet immediately, without any introduction. He shows them the cause of all their troubles. He is going to hold before them the Lord Jesus Christ. If only they could see him as he is and know the truth about him and know their relationship to him, all their other problems would no longer have power over them. They would find themselves back at the very center of this glorious faith, rejoicing in it and overcoming all their difficulties and trials.

That, then, is his method. He goes on to show the superiority of our Lord over the angels, over Moses, over Aaron, over everybody. That is the one great theme running through this long epistle from the very beginning to the very end. This man's whole thesis is that only one thing matters in life, and that is that we have faith in the Lord Jesus Christ.

This is, in fact, the teaching of the New Testament everywhere. This is what differentiates the gospel from all the various teachings that are offered to men and women to help them over this and that problem or difficulty. The glory of the gospel is that it brings us back to the one thing that matters—the Lord Jesus Christ and his preeminence. In this verse we are considering now (2:11), this great theme is put to us in a very wonderful, very beautiful, and very tender manner. Many people are in trouble or perplexity or have major problems and urgent burdens. The answer given to them is this: "for which cause he [the Lord Jesus Christ] is not ashamed to call them brethren."

That is the answer to every problem, every perplexity. Jesus is not ashamed to call us his brothers and sisters. Do we realize this is true? Do we realize what this means? Are we conducting ourselves in the way one should who realizes that this blessed Person is not ashamed to call us his brothers and sisters? Do we realize the privilege of all this? Do we realize that if we were clear about this we would indeed be in the happy position of being able to say, "The LORD is on my side; I will not fear: what can man do unto me?" (Ps. 118:6)? The author quotes this psalm later on (Heb. 13:6). He is our helper; even more, he is not ashamed to call us his brothers and sisters.

I want to hold this wonderful phrase before you for a while so we can look into its riches. This is the answer to our every need; there is no need for anything else. If we are right about this, the other problems will look after themselves. If we are right about this, we know we will have no trouble in prayer, we will have no trouble about life or death or eternity or anything else. The writer of this letter is saying, "Why are you looking back to your old religion? Why are you even thinking for a second that it can help you and that it can supply something better than what you have now? Why are you so blind, why are you so darkened in your understanding? Don't you realize the truth about Jesus Christ and your relationship with him?" "He is not ashamed to call them brethren" (2:11).

One of the great literary characteristics of this epistle is that it contains passages of marvelous exposition of encouraging doctrine and threatening, condemning passages. "We ought to give the more earnest heed to the things which we have heard," says the author, "lest at any time we should let them slip [or slip away from them]. For if the word spoken by angels was stedfast, and every transgression and disobedience received a just recompence of reward; how shall we escape, if we neglect so great salvation?" (Heb. 2:1–3). Do we think of it like that? Do we realize that we are sharers in "so great salvation" (Heb. 2:3)? Are we full of triumph and confidence? In spite of the world being as it is and anything that may be happening to us, do we realize that we have "so great salvation"? The essence of it all is that he is not ashamed to call us his brothers and sisters. Let us look at this carefully in order that we may make certain that we are in this position and have hearts full of praise and thanksgiving and rejoicing.

Let us start, then, with the truth concerning his person. There is no greater fallacy in the world than the foolish notion that theology does not matter. The whole epistle to the Hebrews is theology! The author tells these people that they must be clear about this person because they had become muddled in their thinking about him. They had been listening to the Judaizers, Jews who were saying that Jesus of Nazareth was only a man. So the addressees of this letter had become uncertain of the doctrine concerning the Lord Jesus Christ. Foolish people who say that it does not matter what you believe or think are denying the truth. Not only will they not do anything of value, they will be miserable and unhappy and will miss all the consolation of the Scriptures. So we must start with the person of Christ.

Notice the terms that are used. "For both he that sanctifieth and they who are sanctified are all of one: for which cause he is not ashamed to call them brethren" (2:11). Here are terms indicative of the fact that there is a sameness, a unity. The very terms "all of one" and "brethren" suggest this unity, sharing something in common. If you merely glance at those terms, you might very well go away with the notion, as many have done and are still doing, that Jesus of Nazareth is only a man. They say, "Scripture says they are both one, and he calls them brethren. So that means that Jesus is just a man. He is perhaps the greatest man the world has ever known, but he is nothing more than a man, a man like other men." People say Jesus is a great religious teacher, a great moral example, a man who is concerned about politics and things like that; he taught in his day and generation and his teaching still has value for us.

But the moment you examine those terms more carefully, you see that view is quite wrong. These people had been losing sight of the truth concerning him. The Pharisees and scribes and others had said he was but a man. And these poor Hebrew Christians had been influenced by that. But they had not paid attention to the terms we are discussing. Yes, we are told that he and we are all one, and he calls us his brothers and sisters, but there is a difference also—"he that sanctifieth and they who are sanctified" (2:11). Immediately we are confronted by a distinction. They are being sanctified; he is not. He is the one who is sanctifying them. There is a difference here, and this man's whole argument is to bring out the distinction. We cannot see the glory of it all unless we grasp this.

Notice too this other interesting phrase: "He is not ashamed to call them brethren" (2:11). Again we are aware of a difference. If the Lord Jesus Christ is but a man, there is no need to say that "he is not ashamed to call them brethren." The very phrase tells us that he is not the same, though in one respect he is. It is an astonishing thing, says the author, that "he is not ashamed to call them brethren." Why is this marvelous, and why should it make us praise God? The answer is that though he is the same, yet he is eternally different. If you are dealing with a number of men you would not say it is wonderful that they are not ashamed to call their fellow men and women brethren. They would be cads if they did not do so. If such a man sets himself up on a pedestal and says, "I am essentially different from you," what would you think of him? But here is one of whom it can be said that it is amazing that "he is not ashamed to call them brethren."

We have to take all these terms together—"all of one," "he that sanctifieth and they who are sanctified," and "he is not ashamed to call them brethren" (2:11). What does all this mean? We are standing face-to-face with the greatest marvel and mystery the world has ever known or ever will know—the great and central doctrine of the incarnation. The Son is a man; he shared human nature with us. That is what the author of Hebrews means. He is "all of one" with us in the respect that Jesus of Nazareth, the Lord Jesus Christ, is truly human just as we are. It is put very plainly in Hebrews 2:14: "Forasmuch then as the children are partakers of flesh and blood, he also himself likewise took part of the same." We must never lose sight of this fact. He has a human nature just as you and I have. Ah, yes, but there is an eternal difference. He could not call us brethren as he was prior to the incarnation because he was not one with us then. But he has become one with us, and so he calls us brethren.

This is the argument of the whole epistle, but it is brought out with particular clarity in this second chapter. So we start by looking at Jesus. There is no point in going any further unless we are perfectly clear about him. The glory and preeminence of this blessed person lies in this: He is fully God, and he is truly man—two natures in one person. Though he is eternally different from us, he is one with us in certain respects, and for that reason "he is not ashamed to call them brethren" (2:11).

We have considered him; now let us look at ourselves for a moment. Who is the Lord Jesus Christ not ashamed to call his brothers and sisters? Here is another vital point about which there is great confusion today, just as there was nearly two thousand years ago. But again the terms give us the key to the solution. Jesus does not say this to all men. We do not say to the whole world, "Jesus Christ, the Son of God, is not ashamed to call you his brothers and sisters." Who, then, are these of whom it is true? The answer is "they who are sanctified." "For both he that sanctifieth and they who are being sanctified are all of one" (2:11).

This does not apply universally to the whole of mankind but only to certain people who have been separated from the world. This applies only to Christian people. We find the same thing repeated many times: "Behold I and the children which God hath given me" (Heb. 2:13). He has not given Jesus to the whole world. Christ regards as brethren only those who believe in him. Amen.

11

Fully God, Fully Man

Forasmuch then as the children are partakers of flesh and
blood, he also himself likewise took part of the same.

The second chapter of the epistle to the Hebrews is a message concerning the great salvation that is to be found in our Lord and Savior
Jesus Christ. We are doing this because the author of this epistle urges
us to give more earnest heed to the gospel and to be careful not to let
ourselves slip away from it. In fact, he tells us that if we neglect it we
do so at our peril. In other words, his theme is the great salvation we
have in Jesus, and we have already looked at certain aspects of this.
We have considered its purpose, which is to redeem man and to raise
him to the height of glory in which the Son of God himself dwells. We
have seen that it had to happen the way it did because of the being and
nature and character of God himself—it "became" God to do it like
this (Heb. 2:10). Then we considered the price that was paid for this
salvation, the suffering of our Lord by coming into this world and what
he endured and suffered while he was in it.

There is a sense in which we cannot understand all that our Lord
suffered and endured. We cannot fully understand the meaning of his
incarnation unless we have some conception of his person. This is

emphasized in this great epistle to the Hebrews—"consider him" (Heb. 12:3). Its whole purpose is to show the preeminence of this person over everything and everyone that has gone before him, and it is absolutely essential that we do so.

I want therefore to concentrate attention on a number of statements and expressions in this second chapter of Hebrews that will help us look into and understand something of this mystery. We are told that he was made "a little lower than the angels" (Heb. 2:9) for a little while; we are told he was made "perfect through sufferings" (Heb. 2:10); we are told in the eleventh verse that "both he that sanctifieth"—that is to say Christ—"and they who are sanctified"—that is ourselves—"are all of one" (Heb. 2:11), and we must consider the meaning of that statement. We are told likewise that he is not ashamed to call us and all who belong to him "brethren." We also have the specific statement in the fourteenth verse, "Forasmuch then as the children are partakers of flesh and blood, he also likewise himself took part of the same," and we read in verse 17 that "in all things it behoved him to be made like unto his brethren," and finally we are told that "he himself hath suffered being tempted" (Heb. 2:18).

So a number of statements are made about this Person at whom we are looking, the Lord Jesus Christ, and what we are attempting to do is to understand something of their meaning. Perhaps the best way to approach and to interpret them is to consider the argument that the author is using in this chapter, which is this: "For verily he took not on him the nature of angels; but he took on him the seed of Abraham" (Heb. 2:16). It is generally agreed that the King James rendition of this verse is not a good translation; it would be better rendered, "For verily he lays not hold of angels, but he lays hold of the seed of Abraham." It is not so much a statement about taking on the nature of men or of angels, but rather that he *lays hold* of men. The Son of God came into this world in order to lay hold of mankind and raise it into the heights. The writer reminds us here that he has not done this for angels but with men and for man. That must be the starting point of any consideration of the incarnation.

We are again face-to-face with a great mystery. It is not only man who has fallen; it is not only man who has sinned against God. Before man had ever fallen, before man was ever made and created, certain angels had fallen. The Devil is a fallen angel, and the Scriptures tell us that other angels listened to him and rebelled against God, and they also fell. So when we begin to consider the fall and sin and evil, we must not think only in terms of man; if we do we are going to miss something very wonderful. Man has fallen, certain angels have fallen, but the astounding message of the gospel is that the Lord Jesus Christ does not lay hold upon the angels in order to rescue and redeem them— he does it only for the seed of Abraham. The seed of Abraham are the children of faith, those who believe on the Lord Jesus Christ, those whom the author of Hebrews describes as the "heirs of salvation" (Heb. 1:14). Why did he not save the angels? Why are we told that they are "reserved unto fire against the day of judgment" (2 Pet. 3:7)? We stand face-to-face with a mystery, but what I am concerned about is that we realize the amazing message that comes to us. It is not angels that he lays hold on but you and me, the seed of Abraham, fallen man. The argument here is that it was because of that decision and that de-termination that he takes upon himself the nature that belongs to you and to me, and that is the meaning and explanation of the incarnation.

So what do these statements suggest to us? In the first place, they as-sert that he has come into this world in a different way from anybody else who was ever born into this world. They impress upon us his uniqueness, his separateness, the difference between him and everybody else. Take this idea of his laying hold upon us. That in itself suggests someone com-ing from the outside into our world to do something for us. Someone has come from somewhere, saw us in our plight, and did something about it. That is the very essence of the New Testament teaching about this. The first chapter of this epistle to the Hebrews sets the background, where extraordinary statements are made concerning him: "God . . . hath in these last days spoken unto us by his Son, whom he hath appointed heir of all things, by whom also he made the worlds; who being the brightness of his glory, and the express image of his person, and upholding all things by the word of his power, when he had by himself purged our sins, sat down on the right hand of the Majesty on high" (Heb. 1:1–3).

Consider also those other statements in Hebrews 2. Look again at that phrase about his being made "lower than the angels" (Heb. 2:7, 9).

Something had to happen to him to make him thus. Then take that extraordinary statement about children being "partakers of flesh and blood" and he likewise "took part of the same" (Heb. 2:14). This is a very interesting matter. In these two statements—"the children are partakers of flesh and blood" and "he also himself likewise took part of the same"—the words are not the same in the original, suggesting there is a difference. You and I are sharers together in a common humanity. Jesus Christ comes in from the outside and enters into a partnership with us in this matter. And then we read that "it behoved him to be made [he had to be made] like unto his brethren" (Heb. 2:17). Only one conclusion can be drawn legitimately from all these statements: he was different. The Lord Jesus Christ does not come out of humanity; he comes into humanity. You and I come out of humanity. You and I and everybody else emerge out of human nature, but that is not true of him. He comes into it from the outside. In other words, the teaching of Scripture is that he added human nature to himself.

Here we come to the central mystery concerning Christ. The New Testament tells us that the baby born in Bethlehem was none other than the eternal Son of God, very God of very God, and that when he came into this world he did not come into it like anybody else. He was not born as others were; his birth was a virgin birth. The tenth chapter of Hebrews quotes an Old Testament song that tells us a body was prepared for the Son. He was conceived by the Holy Ghost; the Gospels make that very plain. When this was announced to Mary she said, "How shall this be, seeing I know not a man?" (Luke 1:34). We read in the Gospel of Matthew that Joseph was likewise troubled when the announcement was made to him, but the angel told him that the baby to be born was being conceived by the Holy Ghost (Matt. 1:19–20). The eternal Son of God in this amazing and mysterious manner was born of a virgin in order that you and I might be saved, that you and I might become the children of God. We must lay hold of the amazing thought that he came out of eternity into that. He had to take upon himself flesh and blood, to become a partaker of it. We have to start with the high and exalted and astounding truth that the eternal Son of God humbled himself and that the baby of Bethlehem was God incarnate, the Word made flesh. But we are also emphasizing his difference from us. He is God. He does not come out of ordinary humanity; he comes into it—God descending—and this is where the mystery becomes so great. While he is truly God, he is also truly man.

He was indeed made lower than the angels, and this meant he became capable of suffering and capable of death. Indeed, we read that he was made "perfect through suffering" (Heb. 2:10); that involves his humanity. We have also considered the extraordinary statement, "For both he that sanctifieth and they who are sanctified are all of one" (Heb. 2:11). This is a difficult phrase, and many different interpretations have been put forward. The conclusion to which I have felt compelled to arrive is that the Lord Jesus Christ and all who belong to him are one in nature, and to secure our redemption he had to take upon himself our nature, to come down into ourselves in order to raise us up to him. There is wonderful comfort and consolation in this extraordinary teaching.

Consider again the verse about his not being ashamed to call us "brethren." Various Old Testament Scriptures confirm that. Then we have the specific statement that he took upon himself flesh and blood. We are told that "in all things it behoved him to be made like unto his brethren" (Heb. 2:17), and we are told he "suffered being tempted" (Heb. 2:18) while he was in this world. These things simply assert that while he was truly God, he was also truly man. The history of the church shows that men and women have often gone wrong with regard to this matter. Some have denied his deity and failed to see the Son of God in him, and others failed to see him truly as man. But these statements in Hebrews 2 are typical of what the New Testament asserts. These statements remind us that God did not merely appear to be a man—that is, he did not have some sort of phantom body. He did not appear in this world in a kind of fleshly veil or some kind of covering. Neither must we think of him as being a man only in his body. The teaching of Scripture is that he was truly God and truly man. The phrase "flesh and blood" (Heb. 2:14) should fix this once and forever: "Forasmuch then as the children are partakers of flesh and blood, he also himself likewise took part of the same" (2:14). The term "flesh and blood" in Scripture always stands for human nature. When Peter at Caesarea Philippi made his great confession and said, "Thou art the Christ, the Son of the living God" (Matt. 16:16), our Lord looked at him and said, "Blessed art thou, Simon Barjona: for flesh and blood hath not revealed it unto thee, but my Father which is in heaven" (Matt. 16:17). Flesh and blood means human nature.

Remember, too, the great argument of the apostle Paul in the fifteenth chapter of 1 Corinthians: "Flesh and blood cannot inherit the kingdom of God" (Matt. 16:50). In other words, we have to be changed; something has to happen to us. That is the very phrase used here in Hebrews 2. It is not merely the appearance of humanity that Jesus took on himself; he has it in common with us. Also note again that remarkable statement in verse 17: "Wherefore in all things it behoved him to be made like unto his brethren." This "all things" is qualified in this very epistle itself. "All things" here does not mean that he took upon himself degraded and fallen human nature because we are told he was in all points "tempted like as we are, yet without sin" (Heb. 4:15). There was no evil in him; his nature was pure and perfect. "All things" here applies to his human state and condition, apart from sin. So we see in the light of these statements that he was truly man as well as truly God.

We must try to understand these facts and hold on to them. Take, for instance, what we are told about him in a bodily sense. We are told that he knew what it was to suffer weakness; we are told that he was crucified in or through weakness; we are told that he knew what it was to suffer hunger and to suffer thirst and to suffer fatigue. We are told in connection with the story of the woman of Samaria that our Lord, being tired and fatigued, sat down by the side of the well when the disciples went into the neighboring city to buy provisions (John 4:6–8). On one occasion when they entered into a ship he went to sleep in the stern of the vessel (Luke 8:23). These things are true of men in a bodily, physical sense, and he experienced them as a man; it was not a phantom body that experienced these things. He entered into flesh and blood; in a bodily, physical sense he was a man.

But look at it in terms of the soul as well. We are told that his mind developed and that he grew in wisdom and in stature. It is quite clear from the Scriptures that he was taught by his mother and by Joseph, so that as a child he experienced growth and learning, being truly man as well as truly God. We are told too that he loved Mary and Martha and their brother Lazarus, he loved the rich young ruler, and the apostle John was called the disciple whom Jesus loved. He was the Savior of them all, but he seemed to have a special attachment to John. This personal preference is one manifestation of his humanity. We read too that Jesus was sometimes amazed and that he marveled—he was truly God, yet truly man. We are told that he experienced grief and sorrow. We see him weeping; we hear him say that his soul was exceedingly sorrowful, even unto death. There are indications that he was truly man in his body and in his soul. And in the spiritual realm we find exactly the same thing. He spent a lot of time reading the Old Testament Scriptures, pouring over them and meditating upon them, and thus he could quote them and use them as arguments. But I think there is something in this second chapter of the epistle to the Hebrews that is even more striking and amazing. In verse 13 Jesus says, "I will put my trust in him" (Heb. 2:13). The Lord Jesus Christ, being truly man, exercised faith in God, and he exhorts others to imitate his example. He is one with God and equal with God, and yet here, as a man, he says, "I will put my trust in him."

Even more amazing, look at his prayer life. We often read that he would rise a great while before dawn and go up a mountain alone to pray. When he had the tremendous task of choosing his special disciples he spent the whole night in prayer. There is only one explanation for that, and that is that he was living within the limits of humanity, and so he needed the Father's aid and relied upon it. He was truly man as well as truly God.

We also read that he learned obedience. Read the Gospels and you will find that he constantly said that the words he spoke were not from himself and that the works he did were not his own idea or his own works. He was simply repeating to mankind what God the Father had told him; every work he did was the work God had told him to do and the result of his receiving the Holy Spirit upon him who empowered him for his work. He made the extraordinary statement that he offered himself to God through the eternal Spirit. All of these expressions, including the expression that he was made "perfect through sufferings" (Heb. 2:10; see also Heb. 5:8), emphasizes tremendously for us the fact that he was indeed truly man.

This is the extraordinary mystery of the incarnation—truly God, truly man, yet one individual, one person with two natures. But the two natures are separate and distinct; they are not commingled. He is truly God and truly man. In the light of the teaching of the apostle Paul in the second chapter of the epistle to the Philippians, while living here on earth as a man he did not cease to be God. He was still God, the eternal Son, but he deliberately lived as if he were a man. He did not make use of the prerogatives of deity. Apart from this I see no meaning in his receiving the Holy Spirit, and I do not understand his prayer life and his exercising faith in his Father and putting his trust in him. That is the essence of this extraordinary humiliation. Though he was God, he took upon himself human nature and lived as a man and kept the law in perfect dependence upon his Father, and thus he became the captain of our salvation. The virgin birth is an essential part of all this because he did not take upon him sinful human nature; he was made "in the *likeness* of sinful flesh" (Rom. 8:3). This a mystery we cannot understand, but we do know that the human nature he took upon himself from Mary was a human nature that had been purified and cleansed by the Holy Ghost. I am not saying that Mary herself had been cleansed, but the human nature that he took out of her was cleansed and perfected and purified, and thus he is "the firstborn among many brethren" (Rom. 8:29), the second Adam, and the result of this is that he is the captain, the author, the leader of our salvation.

This mystery of the incarnation and the virgin birth—two natures, distinct and separate in one person—was necessary because he has come to take hold of man, to make atonement for man's sin, to provide a perfect offering, to die for every man in order to satisfy the holiness and the justice of God. The author of Hebrews also tells us Jesus came to be a high priest for us. A high priest represents us in the presence of God and there pleads for us and brings us forgiveness. The law says the high priest had to be like his brethren. So to be our high priest Jesus had to become like us—in the incarnation. Thank God, Jesus Christ is also a sympathetic high priest, One who is faithful, One who is merciful. Having lived the life he lived here on earth he understands us; he is "touched with the feeling of our infirmities" (Heb. 4:15); "he himself hath suffered being tempted" (Heb. 2:18). He knows about the trials of life in this world. He knows about physical needs. He knew what it is to be disappointed by trusted friends. He has gone through all of that.

He is the perfect captain and leader, mighty and powerful. He has conquered evil, and at the same time he can sympathize with us. Mighty as he is, he understands our weakness and can stoop to our level.

There is another suggestion in the second chapter of Hebrews as to why all this was done, and it is that he might forever silence the Devil. "Forasmuch then as the children are partakers of flesh and blood, he also himself likewise took part of the same; that through death He might destroy him that had the power of death, that is, the devil" (2:14). This is God's way of destroying the Devil and silencing him forever. The Devil is God's accuser. If God had forgiven mankind in any other way the Devil would have objected and would have reminded God of the holiness of his own character and would have said, "How can you forgive sin?" But Christ crucified is the eternal answer to the Devil; the enemy is thus rendered speechless. Again if God had redeemed mankind without the incarnation and without sending his Son into this world, the Devil might have said, "The law has been violated. How can you justify man since man has not kept the law?" But the life Jesus Christ lived as man silenced the Devil at that point also. The man Christ Jesus has rendered perfect obedience to the law of God and thus to God himself. He failed at no point. Thus through the incarnation and the life and the suffering and the death of Jesus, the Devil has been silenced, his works have been destroyed, and he himself finally shall suffer eternal perdition.

That is the argument of this second chapter of Hebrews with regard to the meaning and purpose of the incarnation. Oh, that we understood these things as we ought. God so loved you and me that all that happened. The eternal Son took upon himself human nature, flesh and blood. Mystery of mysteries, the eternal Son of God came out of Mary's womb and was laid in the manger. The Son of God endured all those things, and he did it all simply in order to take hold of us and to pull us out of the clutches of Satan, to rescue us from hell and eternal damnation, and to raise us up and make us children of God and prepare us for eternity and a glory that baffles imagination and to share life with him forever and ever. Oh, that we might understand that he came down so that you and I might be lifted up and raised to such glory.

Thanks be unto God for his unspeakable gift. Amen.

12

Our Faithful, Unchanging
High Priest

HEBREWS 2:17-18

Wherefore in all things it behoved him to be made like unto his brethren, that he might be a merciful and faithful high priest in things pertaining to God, to make reconciliation for the sins of the people. For in that he himself hath suffered being tempted, he is able to succour them that are tempted.

The author of the epistle to the Hebrews gives the Hebrew Christians to whom he was writing (and us) great reasons for considering the gospel of Jesus Christ and for being careful never to allow ourselves to slip away from it. His reasons, being summarized, may be put like this: It is a message from God; it is not a human message. It is not a philosophy; it is not ideas put forward by men with regard to our needs in this life and world. God himself is speaking through his Son—not through prophets, not through psalmists, but through his Son, God's final word, the word that is authenticated with signs and wonders and diverse miracles and gifts of the Holy Ghost at the beginning through the Christian church and subsequently. We listen to the gospel message for these reasons, and we listen to it because, as he puts it, "How shall we escape, if we neglect so great salvation?" (Heb. 2:3). If God's final offer is rejected, what can remain but perdition and loss and eternal wretchedness? We consider this message because of the greatness of the salvation that it has to offer us.

We have been looking at that "great salvation" in a more or less objective manner. We have looked at the great scheme and purpose of God in Christ, which is to bring many sons unto glory. The ultimate purpose of God is to form for himself a people who are going to dwell with him in glory, who are going to reign upon the earth. His great plan is to take sinful men and women and turn them into children of God and lead them to that eternal, final glory that we will share with him. We have been considering in great detail why God has worked out that plan in terms of the incarnation and the suffering of our Lord, and especially his death upon the cross—why the incarnation was essential and why it was necessary that the eternal Son should come into this world in the likeness of sinful flesh and for sin. We have been considering all that, confining ourselves mainly to the teaching of Hebrews 2, which is a marvelous summary of the entire epistle and is indeed in itself a compendium of Christian theology. Here is the grand plan and purpose of God and the reasons why it has been worked out in the way it has been worked out. But that is not all. Here we are told something that is so wonderful about this gospel. We must always start with the gospel of Jesus Christ objectively. It is after all the truth of God, and the truth is to be considered objectively. In other words, the fact that people have certain subjective experiences or may undergo great changes in their life does not prove they are Christians. Many agencies in this world can give people significant experiences. Many factors can change a man's life so that he appears to be a Christian, but that does not mean he is a Christian. We must start with the truth; we must know what we are believing. The author of Hebrews starts the second chapter by saying, "Therefore we ought to give the more earnest heed"—to what?—"to the things we have heard," the gospel as it is given in the Bible.

Of necessity we must start with the objective truth with all its grandness glory. But there is a subjective element also in Christian salvation. It is not merely a scheme and plan that you look at; it is something you experience here and now, and we must now move on to consider what the gospel has to give us in the immediate present. There is the vision of what awaits us, the glory for which we are being prepared, but God does not merely give this wonderful vista of that eternal glory and leave us somehow to exist through this world until we get to that. He is actively engaged within us from the very first awakening until he brings us to the final glory. But there are certain aspects of salvation that we experience and enjoy now, things that are incomparably greater than all the wealth of the world put together. This is a vital part of this "so great salvation" (Heb. 2:3). The author of the epistle to the Hebrews was anxious to impress this upon those people, and in a sense that was why he wrote his letter to them. They were having a difficult time, they were suffering persecution, certain problems were besetting them, and this man was anxious to remind them of what they had there and then—not only the things awaiting them, but the things that were available right then.

We must not separate these things; they are all part and parcel of the same thing. The apostle Paul in the epistle to the Romans puts it like this: "[We] have the firstfruits of the Spirit" (Rom. 8:23). The main bulk of our salvation awaits us in glory, but thank God we are given a foretaste, we are given the firstfruits now. What great praise we can offer to God as we consider some of the things that in his infinite grace and kindness he gives immediately here and now to those who believe on the Lord Jesus Christ.

Let me first ask a simple question: Are we experiencing these things which I am going to mention? These things are not theoretical; these things can be experienced. In fact, however great our knowledge may be in an objective and theoretical sense, if these things are not real to us we are not Christians. This is the glory of the Christian faith—it is both objective and subjective, and we must never separate these two things. These things are to be believed and experienced; these things are life and life-giving. So we must ask ourselves whether these things are real to us, whether we are enjoying them, whether we are rejoicing in them. To me the saddest thing in the world is that so many people are unhappy and miserable and wretched because they do not know these things. The New Testament is depicting for us a life that is triumphant, a life that is abundant. You and I are meant to be able to say with the apostle Paul as we look at this dark world, "I am persuaded, that neither death, nor life, nor angels, nor principalities, nor powers, nor things present, nor things to come, nor height, nor depth, nor any other creature, shall be able to separate us from the love of God, which is in Christ Jesus our Lord" (Rom. 8:38–39). We can experience the blessed condition of being able to say "Abba, Father" (Rom. 8:15). We can know something about the glorious liberty of the children of God. I ask again, do we know these things? Are we experiencing them?

What are the immediate blessings that come to those who believe on the Lord Jesus Christ and who can be described as being in Christ Jesus? I am going to try to put them in what I would describe as a kind of theological order. The first thing that is true about the person who believes on the Lord Jesus Christ is that he is reconciled to God and experiences forgiveness of sins. "Wherefore in all things it behoved him to be made like unto his brethren, that he might be a merciful and faithful high priest in things pertaining to God, to make reconciliation for the sins of the people" (Heb. 2:17). That was his great task; that was why he came; that was his purpose. First of all the sinner needs to be reconciled to God, and that is the function and purpose of the high priest. Very well, the author of Hebrews says, Christ has come and has done all this, but for whom has he done it? The high priest is the representative of the people. He makes reconciliation for the people in things pertaining to God; he is the one who represents certain people in the presence of God. Jesus Christ has done this for us who believe. He has done it for those of us who have seen ourselves as unutterable sinners in the sight of God and as deserving hell. He has done it for all of us who know the condemnation of the Law and who when we have tried to stand in the presence of God have seen our unutterable helplessness and hopelessness. He has done it for those of us who having truly seen ourselves know we cannot approach God and have no right to do so. Because of Jesus Christ we can say, "being justified by faith, we have peace with God" (Rom. 5:1).

Does your past life worry you? Is it a burden to you? Do your sins haunt you? Are they ever rising up before you to make you miserable and wretched? Are you afraid of facing God because of them? Do you know God? These are simple, practical, vital questions that are asked by the New Testament itself. The man who has believed and committed himself fully to the Lord Jesus Christ is reconciled to God, and he knows he is reconciled; he has an assurance of his salvation. The New Testament epistles were written in order that men might have that assurance, that they might be delivered from uncertainty, that they might make their calling and election sure, that they might have an abundant entry into the everlasting kingdom. That is the first thing we know, that we are reconciled; that was the message of the first apostles. This ministry of reconciliation was committed unto them, and, says Paul, "We pray you in Christ's stead, be ye reconciled to God" (2 Cor. 5:19–20). That is the message, and we should have enjoyment of a knowledge of sins forgiven and should know that we are reconciled to God. We now approach him with reverence and godly fear, but not with the craven fear that was once in us. We should be aware that we have access through Christ into the presence of God. Take the way this author puts it in the tenth chapter and the nineteenth verse: "Having . . . boldness to enter into the holiest by the blood of Jesus" (Heb. 10:19). Are you able to pray to God with boldness and confidence? Are you able to heed and practice the exhortation, "Let us therefore come boldly unto the throne of grace, that we may obtain mercy, and find grace to help in time of need" (Heb. 4:16)? The Christian is one who knows God and should be able to approach God with this holy boldness and should be certain of this access. He should know God in such a way that he can come into his presence and find needed grace. He begins a life of prayer that he has never known before. Uncertainty and doubt and hesitation should be gone, and the man who comes into the presence of his Father in this way is reconciled by the blood of Jesus and comes with this holy boldness.

The second word we will consider is the word "sanctified." We read in the eleventh verse, "For both he that sanctifieth and they who are sanctified are all of one: for which cause he is not ashamed to call them brethren" (Heb. 2:11). "He that sanctifieth—namely the Lord Jesus Christ—"and they who are sanctified are all of one" (Heb. 2:11). We are the ones who are sanctified. To me this is one of the most wonderful things of all. To be sanctified in the first instance always means to be set apart. We read about the Holy Mount in the Old Testament, the mountain that was set apart for God. Instruments and vessels were sanctified, set apart for the Lord's use; they were never to be used for anything else. We, says Scripture, are sanctified by the blood of Jesus, which means that we are set apart for God. I know of nothing that is of greater comfort to man than that. There are only two views of man: Those whom God has set apart to be his own and those who are not in that company. This is the message of the New Testament gospel. God has taken hold of certain people in this sinful world and has set them apart for himself. He is forming a people who are to be a special possession for himself. Remember Paul's prayer to the Ephesians about "the eyes of your understanding being enlightened; that ye may know what is the hope of his calling, and what the riches of the glory of his inheritance in the saints" (Eph. 1:18). God's "inheritance" is "the saints." We are "a peculiar people," says the apostle Peter (1 Pet. 2:9), by which he means that we are God's special property. He sets us apart for himself, and he is going to glorify himself in us.

If you are a Christian, if you are in Christ Jesus, you are a special object in the sight of God, the Lord God Almighty who made the universe out of nothing and who keeps everything going and by whom everything consists, that almighty, everlasting Being who dwells in a glory that we cannot imagine. He has put his hand on you, and he takes a special interest in you. Have you ever thought of yourself like that? The world may be cruel to you, it may laugh at you, it may spit in your face, it may cast you into prison, as it is doing to many at the present time. But whatever happens to you, remember that God has set you apart for himself. It is wonderful to know that you are in the hand of God, that the eternal and almighty and ever perfect God looks upon you in this way. As our Lord himself put it, God has counted the very hairs of your head. Nothing can happen to you or will be allowed to happen to you apart from God's knowledge and consent. Many things are happening to God's people that we do not understand, and sometimes we are tempted to complain. But "all things work together for good to them that love God, to them who are the called according to his purpose" (Rom. 8:28).

We are "sanctified"—set apart that we may be prepared and purified and perfected for the glory he has prepared for us. He is, as the tenth verse tells us, preparing and leading many sons to glory (Hebrews 2). He sets us apart, and we become the special objects of his care. He "worketh in you both to will and to do of his good pleasure" (Phil. 2:13). Sometimes he chastens us, but only because he loves us. He is scourging his sons because he is bringing them to glory. So in a sense the more we suffer, the more we can thank him because his chastening is proof that we are his children. Because God loves us, he sets us aside for the glory to which he is going to bring us, and he makes us fit for it. Whom the Lord loves he chastens and sanctifies.

But we must also look at some other terms. God has set us aside, but he has done even more. "For both he that sanctifieth and they who are sanctified are all of one: for which cause he is not ashamed to call them brethren" (Heb. 2:11). And before that he said, "For it became him, for whom are all things, and by whom are all things, in bringing many sons unto glory . . . " (Heb. 2:10). The author adds, "Forasmuch then as the children are partakers of flesh and blood, he also himself likewise took part of the same" (Heb. 2:14). These terms describe Christians, children of God, sons of God, brethren of the Lord Jesus Christ. We are of one nature with the Lord Jesus Christ. The Son of God, the eternal Word, was made flesh. Why? He took upon himself the flesh and blood of which the children are partakers in order that he might become a sympathetic high priest. Furthermore, he identified himself with us so that he might identify us with him, "for both he that sanctifieth and they who are sanctified are all of one" (Heb. 2:11). He was made flesh and became man in order that you and I might become sons and daughters of God. He has taken on him our nature in order that he might give us his nature, and thus we become partakers of the divine nature; we receive him, and he comes to dwell within us. If you and I really understood these things, the Christian church would not be as she is today. There would be no fear of man and of the future. We would not be afraid if we grasped that those in Christ have become children of God and that Christ himself calls us his brothers and sisters and that we share his nature, that we are in Christ and are partakers of his glory even here and now, that we sit together with him in heavenly places and eventually will share with him the glory that God is preparing for us. There is only one thing to say about people who laugh at the Christian religion, and that is they are ignorant, they are blind, they do not know these things. Foolish people vie with one another to get earthly honor that will be of no value to them in a few years. Poor, blind, damned souls glory and boast in something like that when they could be the children of God, joint heirs with Christ. The man who is truly Christian, the man who repents and believes on the Lord Jesus Christ, yields himself to God and becomes at once a child of God, and Christ calls him his brother.

The next thing we find here is that we are delivered from the bondage of Satan. "Forasmuch then as the children are partakers of flesh and blood, he also himself likewise took part of the same; that through death he might destroy him that had the power of death, that is, the devil; and deliver them who through fear of death were all their lifetime subject to bondage" (Heb. 2:14). The moment you become a Christian you are no longer in the bondage of the Devil. That is a staggering statement, but the New Testament says this repeatedly. We are no longer under the dominion of sin and of Satan; we no longer belong to the territory of the Devil. We have been translated from the kingdom of darkness into the kingdom of God's true Son. We are no longer slaves, bondservants, captives of Satan. Christ takes hold of a man and takes him out of the realm of Satan and sets him apart in his own dominion and in his own eternal and glorious kingdom. We must not despise the power of Satan, but in Christ we need never fear him. The Christian can say with the Scriptures, "Resist the devil, and he will flee from you" (James 4:7) and "they overcame him by the blood of the Lamb, and the word of their testimony" (Rev. 12:11). We can resist him steadfastly in the faith without fear. This is not foolhardiness; it is the confidence that comes from knowing Christ. We are brethren in Christ who has in the flesh conquered Satan and routed him and put him to an open shame upon the cross, and now he delivers all who are in him and who look to him. We have been delivered from the bondage of Satan.

But surely, says someone, you are not preaching a kind of sinless perfection. No, I am not. Surely, says someone, Christian people still fall into sin. Yes, they do. But they do not have to fall into sin; they do because of their failure to look to Christ. But God in his infinite kindness has even made provision for that. That is the meaning of this great teaching here concerning the high priesthood of Christ. He has entered into the presence of God on our behalf; he ever lives to make intercession for us. In the words of the apostle John, "And if any man sin"—he is talking about Christians—"we have an advocate with the Father, Jesus Christ the righteous" (1 John 2:1). As Christians we enjoy these great blessings, yet in our folly we sometimes listen to Satan, and we fall, and we begin to wonder what we can do. Here is the answer: You have a high priest representing you before the Father, and he ever lives to make intercession for you. He is interceding at the throne of God for you. So if you feel condemned, ashamed of yourself because you have not only let yourself down but you have let Christ and the church down, this is my word to you: you have an advocate, an intercessor, One who understands and knows you, and as you acknowledge your sins and put your case in his hands, he assures you of an abundant, full, and free pardon.

This is one of the blessings that come to those who are in Christ, but there is more. He succors the tempted. We might fall into sin and are depressed and discouraged, but we have a great advocate. Yes, we have been assured of forgiveness, but that does not change the world, and it does not change the Devil and sin and temptation. What if we fall into sin? Is there a way of deliverance? Our Savior is able to succor those who are tempted. He does not leave us to ourselves. He is ever by our side, and as we rely upon him we will not fall into sin. He is able to keep us from falling if we turn to him and live by faith.

> I need Thee every hour;
> Stay Thou nearby;
> Temptations lose their power
> When Thou art nigh.
>
> Annie S. Hawks, "I Need Thee Every Hour"

Remember that he is near you, and he can hold you and strengthen you. Remember too that because "he himself hath suffered being tempted, he is able to succour them that are tempted" (2:18). He is a merciful, faithful High Priest. He is able to stoop to our weakness and have mercy upon our infirmities. He has been in this world. He has lived as a man in it, he knows all about it, and though he never sinned and sin never appealed to him for even a fraction of a second, he felt the devilish force of it all, and he can sympathize with you and bear with you and therefore succor you.

But there is even more. He is always the same and never changes. We live in a changing world, and we are creatures with varying moods and changes. We have a high priest who never changes. That is the great theme of this epistle to the Hebrews. Jesus Christ is "the same yesterday, and to day, and for ever" (Heb. 13:8). He will never change, and because he ever lives to intercede for us he will save us to the uttermost (Heb. 7:25). Some foolish people have explained this by saying that he saves to the guttermost, but this is an infinitely greater truth than that. It means that because he is everlastingly the same, he does not start the process of our salvation and then leave it. He will finish it. He will save us to the very end until we are glorified and perfected and without blot or wrinkle or blemish. He will save to the uttermost all who come to God by him, and the eternal security of the believer is one of the most glorious and assuring things that the New Testament has to tell us.

> The work which His goodness began,
> The arm of His strength will complete;
> His promise is Yea and Amen,
> And never was forfeited yet.
> Things future, nor things that are now,
> Nor all things below or above,
> Can make Him His purpose forego,
> Or sever my soul from His love.
>
> Augustus Toplady, "A Debtor to Mercy Alone"

Our High Priest ever lives and will save us to the uttermost, to the end, until the work is completed. All our needs are provided for; all things that pertain to life and godliness are fully provided. All that you and I need has been foreseen and provided for before we ever realized our need. This includes knowledge of sins forgiven, reconciliation with God, being able to enter into his presence, being set apart for him, being the object of his special interest, becoming a child of God, assurance of help and deliverance from the bondage of Satan, the knowledge that we no longer belong to the realm of sin and of darkness but to the kingdom of God, help when we fail, restoration, peace, strength, succor, help, the confidence and assurance that he does not merely start our salvation but finishes it. Ah, says someone, what about death, the certain knowledge that we are here today and gone tomorrow? Does the gospel say anything about that?

"Forasmuch then as the children are partakers of flesh and blood, he also himself likewise took part of the same; that through death he might destroy him that had the power of death, that is, the devil; and deliver them who through fear of death were all their lifetime subject to bondage" (Heb. 2:14–15). Any man who thinks seriously about death is certain to be afraid of it; any man who has any understanding of what the Bible has to say about death will be alarmed by the thought of death, for its teaching is that death is a door through which we pass to an eternal destiny—an eternal destiny, if we do not know God and Christ, of torment and suffering and sorrow and pain. No man can contemplate that without being afraid of death. Death to the unbeliever is terrifying. It is not merely the physical fact of death that frightens people; it is the consequences that follow death if they have not believed the gospel. If we could know for certain that when we die that is the end of us and nothing happens afterward, nobody would be afraid of death; many people would even welcome it. But the strength and the sting of death is sin, which means this: We have a feeling within us that because we have sinned against God we are going to be punished for it when we die. And that is true—that is the sting of death, and what makes it come to us with power is the law of God that proclaims it. The sting of death is sin, and the strength of sin is the law. That is what makes people alarmed about death. The moment the law makes its announcement, we fear death and are alarmed at the thought of it.

The good news is, Christ delivers us from that because he has dealt with our sin. He has taken the sting out of death because he has dealt with the guilt of our sin; he has dealt with the law. By dying for our sins, and by his active obedience to the law, the law is satisfied, and now there is no strength in the sting of death. In other words, the Christian does not need to fear death, and Satan only has power over those who are condemned by the law and belong to the kingdom of Satan that he controls and therefore controls their death and their fear of death. But the moment a man sees what Christ has done about the law, he knows the sting is gone, and with Paul he can say, "O death, where is thy sting? O grave, where is thy victory?" (1 Cor. 15:55). Thanks be to God—Christ has conquered death and the grave and has taken the sting out of it all because he has satisfied God's perfect and holy law. He has thus destroyed the main work of the Devil, and he delivers us from the bondage of death and from the fear of death that we experienced when we saw ourselves condemned by the law. So the Christian is not only not afraid of death—its terrors for him are gone. The Christian knows that for him death means being with Christ, which is far better.

My dear friends, do you know these things? Are these things realities to you? To be a Christian doesn't mean doing something yourself; it means giving yourself to the One who does it for you. These things we've been considering are gifts from God. Are you enjoying them? Are you living in the light of them? Is this the way you are facing your future life in this dark world? These are the blessings Jesus Christ offers, the foretastes, the firstfruits of that wondrous glory that we will enjoy in all its fullness and perfection someday. Amen.

13

Full Maturity

Therefore leaving the principles of the doctrine of Christ, let
us go on unto perfection; not laying again the foundation or
repentance from dead works, and of faith toward God, Of
the doctrine of baptisms, and of laying on of hands, and of
resurrection of the dead, and of eternal judgment. And this
will we do, if God permit.

I want to call your attention in particular to that great and ringing
exhortation, "Let us go on unto perfection" (6:1), or "Let us advance
to maturity, to full development."

Here the author of this epistle puts before the Hebrew believers to
whom he was writing the very word that they needed above all else.
These people, let me remind you, were Christians. They have been
brought up as Jews in the Jewish religion, but they had heard the
preaching of the gospel, as we are reminded in the second chapter, and
they had believed it, and for a while everything seemed to have gone
well. But now they are in a condition of unhappiness and uncertainty.
They have not renounced the Christian faith, but it is quite clear that a
number of them are looking back to the old Jewish religion, and they
are thoroughly depressed.

That is why the writer takes the trouble to write his letter to them, and the great thing that he does, as we have seen, is to show the sufficiency and the preeminence of the Lord Jesus Christ. This epistle is one of the greatest expositions of our Lord in his person, in his work, and in his glory in the whole New Testament. But at this particular point and juncture he puts it in a very practical manner and exposes what is, after all, their central and chief cause of trouble.

He had already been leading up to that at the end of chapter 5. He wants to comfort them; he wants to give them consolation in our Lord. But there are great profundities in the truth, and he is anxious to explain some of these to his readers. But there is a difficulty here.

> We have many things to say, and hard to be uttered, seeing ye are dull of hearing. For when for the time ye ought to be teachers, ye have need that one teach you again which be the first principles of the oracles of God; and are become such as have need of milk, and not of strong meat. For every one that useth milk is unskillful in the word of righteousness: for he is a babe. But strong meat belongeth to them that are of full age, even those who by reason of use have their senses exercised to discern both good and evil. (Heb. 5:11–14)

He says in essence, "I have wonderful comfort and consolation to give you, but I am convinced that at this time you are not able to receive it." So he makes this great appeal to them: "Let us go on unto perfection" (6:1).

This, it seems to me, is the very exhortation that many need today. We are living in an age that is characterized by confusion and uncertainty. This is obvious in the world. Standards are disappearing; nobody seems to know what to do or what to say. Alas, it is even an age of confusion in the church. Until recently everybody agreed about certain things, but this is no longer so. This age of utter confusion is the result of immaturity, superficiality, and a lack of knowledge.

This is not a new complaint against God's people. The prophet Hosea was given a message by God to deliver to the children of Israel: "My people are destroyed for lack of knowledge" (Hos. 4:6). That was true then, and it is true now. If you do not have knowledge, you will not have standards, and thus you cannot evaluate anything, you cannot judge anything. So it seems to me that it is as necessary as ever for us to face this exhortation: "Let us go on unto perfection!" Let us go on to maturity. Let us cease to be children. "In malice be ye children," says the apostle Paul to the Corinthians, "but in understanding be men" (1 Cor. 14:20). Grow up! Go on to perfection and to maturity.

We do well to ask ourselves this simple yet profound question: Are we growing? Are we advancing? How do we find ourselves as compared with a year or ten years or twenty years ago? Are we more mature than we were at any given point in the past? This is an urgent matter, so let us look at the reason why the writer gave this exhortation to these Hebrew Christians and why it is needed by all of us at the present time.

The first reason is that the Christian life, by definition, is a developing and an advancing life. I have referred to it as a life, and that is what it is. That puts it into an entirely different category from all philosophies and teachings, political and social ideas, and so on. It is a teaching, of course, but it is more than that; it is a life! That is what we are reminded of everywhere in the Bible and particularly in the New Testament. When one becomes a Christian, one receives new life.

The characteristic New Testament terms make this clear. For example, "He is a babe" (Heb. 5:13). This suggests life. A child is born; a child is alive. A child is not a machine; it has life, and wherever there is life there is growth. The gospel and the Bible are both often referred to as a seed. Our Lord gave us his parable of the sower, and the seed, he says, is the Word of God. It has life inside it. It is not something stagnant or inert, something that cannot grow and develop and that you would expect to find in exactly the same condition in a year's time as you find it now. There is life in it and power, all of which suggests growth and development. A Christian is one who is born again, regenerated, a new creation, one who has been given life.

It is a great tragedy when a child never develops because he is deficient or defective and remains in an infantile condition. It is equally a tragedy in the spiritual life. "Grow in grace, and in the knowledge of our Lord and Saviour Jesus Christ" (2 Pet. 3:18). This is the characteristic of the Christian life just as it is the characteristic of natural life. There is always growing and developing and advancing; there are always evidences of growth.

The apostle Paul reminds believers in Ephesians 4 that they are born again, they have life, and they are all growing together. He says they must go on growing together until they arrive at that "perfect man, unto the measure of the stature of the fulness of Christ" (Eph. 4:13). This is taught throughout the New Testament. Life must develop and mature; we must keep going on in the direction of ultimate perfection.

Let us now face a second question, a practical one. Why is the author of Hebrews so concerned that we should be thus maturing? Why does he make this appeal to these people? "Leaving the principles [the elements, the first beginnings] of the doctrine of Christ," he says, "let us go on unto perfection. . . . And this we will do, if God permit" (6:1, 3). Why is this so important? I have already given one answer: we have been given life, and for life not to grow and develop is a contradiction in terms.

But we must add, to fail to mature and develop like this would dishonor God. The apostle Paul in writing to the Ephesians says that his work as a minister is "to make all men see what is the fellowship of the mystery, which from the beginning of the world hath been hid in God, who created all things by Jesus Christ: to the intent that now unto the principalities and powers in heavenly places might be known by [or through] the church the manifold wisdom of God" (Eph. 3:9–10). That is a tremendous statement. It means that through the church, through you and me and people like us, God is manifesting his wisdom and glory, even to the principalities and powers in heavenly places (the angels and the archangels, the good angels). So it follows of necessity that if you and I remain as undeveloped children, or if our condition is poor or undernourished, that is a reflection upon God. God is, as it were, leaving his reputation in our hands. He uses us in order to prove his greatness, his glory, and the wonders of his ways.

We often give the impression that we are much more troubled than the people in the world, that the main effect of our religion is to fill us with problems and difficulties and perplexities. How does that reflect upon the purpose and the plan of God and his glory in the salvation of men and women? God is saying through the gospel that he is going to produce a new humanity, that what failed in Adam will succeed in

Christ, and you and I are to manifest this. So it is not just a question of ourselves—it is a question of the honor and glory of God.

If then you are a member of the Christian church, you are claiming that you are one of God's people, and the world and the principalities and powers in the heavenly places are entitled to look at you and say, "Is this the sort of work that God does? Is this the kind of individual that God claims he has produced in a miraculous manner through sending his Son into the world?" That is why we should "go on unto perfection" (Heb. 6:1). It is a very poor recommendation of the grace of God and the power of the Spirit if you and I are exactly the same as we were a year ago or ten years ago, if we have not advanced at all, if we are not able to cope with life in a stronger, firmer, more triumphant manner than before. The honor of God is involved.

Let's look at this from our own standpoint. The author appeals to them to go on to perfection and to maturity *for their own sakes*, because if they do not, they will remain babies, children. This is as true in the spiritual realm as it is in the natural. Children are victims of fears because of their ignorance; they imagine things. All people who are ignorant and underdeveloped are full of superstitions and are victims of fears. That was the condition of the pagan world at the time of our Lord, and this still persists where paganism is rampant. People are fearful, terrified, wondering what is going to happen. But the apostle Paul says to the Romans, "ye have not received the spirit of bondage again to fear"—we have been delivered from that—" but ye have received the Spirit of adoption, whereby we cry, Abba, Father" (Rom. 8:15). He writes to Timothy, "God hath not given us the spirit of fear; but of power, and of love, and of a sound mind" (2 Tim. 1:7). Fear is a child-like condition, says the author of Hebrews, so leave it behind, "go on unto perfection" (6:1). Grow, and you will get rid of that childish fear.

Furthermore, children, again because of their ignorance, are ready victims of false teaching. The apostle wrote about this to the Ephesians: "Till we all come in the unity of the faith, and of the knowledge of the Son of God, unto a perfect man, unto the measure of the stature of the fulness of Christ" (Eph. 4:13). He then says, "that we henceforth be no more children, tossed to and fro, and carried about with every wind of doctrine, by the sleight of men, and cunning craftiness, whereby they lie in wait to deceive" (Eph. 4:14). Children are at the mercy of any plausible person who comes along. They do not understand or discern, and if anybody is nice and ingratiating, they take him at face value and believe all he says. Thus they are duped and misled and led astray.

This is equally true of spiritual children. One of the last things we develop is a sense of discrimination and understanding. There is a great lack of this at the present time. However smiling and ingratiating, however nice people may appear to be, the question is, what are they teaching? What is their doctrine? What do they stand for? It is alarming to notice the way in which people are misled because they see a smiling face on television. They are like children—"tossed to and fro, and carried about with every wind of doctrine" (Eph. 4:14).

Why is this? It is because they do not have a standard; they do not know how to test doctrine; they do not have knowledge. You cannot test anything without knowledge. Some people earn a living by testing—testing tea, testing wine, testing various foods. They must have knowledge to do that; they must have a standard. It is exactly the same with respect to truth. The person who does not know much but has just had some experience does not have a standard. You must have something objective; you must have knowledge. If you do not, you will be the victim of all kinds of false teaching.

There is another reason for growing and for ceasing to be children. Children never know how to react to circumstances and to what happens to them, and again this is because they do not understand. They are not only victims of imaginary fears, not only victims of false teachings, but when things go wrong they have nothing to fall back on. We should not expect them to—they are children. That is why we who are older and are parents and so on must protect and guard them. When something goes wrong with a little child, it is the end of the world. He has no comfort, no consolation. That is because he lacks knowledge, understanding, maturity. He doesn't know how to evaluate things or how to put things in perspective; he is entirely cast down. He becomes panicky, frantic; he feels utterly hopeless and does not know what to do or where to turn.

It is exactly the same with regard to the spiritual child. Nothing tests us as much as our reaction to circumstances. How do we react when things go wrong? These are practical matters. Some people seem to be good Christians until something goes wrong, and then they seem to be shattered; they have nothing to fall back on. They do not seem to have any consolation; they are victims. Is not this a great tragedy? What are we like when we are taken ill? What are we like when our circumstances suddenly turn against us? What are we like when we are disappointed? What are we like when we look into the face of death?

What is the point of our saying that we believe this or that and the other and that we are Christians and are different from people outside the faith if when the same trials come to us that come to them we do not react differently? What is the value of our Christianity then? Thus we not only fall short of living out the gospel—we bring the very name of God and of Christ into disrepute.

In the immediate context that we are dealing with here, a further reason is given for our advancing unto maturity and perfection. A great principle was laid down by our Lord himself when he said, "Take heed therefore how ye hear" (Luke 8:18). Then he adds, "For whosoever hath, to him shall be given; and whosoever hath not, from him shall be taken even that which he seemeth to have" (Luke 8:18). The more we have, the more we can receive. This is a peculiar thing, but it is very important. The more knowledge you have, the more knowledge you will be able to receive. Without a given substratum of knowledge and understanding you can never be introduced to deeper truths. The man or woman who knows a lot will always learn more. The man who does not know anything is never going to know more and is never going to grow in his knowledge and understanding.

That is the writer's whole argument. He says, "I would like to give you great comfort and consolation with regard to your position, in terms of understanding about our Lord being a 'high priest after the order of Melchisedec, of whom we have many things to say, and hard to be uttered, seeing ye are dull of hearing. For when for the time ye ought to be teachers, ye have need that one teach you again which be the first principles of the oracles of God'" (Heb. 5:10–12). "You know," says the author, "this is the tragedy of the position. I could put you right at once if only I could tell you about Jesus as the high priest after the order of Melchisedec. But I cannot do it because you have not sufficiently grasped the groundwork and the framework for me to teach this to you."

If we remain babies we are going to miss the most glorious things in the gospel. We are going to miss its most wonderful comfort, and we are going to remain weak. The world says knowledge is power, and to a point that is true in the natural sense, but it is even more true in the spiritual sense. The more we know, the more powerful we will be. The apostle Paul says this in every one of his epistles in some shape or form. In the third chapter of the epistle to the Ephesians he says he is praying that they might "be strengthened with might by his Spirit in the inner man" (Eph. 3:16). What for? That they "may be able to comprehend with all saints . . . " (Eph. 3:18). We need to be strengthened in order to receive the knowledge that we are meant to be "filled with all the fulness of God" and that he is able to do for us "exceeding abundantly above all we ask or think" (Eph. 3:19–20). It is possible for us to not know that we are miserable and unhappy and frightened and alarmed, but if we knew, we would be made strong. Knowledge is power. The more we know and the more we understand of God's ways, the stronger we will be.

It is like the difference between a sapling and a full-grown oak. The sapling has the potentiality in it, but it has not developed yet, and it cannot stand up to the gales and the hurricanes and the storms and the downpours. Do not remain as saplings, the author of Hebrews is telling us; grow, develop, mature; develop strength so that whatever happens you will stand. "The trees of the LORD are full of sap; the cedars of Lebanon, which he hath planted," says one of the psalmists (Ps. 104:16). The New Testament puts it like this: "rooted and grounded" (Eph. 3:17), "building up yourselves on your most holy faith" (Jude 20). Rooted! Grounded! Built up! Established! Made mature! In other words, the author of Hebrews is trying to persuade us to go on "to know the love of Christ, which passeth knowledge" (Eph. 3:19).

Let me give you one final reason for going on to perfection and maturity. Remember those who are outside. With all the present muddle and confusion I believe that one of the greatest evangelistic factors in the future is going to be the life of the individual Christian. We go to church on Sunday or to other meetings, but that is not going to influence unbelievers. But when they see a life that is absolutely different, they will pay attention.

"Let us go on unto perfection" (Heb. 6:1), says the author. But how do we do it? Of course he answers the question for us, and here is the first point: "Therefore leaving the principles of the doctrine of Christ, let us go on unto perfection" (6:1). What does he mean by "the principles"? He means the first principles, the elementary teachings, the foundational truths and principles. This is of vital importance. These Hebrew Christians were in trouble because they had become uncertain in their minds as to the basis and foundation of the Christian faith and their Christian position. They were in trouble about how men and women are saved. The very fact that they were looking back with longing eyes to their old Jewish religion is proof of that. The teaching they had been brought up under was that a man saved himself by keeping the Law. He presented his burnt offerings and sacrifices, and thereby he justified himself by his works, by his religion.

That was the cause of their trouble. So this man writes to them, and he puts it quite plainly. "When for the time ye ought to be teachers, ye have need that one teach you again which be the first principles of the oracles of God" (Heb. 5:12). He says, "I have to give you milk again. You have gone back, as it were, to the beginning, and you have become uncertain about the whole question of how a man is saved." He puts it here in specific terms. He says, " . . . not laying again the foundation of repentance from dead works, and of faith toward God, of the doctrine of baptisms, and of laying on of hands, and of resurrection of the dead, and of eternal judgment" (6:1–2). That is the evangelistic message. He says in essence, "You are a church, you are Christian people, and I do not want to give you milk any longer. I want to give you strong meat, because it is so full of comfort and consolation and strength. But I have to give you milk again, I have to go back and make sure that you really are Christians."

Then follows perhaps the most frightening passage in all of Scripture: "For it is impossible for those who were once enlightened, and have tasted of the heavenly gift, and were made partakers of the Holy Ghost, and have tasted the good word of God, and the powers of the world to come, if they shall fall away, to renew them again unto repentance; seeing they crucify to themselves the Son of God afresh, and put him to an open shame" (Heb. 6:4–6).

That passage just means this: a man who denies the Lord Jesus Christ and his atoning death and justifying resurrection, a man who does not lean absolutely and entirely upon him, is a man who is lost. He is a man who puts Christ to an open shame by denying him; he crucifies to himself the Son of God afresh. This does not refer to his actions; it does not refer to sins. This is a person who denies the whole gospel and rejoices in his denial. He is without hope.

That is the problem with which the author of Hebrews is confronting these people. He says, "You must be absolutely certain about this. You must not say, 'Yes, I believe in Christ,' then 'I am not so sure.'" He continues in essence, "Are you not certain yet as to the way of salvation? Do you not realize that all your works are 'dead works' (6:1)? It does not matter how good they may be. It does not matter what your obituary notice in the newspaper will be. In the sight of God they are dead works; there is no value in them at all. 'All our righteousnesses are as filthy rags' (Isa. 64:6). Are you not clear about that? Must I come and tell you all this again? Must I tell you that the blood of bulls and of goats and the ashes of a heifer can never make the unrighteous and the ungodly and the sinful clean in the sight of God? Are you going back to the types? Have you not realized that the antitype has come? Are you still unclear as to the one and only way of salvation? If so, you cannot grow, you cannot develop. I cannot even teach you until you are absolutely clear about this."

This is a great issue at the present time. Certain gatherings of Christians are always arguing about these fundamental principles; that is why they do not grow. There must be agreement about certain foundational principles. There is no hope for the Christian church until she is clear about the person of Christ and about the one and only way of salvation in him and by his precious blood as the result of repentance and new birth. That is the foundation. We must be absolutely clear about that.

My experience as a pastor enables me to say exactly the same thing. I know of nothing more tragic than that people should come to me, as they do, and wonder whether they are Christians at all, simply because they have fallen into a certain sin. Because they have sinned, they question the whole basis of their position. They are justifying themselves by their works and are not trusting absolutely in the Lord Jesus Christ and his death for them.

Are you sure that you are not trusting in yourself in some shape or form? If you are, you are in trouble because you are still a baby spiritually. You are confused; you are perplexed by your difficulties, and you do not know what to do or where to turn. We must be certain of these things before we can move on.

Even if we are certain about these things, we must not stop there, and here is the trouble with another large group of Christian people. They are quite clear that they are saved, they are quite clear about the way of salvation in Christ, and they are trusting only in him and in his precious blood. But many Christian people have been doing that for fifty years and have never advanced a single step further. There is no evidence of growth, no evidence of development, no increased understanding. They are exactly where they were twenty years ago, with no sign of advance at all. They have stopped at the first principles. They understand them, but they have never advanced beyond them. There is no deepening, no developing, no evidence of maturing or growth in understanding and knowledge. They have not advanced in the direction of perfection.

This is a fundamental point, and again we must test ourselves by it. You who are clear about the fact that you are Christians and that you are saved only by the blood of Christ, are you developing, are you maturing, is there a fullness about your understanding that was not there a year ago or ten years ago? You must be clear about the first principles, but you must leave them behind; you must go on and advance.

How? The writer gives us the next step: "strong meat." "Every one that useth milk is unskilful in the word of righteousness: for he is a babe. But strong meat belongeth to them that are full of age, even those who by reason of use have their senses exercised to discern both good and evil" (Heb. 5:13–14). What is "strong meat" (Heb. 5:14)? This is, in reality, the teaching of the New Testament epistles—those mighty epistles and their doctrines and their arguments.

The apostle Peter puts this in an almost plaintive way in his second epistle when he refers to the epistles of the apostle Paul: "And account that the longsuffering of our Lord is salvation; even as our beloved brother Paul also according to the wisdom given unto him hath written unto you; as also in all his epistles, speaking in them of these things; in which are some things hard to be understood, which they that are unlearned and unstable wrest, as they do also the other scriptures, unto their own destruction" (2 Pet. 3:15–16). Because they are "unlearned and unstable" (2 Pet. 3:16) they twist the Scriptures to their own destruction. They have not become mature; they have not gone on.

The apostle Peter says that in the epistles of the apostle Paul some things are "hard to be understood" (2 Pet. 3:16). Indeed many things in the Bible are hard to understand. But the question is, how do you react to that, what do you do about it? Do you say, "I cannot be bothered. I am much too busy for this"? Is that your attitude? Then you are a spiritual infant, and it is not surprising that you are in trouble, that you do not quite know what you believe, and that you believe that everything is Christian that calls itself Christian. We need strong meat if we are to grow.

These days Christian people are crying out for more and more singing and entertainment. Everything must be done in the modern fashion. But gospel truth is "strong meat" (Heb. 5:12), not mere entertainment. We must cease to be children wanting to be constantly pampered, spoon-fed, and entertained. We must be ready to use our intellects and gird up the loins of our mind and be strong and hope to the end for the salvation that is about to be revealed to us.

But we must realize that this is going to be difficult. There are difficult passages in the Scriptures, and we must patiently apply ourselves to their study. There is "strong meat" (Heb. 5:14) there—all the promises of God, all the great purposes of God, all the great doctrines, telling us about the Lord in his fullness. Thank God for strong meat, for the riches of his grace, for food for the soul that will build us up and make us strong and enable us to resist everything that comes against us.

This "strong meat belongeth to them that are of full age, even those who by reason of use have their senses exercised to discern both good and evil" (Heb. 5:14). We must "have [our] senses exercised" (Heb.

5:14). We must make use of the faculties that have been given to us; we must be diligent. He says this again in the sixth chapter, verses 11–12: "And we desire that every one of you do shew the same diligence to the full assurance of hope unto the end: that ye be not slothful, but followers of them who through faith and patience inherit the promises" (Heb. 6:11–12). Diligence! Application! Effort!

Are you troubled about the moral state today? Do you feel something must be done? It can only be done by you and by me as individuals. The church makes her pronouncements, but nobody listens. The church needs revival, reawakening, and that will never happen until every one of us begins to put diligence into this matter. Less time with the world, more time with God; more time with the Word of God; more time in prayer; more time in self-examination—"senses exercised to discern both good and evil" (Heb. 5:14).

Our fathers could tell what was true and what was not; they talked about heresy and truth. We do not. The trouble today is that people cannot discern the difference between good and evil. We do not have our senses exercised, and that is because we lack knowledge. So let us give ourselves to this. Let us use the powers that God has given us. Consider the powers and the faculties that you have in your profession or work; apply the same diligence here. Read books about it, discuss it together, ask questions. Do everything you can until you feel that you are laying hold upon the needed spiritual knowledge.

The apostle Paul told the Philippians exactly the same thing: "And this I pray, that your love may abound yet more and more in knowledge and in all judgment; that ye may approve things that are excellent; that you may be sincere and without offence till the day of Christ" (Phil. 1:9–10). There it is! If we really are Christians, and if we do bemoan the state of the church and the terrible state of the world and of society, then the call to us is this: "Let us go on to perfection" (Heb. 6:1). Let us grow in grace and in the knowledge of the Lord. Let us become spiritually mature men and women. Let us in understanding be men. Let us exercise our senses and together go on to full maturity, which will ultimately in the eternal state be even to the measure of the stature of the fullness of Christ himself. God, enable us to do so! Amen.

14

The Pattern

HEBREWS 8:1-5

Now of the things which we have spoken this is the sum:
We have such an high priest, who is set on the right hand
of the throne of the Majesty in the heavens; a minister of
the sanctuary, and of the true tabernacle, which the Lord
pitched, and not man. For every high priest is ordained to
offer gifts and sacrifices: wherefore it is of necessity that this
man have somewhat also to offer. For if he were on earth,
he should not be a priest, seeing that there are priests that
offer gifts according to the law: who serve unto the example
and shadow of heavenly things, as Moses was admonished
of God when he was about to make the tabernacle: for, See,
saith he, that thou make all things according to the pattern
shewed to thee in the mount.

In these words the author of the epistle to the Hebrews reminds us of
the great commission that was given to Moses, the servant of God, the
great leader and teacher of the children of Israel. But I want to suggest
to you that this great commission is also given to all who claim to be
preachers of the Christian gospel. What are we to preach? What is the
Christian message?

In other words, the fundamental question facing everybody who is interested in these things is the question of *authority*. It must be extremely difficult for those outside the Christian church to know what the gospel is; they hear so many different things. They hear people claiming "This is the gospel" and others saying, "That is not the gospel." Different people are using the name "Christian" and yet are saying things that are obviously contradictory of one another. So those who are outside the church rightly ask, "Who am I to believe? What is one to believe?"

This question of authority is the source of all modern-day confusion, and there is only one answer to that question—*revelation*.

The author of the epistle of Hebrews was writing to Christians who had become confused about the faith. There were false teachers even in the first century, and people often wondered what they should believe. This man writes to them for that reason, and he gives them this great declaration of the Christian gospel and the way of salvation. In doing this he constantly emphasizes the matter of authority, and he puts it in a most interesting manner. He is writing to Jews who had become Christians, and he says in essence, "Do you Jews not see that your position is similar to how it was in the days of your great national hero and leader Moses?" That man stood out in the history of Israel as the great lawgiver, the teacher greater than all other teachers, the man who was given the particular task of leading the children of Israel out of the captivity of Egypt and into the land of Canaan, the great picture of salvation that runs through the entire Old Testament.

Where did Moses get his message? Why did he do what he did? How do you explain the character of Moses and his teaching? Was he just a nationalist? Was he merely an astute politician? Was he just a clever and able man? He addressed his contemporaries and called them to do certain things at great risk and gave them detailed instruction with respect to their worship and their ceremonies and various other matters. How did he do all this? What enabled him to do it? What was the source of his message and of his authority? The author of Hebrews gives us the answer.

Moses was not just a great religious teacher. Moses was not just one of those geniuses that arise from time to time and seem to be endowed with unusual ability. He was not a natural-born leader. Moses did not appear before the people and say, "I have been meditating upon this problem, and I have formed a plan, and now I want to present it to you." He was not a statesman who said, "Here are my proposals for you. Are you ready to accept them and to act upon them and to follow me?" That was not what Moses said at all. What he said and did was the exact opposite. Moses had become a shepherd, and he really did not want to be disturbed. He became the man that he was for one reason only: God called him and gave him a commission (read the story for yourself in the early chapters of the Book of Exodus). He said, "I am not a speaker; what shall I say to them?" God said to him, "Go and say, 'The God of your Fathers has sent me unto you.' Say to them, 'Jehovah has sent me, and this is the message that he has given me.'" Moses, trembling, went and did this very thing (see Exodus 3–4).

Later Moses gave that great Law, the Ten Commandments, and the moral law and the ceremonial law and the laws of behavior and all those matters that you can read of in the early books of the Old Testament that are so interesting and so important. Where did he get all that from? Was he just an exceptional lawyer? How did this man get all these ideas? The answer is given to us in the Bible, and the man writing to these Hebrew Christians is simply quoting what you can find in Exodus 25:40.

God called Moses onto a mountain, and he kept him there forty days and forty nights. During that period he told him exactly what he was to do, what he was to say, how he was to build the tabernacle, and how he was to furnish it. God told him the color of various materials that were to be used, the measurements, the various types of wood that were to be used, and the amount of gold that was to be used. Everything was given to him in exact detail. For forty days and forty nights God gave this man his commission and told him exactly what he was to do, and then he sent him down to do it. As God finished giving him this detailed plan, he uttered this final word to him: "And look that thou make them after their pattern, which was shewed thee in the mount" (Ex. 25:40).

So the writer is reminding these Hebrew Christians of that, and this is what we need to consider as well. God gave to Moses not only a general idea, but a detailed plan. Everything in the most minute detail was to be done exactly as God had told Moses. I emphasize that because the great message of the Bible is one, and every detail is of importance. We are totally incapable in these matters, and we need detailed instruction given to us by God himself. What are the most important matters? First of all, how is God to be approached? That was the problem confronting the children of Israel. They have come out of Egypt, the hosts of Pharaoh are after them, but now what are they to do? They have come against the Red Sea, there is a mountain on each side of them, and they are hemmed in. Are they are finished? Not at all! "Speak unto the children of Israel," says God to Moses, "that they go forward" (Ex. 14:15). The sea opens, and through it they go. Then they are traveling in a wilderness. Now what are they to do, how are they to live, what can they eat? How are they, above all, to keep in contact and communion with God? God answers all those questions in the detailed pattern and plan that he gives to Moses when he is forty days and forty nights upon the mountain. This is the way to approach God; this is the way to worship God; this is the one and the only way of blessing.

There is only one way to worship God and to be blessed of God, the way that was given to Moses. Certain people disputed this. Among them were even some of the sons of Aaron, the brother of Moses, who was made the high priest. They thought they could find a better way, and they introduced what is called "strange fire," and they were killed because of it (Leviticus 10). Later three clever men named Korah, Dathan, and Abiram, princes of Israel, objected to God's way. "Why should it only be the way of Moses and Aaron?" they said in essence. "We have better ideas; let us put them into practice." They tried it, and they were destroyed in a most calamitous manner (Numbers 16). God's pattern, God's plan, must be followed. "See . . . that thou make all things according to the pattern shewed to thee in the mount" (Heb. 8:5).

The writer reminds these Hebrews of this. He says in summary, "That is how it was under Moses, and if it was that way with respect to 'the . . . shadow of heavenly things' (v. 5), how much more is it true with regard to the heavenly things themselves." The tabernacle and the temple and all that was only a pattern, a shadow, a type, but not the real thing. So if obedience is necessary with regard to the "pattern," how infinitely more is it necessary with regard to the great fact itself. "So," he concludes in essence, "there must be no argument or disputation. All things must always be done according to the pattern that God revealed on the mount."

This is where the church generally has gone astray. According to popular teaching we must start with man's needs, with man's ideas. Religious journals and books tell us, "We must realize that modern man is not what man has been in the past. We are living in an entirely new age—the scientific age! Man has grown up! The old forms may have been all right in the past, but no longer. To address modern man we must understand him, we must use his idiom, we must get hold of his modes of thinking, and if we do not do that, we can do nothing at all." They start with man, the modern man of science and knowledge.

We have been told for so long that we must set out in the great search for truth. That is people's idea of Christianity and of religion. We exalt philosophy and speculation and human thinking. What man thinks, what man says—that has been the approach. It is not surprising that we are in utter confusion. The Bible has told us from the very beginning that a man cannot find God merely by searching for him (Job 11:7). Paul tells us, "For after that in the wisdom of God the world by wisdom knew not God, it pleased God by the foolishness of preaching to save them that believe" (1 Cor. 1:21). But we have reversed that, and our thinking is all wrong.

There is only one thing for us to do: we must come back to the pattern shown in the mount. I invite you to come back to this mount of revelation, the mount of God. We must cease from our own wisdom and consult again the pattern that God has been graciously pleased to give to us. This is proclaimed throughout Scripture. Here the writer reminds us how it was in the case of Moses, but it was exactly the same with all the prophets, with all the great teachers of Israel. The apostle Peter writes, "No prophecy of the scripture is of any private interpretation" (2 Pet. 1:20). The teaching of the prophets was not the result of their own meditation and cogitation; they did not suddenly get a bright idea. "The prophecy came not in old time by the will of man." How did it come then? "But holy men of God spake as they were moved by the Holy Ghost" (2 Pet. 1:21). They were not voicing their own opinions and ideas. They were vehicles communicating the message of God. Read them for yourselves. They say, "The Spirit of God came upon me"; "Thus saith the Lord." God gave them the pattern, God gave them the message and the revelation, and they wrote it down or spoke it. They were giving God's thoughts; they were transmitters of what God had revealed to them.

When you come to the New Testament the first preacher we see is John the Baptist. At a certain historical point we are told, "The word of God came unto John the son of Zacharias in the wilderness" (Luke 3:2). The Word of God came to him! He did not arrive at anything— it took hold of him.

The apostle Paul says the same thing about himself: "[we are] stewards of the mysteries of God" (1 Cor. 4:1). We are only stewards; the mysteries have been given to us. In writing to the Corinthians, in order to show his authority as an apostle, he says, "Moreover, brethren, I declare unto you the gospel which I preached unto you, which also ye have received, and wherein ye stand. . . . I delivered unto you first of all that which I also received" (1 Cor. 15:1, 3). They and he had *received* it. He puts it even more explicitly in writing to the Galatians: "I certify you, brethren, that the gospel which was preached of me is not after man. For I neither received it of man, neither was I taught it, but by the revelation of Jesus Christ" (Gal. 1:11–12). He is merely a custodian, a guardian, a herald. He is an ambassador. He does not give his own opinions; he gives the opinion of the King who has sent him and appointed him. He does not use his own authority; it is delegated authority.

It is still the same today. I have no authority in the pulpit apart from the Word of God. I do not understand more than anybody else. I have nothing to say except to deliver God's message, the "pattern" God has been pleased to show on the mount of revelation. What is God's pattern for men and women and their well-being in time and in eternity? What is the message of the Christian gospel? Let me put it in terms of certain mountains, certain peaks on which the pattern has been given so plainly and so clearly.

Let us go first of all to the Mount of Transfiguration, the particular account of which is given in the seventeenth chapter of the Gospel according to Matthew. Why do I start with this mount? This mount tells us clearly about the blessed person, Jesus of Nazareth, the central figure of the New Testament. Here is the one whose portrait we have in the pages of the four Gospels; here is the one about whom the apostles preached. The great question is, who is he? The greatest and the most momentous question for the world tonight is, who is this blessed person?

"And after six days Jesus taketh Peter, James, and John his brother, and bringeth them up into an high mountain apart, and was transfigured before them: and his face did shine as the sun, and his raiment was white as the light" (Matt. 17:1–2). One of the other Gospels says that his clothing was white "as no fuller on earth can white them" (Mark 9:3). He was transfigured before them, a glory suddenly flashed upon them, and they saw his majesty.

Peter, writing the first chapter of his last epistle as an old man on the verge of the grave, puts it like this: "We have not followed cunningly devised fables, when we made known unto you the power and the coming of our Lord Jesus Christ, but were eyewitnesses of his majesty. For he received from God the Father honour and glory, when there came such a voice to him from the excellent glory. . . . And this voice which came from heaven we heard, when we were with him in the holy mount" (2 Pet. 1:16–18). Suddenly he became transfigured, and his face was shining like the brightness of the sun. His very clothing was entirely transformed, and a glory seemed to cover the whole place. "Behold a voice out of the cloud . . . said, This is my beloved Son, in whom I am well pleased; hear ye him" (Matt. 17:5). This is the One to whom we must listen. "This is my beloved Son; he is the one I am sending; he is the one to listen to."

So it is not surprising that the author of the epistle to the Hebrews starts his great epistle with these words: "God, who at sundry times and in divers [various] manners spake in time past unto the fathers by the prophets, hath in these last days spoken unto us by his Son, whom he hath appointed heir of all things . . . who being the brightness of his glory, and the express image of his person . . . " (Heb. 1:1–3). This is the vital point. The world is in trouble, and we have listened to men, we have listened to philosophers, we have listened to politicians and statesmen and poets and all the people who claim to be experts, but they do not help us, they do not understand. They do not even know themselves. They are failures in their own personal lives, and none of them can solve the problem of death and the grave; none of them can teach us how to live. Listen instead to the voice of the holy mount: "This is my beloved Son, in whom I am well pleased" (Matt. 17:5). We do not gather as Christ's church to put forward our own theories and ideas or to propound some new morality or whatever. We gather to say that God has spoken, and spoken finally, in his Son. Hear him, says God himself, "from the excellent glory" (2 Pet. 1:17). Peter and James and John heard these words when they were with him on that holy mount.

Oh how vital, how essential this is! Jesus of Nazareth is not just a great religious teacher. He is not just a moral reformer. He is not just the first great socialist, nor the first great pacifist. He is none of these things. You must not reduce him. He is the Son of God. He has come from heaven. He is "the brightness of God's glory, and the express image of his person" (Heb. 1:3). These apostles were eyewitnesses of that majesty and glory, and this is their conclusion: "There is none other name under heaven given among men, whereby we must be saved" (Acts 4:12). He is unique; there is none like him. He himself said, "I am the light of the world: he that followeth me shall not walk in darkness, but shall have the light of life" (John 8:12). On that Mount of Transfiguration we see that he is indeed the Son of God—God is speaking to us in the person of his only begotten Son.

No one else will ever bring you to the knowledge of God apart from Jesus Christ. And no one else will ever give you a true knowledge of yourself. "The heart is deceitful above all things, and desperately wicked: who can know it?" (Jer. 17:9). Only he can tell us the truth about ourselves; only he can tell us how to live; he alone can tell us how to die; he alone can tell us about the eternity that lies ahead of us. "Hear ye him" (Matt. 17:5). Here is the essential thing about this pattern: it is all found in this one blessed Person and in no other.

Let us now consider the Sermon on the Mount (Matthew 5–7). This sermon was delivered by the blessed person who was transfigured on the Mount of Transfiguration: "Hear ye him" (Matt. 17:5), said God from heaven. So let us listen to him. What is his teaching? Let me try to give you a summary of the Sermon on the Mount.

Our Lord starts with the Beatitudes. These are descriptions of what a Christian really is, and if the world ever needed to know that, it is at this present time. The idea today is that anybody who is nice and good and friendly is a Christian. People are saying from Christian pulpits and in best-selling religious books that whether you believe any of the doctrines of the Christian faith or not does not matter—you can deny them all. If you are good and kind and loving, they claim, you are a Christian, you have the love of God in you; wherever you find kindness and goodness and love, there you find God.

But if you really want to know what a Christian is, examine the Sermon on the Mount, and this is what you will find: "Blessed are the poor in spirit" (Matt. 5:3). That means that you think nothing of yourself, that you know you have no hope. "Blessed are they that mourn" (Matt. 5:4). You are grieved because you are a sinner. You are not always justifying yourself and showing what a good fellow you are, though you deny Christ. "Blessed are the meek" (Matt. 5:5). Is the modern man a picture of meekness? Considering the confidence and assurance and the pomp and the show of it all, modern man is obviously filled with a spirit of self-confidence and assurance. He despises everybody who has lived before him; he has arrived.

Jesus goes on to make other contrasts. "Blessed are they which do hunger and thirst after righteousness" (Matt. 5:6). Is the modern world hungering and thirsting after righteousness? Is the man who thinks that as long as he lives a fairly good and clean and decent and moral life and gives a bit of help to other people he is a fine Christian and that if he goes to church once a year he is hungering and thirsting after righteousness? "Blessed are the merciful . . . blessed are the pure in heart . . . blessed are the peacemakers . . . blessed are they which are persecuted for righteousness' sake" (Matt. 5:7–10). That is a portrait of Christian men and women. They are not just nice and good and decent people. They are deeply spiritual, in the way that is described so perfectly in the Beatitudes.

The next thing we are told is that the Law of God is absolute. The modern world hates that. It says, "We do not believe in the law. We believe in Jesus, but we do not believe in the God of Sinai. We believe in the love of God in Christ, the God of Jesus." But listen to what Jesus says, the One God tells us to listen to. "Think not," he says, "that I am come to destroy the law, or the prophets: I am not come to destroy, but to fulfil. For verily I say unto you, Till heaven and earth pass, one jot or one tittle shall in no wise pass from the law, till all be fulfilled" (Matt. 5:17–18). The law given through Moses was the law of God, and it is absolute, and it stands. The whole law matters; it is not enough to keep bits of the law. If you break one section of the law, you have broken the whole law. God demands that the whole law be kept, and it is this: "Thou shalt love the Lord thy God with all thy heart, and with all thy soul, and with all thy strength, and with all thy mind; and thy neighbour as thyself" (Luke 10:27). That is what Jesus teaches. Not a little bit of goodness and kindness and compassion, but loving God with the whole of your being and living to his glory and to his praise.

Then Jesus goes on to tell us the spiritual character of this law. He says it is not external, it is something in the heart. It is not enough that you have not committed murder; if you have hated and murdered a man in your heart or in your imagination you have murdered him. If you say "Thou fool" (Matt. 5:22) about a man, you have murdered him. It is the same with adultery. The Pharisees said, "We have never committed adultery." But Christ said, "Whosoever looketh on a woman to lust after her hath committed adultery with her already in his heart" (Matt. 5:28). God does not judge by external appearance; God judges the heart. Our Lord says to the Pharisees later on, "Ye are they which justify yourselves before men, but God knoweth your hearts: for that which is highly esteemed among men is abomination in the sight of God" (Luke 16:15). He goes on to point out that the Law is not a matter of observing certain externals—it is the heart that matters. God wants the heart—the whole heart.

Our Lord goes on to tell us that we must be absolutely honest with God. He says in effect, "When you fast, do not make a show of it and parade it in order to be thought of highly by men; instead go wash your face and give the impression that you are not doing anything at all" (Matt. 6:16–18). He says further, "If therefore thine eye be single, thy whole body shall be full of light. But if thine eye be evil, thy whole body shall be full of darkness" (Matt. 6:22–23). You must be true within. Our Lord continues, "Judge not, that ye be not judged. For with what judgment ye judge, ye shall be judged: and with what measure ye mete, it shall be measured to you again. And why beholdest thou the mote that is in thy brother's eye, but considerest not the beam that is in thine own eye?" (Matt. 7:1–3). He unmasks hypocrisy and pretense and sham. He says we must be absolutely honest, for we are under the eye of God.

He goes on to say that the way to life is a narrow way. "Enter ye in at the strait gate: for wide is the gate, and broad is the way, that leadeth to destruction, and many there be which go in thereat: because strait is the gate, and narrow is the way, which leadeth unto life, and few there be that find it" (Matt. 7:13–14). Believers will be derided and condemned, perhaps even persecuted. It is a "strait gate . . . [a] narrow . . . way" (Matt. 7:13–14) to follow him.

He ends the sermon by telling us about judgment. The wolf thinks he is very clever when he covers himself with "sheep's clothing," but he will be unmasked. The fruit that appears to be right will be judged by the eye of the eternal God. "Do men gather grapes of thorns, or figs of thistles?" (Matt. 7:15–16). A final judgment is coming. "Many will say to me in that day, Lord, Lord, have we not prophesied in thy name . . . and in thy name done many wonderful works? And then will I profess unto them, I never knew you: depart from me, ye that work iniquity" (Matt. 7:22–23). He sums it all up in that tremendous parable of the two houses, one built on the rock and one on the sand, both looking the same. "Therefore whosoever heareth these sayings of mine, and doeth them, I will liken him unto a wise man, which built his house upon a rock" (Matt. 7:24). That house did not fall. The man who built his house on the sand, which he had put up so quickly, the jerry-built house, thinks he is all right. But, says our Lord, "And everyone that heareth these sayings of mine, and doeth them not, shall be likened unto a foolish man, which built his house upon the sand: and the rain descended, and the floods came, and the winds blew, and beat upon that house; and it fell: and great was the fall of it" (Matt. 7:26–27). This the judgment of God! This is Christianity.

"Listen to him," says God on the Mount of Transfiguration. In the Sermon on the Mount we are listening to him. A modern man might write in a newspaper article or in his book or might preach from a pulpit that Jesus is just love and that God loves everybody. But in the Sermon on the Mount Jesus condemned every one of us, showing that we have all broken the holy Law of God. We are all unclean; we are all hypocrites; we are all under the judgment of God. That is the pattern that we see in the Sermon on the Mount.

I thank God that we can flee to yet another mount, a hill called "Calvary" (Luke 23:33). Blessed be the name of God—the pattern here is more glorious than anywhere else. On the Mount of Transfiguration Moses and Elijah came and spoke to him, and what did they talk to him about? " . . . his decease [literally exodus] which he should accomplish at Jerusalem" (Luke 9:31). The great representatives of the Law and the Prophets discussed with him his fulfillment of all they had taught and said. He is the fulfillment of all that we read about the burnt offerings and sacrifices and many other things in the Old Testament. He is the one about whom the prophets had been speaking. For example, "Comfort ye, comfort ye my people, saith your God" (Isa. 40:1). Why? A great person, the Messiah, is coming. "Make straight in the desert a highway for our God. Every valley shall be exalted, and every mountain and hill shall be made low: and the crooked shall be made straight, and the rough places plain" (Isa. 40:3–4). What is happening? He is coming! "And the glory of the LORD shall be revealed, and all flesh shall see it together" (Isa. 40:5). Now here is this blessed person, the one who flashes the glory of God into the eyes of Peter and James and John on the Mount of Transfiguration. This one "taught them as one having authority, and not as the scribes" (Matt. 7:29). This one lived a perfect life, worked miracles, gave sight to the blind and power to walk to the lame, raised the dead, and silenced the tempest.

But we also see him on the Mount of Calvary crucified on a tree in utter weakness and apparent helplessness. What is he doing there? How did he get there? The answer is, "He stedfastly set his face to go to Jerusalem" (Luke 9:51). Some Pharisees tried to dissuade him, saying in effect, "Don't go near Jerusalem. Herod is determined to kill you" (Luke 9:31). But he insisted upon going. Then at the scene of Jesus's arrest one of his disciples was prepared to defend him with his sword. "Put it back," he said in essence. "If I wanted to escape I could summon twelve legions of angels and go straight to heaven. But I have come to fulfill all righteousness" (Matt. 26:51–53). "The Son of man came not to be ministered unto, but to minister, and to give his life a ransom for many" (Matt. 20:28). He said, "As Moses lifted up the serpent in the wilderness, even so must the Son of man be lifted up: that whosoever believeth in him should not perish, but have eternal life" (John 3:14–15). That is why he was on the cross.

What do we see on this blessed mount? Would you know God, would you have new life, would you lose the fear of death and the grave, would you make certain of your eternal bliss in heaven? Then listen to the message of this mount. What is the message of Calvary?

First, it is a message concerning the holiness of God. The author of the epistle to the Hebrews makes a great deal of this. In many ways it is his central theme. It was essential that he should do so because there was great confusion on this point. The message is this: "Without shedding of blood is no remission [of sin]" (Heb. 9:22). Of course, that was the message given through Moses. When God gave that pattern to Moses on the mount, he told him how to build the tabernacle and its various compartments. He told him how he was to set up priests and the high priest and how they were to take a certain animal, put their hands on its head, kill the animal, take the blood, do this and that with it, then burn the carcass, and so on. Bulls and goats, ashes of a heifer, a paschal lamb, a lamb offered day by day—what does it all mean? It was God who told Moses to instruct the children of Israel to do all this. Why? "Without shedding of blood is no remission [of sin]" (Heb. 9:22).

God is a holy God, and he has told us in so many places that he cannot abide sin. He is the governor of the universe, the great law-giver, and he has made it plain that sin must be and will be punished. Through Moses he taught the people to take bulls and goats and to kill them and to apply the blood. But the great message of the epistle to the Hebrews is this:

But Christ being come an high priest of good things to come, by a greater and more perfect tabernacle, not made with hands, that is to say, not of this building; neither by the blood of goats and calves, but by his own blood he entered in once into the holy place, having obtained eternal redemption for us. For if the blood of bulls and of goats, and the ashes of an heifer sprinkling the unclean, sanctifieth to the purifying of the flesh: how much more shall the blood of Christ, who through the eternal Spirit offered himself without spot to God, purge your conscience from dead works to serve the living God? (Heb. 9:11–14)

The writer continues to argue this great theme. He says in a later chapter, as he has said in earlier chapters, that the blood of bulls and goats could not take away sins. Why? Because they were only animals. They were merely figures pointing forward to something that was going to happen. The blood of bulls and of goats is not sufficient, but they have a great function—they pointed forward to a blood that would be enough.

What blood is this? John the Baptist said the first thing about it. He was with his followers, and they thought the world of John, this great teacher, this remarkable man in the desert. But as John is talking to them he suddenly sees the Lord Jesus Christ pass by, and he turns to his followers and says, "Behold the Lamb of God, which taketh away the sin of the world" (John 1:29). "The Lamb of God"! What does he mean? He says in effect, "This is the fulfillment of all that was taught by Moses and the prophets. We have been using lambs, but they were only temporary. Their blood was not sufficient, but here now is the Lamb of God himself. God has provided his own Lamb, his own sacrifice." So the author of the epistle to the Hebrews tells us that when our Lord went into heaven he did not offer the blood of bulls and goats. He offered "his own blood" (Heb. 9:12). He is God's sacrifice; he is God's Lamb! "Without shedding of blood is no remission" (Heb. 9:22), but God has shed the blood of his own dear Son in order that you and I might be forgiven. The hymn-writers tell us:

His blood can make the foulest clean,
His blood availed for me.

Charles Wesley, "O for a Thousand Tongues to Sing"

There is a fountain filled with blood
Drawn from Immanuel's veins;
And sinners, plunged beneath that flood,
Lose all their guilty stains.

William Cowper, "There Is a Fountain Filled with Blood"

That is the message from the hill of Calvary.

It follows inevitably that this is the only way whereby we can ever be forgiven. Is it conceivable that a holy, loving, righteous, just God should ever have allowed his Son to suffer what he suffered upon that cross—the agony and the shame, the broken heart, the cry of dereliction—is it conceivable that God would ever have allowed him to suffer all that if there was any other way whereby man could be saved and forgiven and redeemed and reconciled to God? Absolutely not!

There was no other good enough
To pay the price of sin,
He only could unlock the gate
Of heaven and let us in.

Cecil Frances Alexander, "There Is a Green Hill Far Away"

"For other foundation can no man lay than that is laid, which is Jesus Christ" (1 Cor. 3:11). "For I determined not to know any thing among you, save Jesus Christ, and him crucified" (1 Cor. 2:2). There is no other way. Calvary tells me that. The Son came to earth to die. "Thus it becometh us to fulfil all righteousness" (Matt. 3:15). "He set stedfastly his face . . . " (Luke 9:51). If he had not done so, there would be salvation for none. Salvation comes only through the shed blood of the Son of God, through his sacrifice for us on the hill of Calvary, making his soul an offering for us.

So the message of this hill is a message about the love of God— "Love so amazing, so divine." The innocent, pure, guiltless Son of God went willingly as a Lamb led to the slaughter, God the Father laying "on him the iniquity of us all" (Isa. 53:6) Here is love! This modern sentimental notion of love is an insult to real love and an insult to God. If you want to know the measure of God's love, you must go to Calvary's hill, and there you see it—God giving up his own Son to bear the punishment and the shame and the agony of all our sin, to "taste death for every man" (Heb. 2:9). "God so loved the world, that he gave"—gave up to the shame and the death of the cross—"his only begotten Son, that whosoever believeth in him should not perish, but have everlasting life" (John 3:16). My friends, that is the message of this hill; here is the pattern shown us on the mount by the person who was transfigured, by the One who preached the sermon, by the One who died upon the cross.

We will now consider Mount Olivet. Our Lord died upon the cross, his body was buried, and he rose again, bursting asunder the bands of death as he arose triumphant over the grave. He then revealed himself for forty days to certain of his chosen disciples and certain other people. On one occasion five hundred saw him alive. You will find the evidence for this in 1 Corinthians 15:6. He asked his disciples to meet with him on a mount called Olivet, and there he gave them the great promise of the coming baptism of the Holy Spirit, the baptism of power without which even these apostles, who had been with him for three years and knew all his teaching and had seen his death and resurrection, could do nothing. This baptism gives conviction and power to the Word. "And when he had spoken these things, while they beheld, he was taken up; and a cloud received him out of their sight. And while they looked stedfastly toward heaven as he went up, behold, two men stood by them in white apparel; which also said, Ye men of Galilee, why stand ye gazing up into heaven? this same Jesus, which is taken up from you into heaven, shall so come in like manner as ye have seen him go into heaven" (Acts 1:9–11). Having been told that, "Then returned they unto Jerusalem from the mount called Olivet, which is from Jerusalem a sabbath day's journey" (Acts 1:12).

Thank God for this message in this modern, evil, arrogant world, the world that is so proud of its atomic power and its own abilities and thinks that it can control history. Consider the pride of the politicians who think they really are going to make a difference. Of course they are not. Here is the answer to it all: "This same Jesus, which is taken up from you into heaven, shall so come in like manner as ye have seen him go into heaven" (Acts 1:11). This is as essential a part of the gospel as all the others. When we come to the Communion table what are we doing? We are declaring "the Lord's death till he come" (1 Cor. 11:26). He is going to come, and we are waiting for him! The message of the mount of Olivet proclaims this. He has taken his seat at the right hand of God, he has all power in his hands, and he is "expecting till his enemies be made his footstool" (Heb. 10:13). Then he will come the second time, as the author of the epistle to the Hebrews puts it, "without sin unto salvation" (Heb. 9:28).

What is the future of the world? Will it be one of gradual improvement? Is it one of increasing reform? Will men will be so educated and so nice and good and kind that they will banish war and never fight again? Will the whole world be increasingly perfect, and are we all going to have a great time, no work, plenty of money, great enjoyment, everything perfect? Oh, the blindness of those who believe in such folly. Here is what the apostle Paul says: "Evil men and seducers shall wax worse and worse" (2 Tim. 3:13). Jesus said there will be "wars and rumours of wars" (Matt. 24:6) and also, "But as the days of Noah were, so shall also the coming of the Son of man be. For as in the days that were before the flood they were eating and drinking, marrying and giving in marriage, until the day that [Noah] entered the ark . . . " (Matt. 24:37–38). It was the same with Sodom and Gomorrah. In its amazing symbolism of extraordinary beasts the Book of Revelation tells us that evil men shall indeed wax worse and worse. There we see pictures of great world powers arising, military powers, governmental powers, church powers—beasts with power and authority controlling the whole world, killing people who do not have the mark of the beast on their hands or foreheads, mighty power shaking the universe and dominating civilization.

God in his inscrutable wisdom permits this, but only for a while. When least expected the One who ascended into heaven from the mount of Olivet comes riding the clouds of heaven, surrounded by the holy angels. He is the King of kings and Lord of lords, riding upon his white horse. He is coming back into this world to complete what he began—to judge the world in righteousness, to destroy all the enemies of God, to cast the Devil and all his followers, whether they be angelic spirits or human beings, into the lake of perdition, to cast them eternally out of the presence of God.

He also comes to set up his glorious kingdom of light and knowledge and truth. The whole cosmos will be purged of all evil and every relic of sin and wrongdoing. "The earth shall be full of the knowledge of the LORD, as the waters cover the sea" (Isa. 11:9). Christ will reign over all and will hand the kingdom back to his Father, and God will be all and in all. That is the pattern we see on the mount of Olivet.

Do you realize that that is the pattern? Are you unhappy, are you conscious of failure, are you "poor in spirit" (Matt. 5:3)? Are you a failure because you are looking for but have not found life, peace, power, hope? Is that your position? The pattern we have been studying is all you need, in fact infinitely more than you need. But here is the vital question: Do you accept this as the pattern, or are you still trusting in your own opinions and the opinions of men and women like yourselves, clever people who talk on the radio and television and write their articles and think they know a thing or two? There are not many choices here. We either do things according to God's pattern or we do not. Have you submitted to that pattern? Do you realize that this is the pattern outlined by the Son of God himself, the One whom God the Father sent and of whom he said, "This is my beloved Son, in whom I am well pleased; hear ye him" (Matt. 17:5)? Have you listened to him? Have you listened to him on the cross? Look into that face; see the suffering, the agony; listen to him. He is telling you, "This is the only way whereby you can be saved. I would not be here but for that. I am dying for you. You have nothing to do except to believe in me and to trust in the efficacy of my blood and resurrection and intercession."

He is coming again, and believing in him will usher you and all who believe into the joy that is without equal in its glory. But if you do not accept this pattern, that coming again will be to you the beginning of everlasting destruction. Believe on the Lord Jesus Christ, and you will be saved. Simply come just as you are and say, "I see my folly, I believe the pattern, I submit myself to God's salvation." Just go to him and say that, and he will receive you, and you will begin to know that you are a part of the great plan and purpose of God, and you will be amazed day by day at the outworking of this glorious plan in your own personal life. And as you go on with him, your wonder will increase more and more until at last you find yourself in his glorious presence beginning to enjoy glory everlasting. Amen.

15

God's Own People

Then verily the first covenant had also ordinances of divine service, and a worldly sanctuary. For there was a tabernacle made; the first, wherein was the candlestick, and the table, and the shewbread; which is called the sanctuary. And after the second veil, the tabernacle which is called the Holiest of all; which had the golden censer, and the ark of the covenant overlaid round about with gold, wherein was the golden pot that had manna, and Aaron's rod that budded, and the tables of the covenant.

I want to call your attention in particular to that last statement about the ark of the covenant "wherein was the golden pot that had manna, and Aaron's rod that budded, and the tables of the covenant" (9:4).

One of the troubles with the Christian church throughout her long history, and especially perhaps at the present time, is a failure to realize who and what exactly she is. The same is equally true of the individual Christian. We somehow fail to realize who we are as Christians and all the glorious possibilities that exist for us. This tendency is shown particularly in the long and checkered history of the children of Israel as we find it depicted in the pages of the Old Testament. These were

God's people, a unique people, and yet they were constantly unhappy and perplexed and in troubles and difficulties.

What was the matter with them? In a sense it can all be reduced to this: They would persist in forgetting who they were. They forgot their own greatness; they failed to realize that they were God's own people. They forgot what God had provided for them and what God was ready to do for them. Constantly they were looking at the other nations and thinking of themselves as if they were like these other nations. They envied the other nations for certain things they had; they envied those kingdoms and desired a king for themselves, not realizing that to be in a theocracy is more wonderful than to have a king. The children of Israel constantly looked upon themselves as if they were merely one nation among others. They never saw their true uniqueness, and as a result their history was one of mourning, rebellion, unhappiness, and wandering away from God and being called back. The whole story of the Old Testament can be explained by the fact that these people did not realize their true nature but persisted in conceiving of themselves in an earthly and human manner.

Now they were entirely without excuse for all this because wherever they were and wherever they went they had a permanent reminder of the very essence of their being, as we see in these words we are going to consider now. Wherever they went, the ark of the covenant went with them. God had commanded this. It was placed first of all in a tabernacle that could be moved about, and eventually it was placed in the great temple that was built in Jerusalem. This ark of the covenant was the agreement between them and God, and God commanded that in that very ark of the covenant certain things should be placed. These included the golden pot that contained manna, Aaron's rod that budded, and the tables of the covenant. God commanded his people to place these things in the ark in order that they might have a permanent reminder of certain things. Every time they looked at the temple, every time the high priest went into the Holiest of All, they were reminded of the ark of the covenant and what it contained. That in turn would remind them of their whole being, their essential nature, and that should have delivered them from the constant tendency to conceive of themselves in a purely earthly, human manner and to find themselves so constantly overwhelmed by troubles and disasters.

I suggest that this reminder is as essential today as it has ever been. If you look at the state of the Christian church, you find a condition of which no Christian can be proud. What is the matter with the Christian church? Why is she so ineffective and powerless? Why does she count for so little in the modern world? Why is she laughed at and derided and dismissed? Why is the church resorting to human means and methods of organization? Why is there such a contrast between the bride of Christ depicted in the New Testament and the church as she is today?

On the personal level, why are we individual Christians such poor specimens? As you read about the new men and women in Christ Jesus in the New Testament, as you read the glowing words of a man like the apostle Paul as he describes his own experience and that of the first Christians and then look at yourself, you are conscious of a great difference. "Whom having not seen," says Peter to those first Christians, "ye love; in whom, though now ye see him not, yet believing, ye rejoice with joy unspeakable and full of glory" (1 Pet. 1:8). Can we say that we are like those first Christians and that if suddenly it was announced that we were to be thrown into the arena with the lions and our lives were to be destroyed, we would thank God that we were "counted worthy to suffer shame for his name" (Acts 5:41)?

It is the same with us as it was with the children of Israel. We persist in having our own ideas about Christianity instead of coming back to the reminders that we have in the New Testament. Of old in the ark of the covenant in the temple and now in the New Testament we find everything that we need, and yet how ready we are to live on a lower level, how ready to conceive of the Christian life in terms that are derived much more from human thinking and philosophy and the common idea of man than from the Bible itself. The way to correct all that tendency is to do what the children of Israel should have done. We must remind ourselves of the memorials that God himself has given his people. He said to the children of Israel in essence, "I want you to keep these things as a permanent reminder. In that ark I want you to put a golden pot with an omer of manna. I want you to put in the ark Aaron's rod that budded and the tables of the covenant. Wherever you go and whatever happens to you, always remember those three things. They will hold before you the basic principles that are absolutely essential to your whole life and well-being and welfare." We must go back to these things today.

Let us look at these things carefully, for what is described in the case of the children of Israel is a type of what is true of us. They were given a material form and we a spiritual form, but the truth conveyed is absolutely identical. Here are three things that we must never forget, for they are absolutely basic to our whole position. My whole thinking about myself as a Christian, my whole conceiving of the Christian church, her nature and her foundation, must always be in terms of these things.

Think, first of all, of the golden pot that had manna. The children of Israel, having crossed the Red Sea, were going forward on their journey and began to hunger after the delicacies of Egypt. They felt they did not have sufficient food. God told them that he would supply food, and one morning they woke up and saw upon the ground something that looked like a little pearl of dew. When they picked it up they called it *manna*, bread from heaven. God continued to send it to them until they came to the end of their pilgrimage (Ex. 16:15–35). Then God told them to take a certain measure of that manna and to put it into the ark of the covenant (Ex. 16:33). What is the significance of that? It is a permanent reminder of the miraculous and the supernatural element in our Christian life. In other words, the first thing we must realize about ourselves as Christians is that the type of life we have is entirely different from everything else known to mankind; it is unique. Look at those children of Israel traveling in the wilderness. Something was happening to them there that had never happened to any other nation. All other nations had to work and to provide for themselves; all the children of Israel had to do was gather the manna. This is supernatural provision; you cannot explain it in ordinary human terms. It is the direct action of God, God working miraculously, and that is the essential nature of the life of his people. It was true of Israel, and it is true of the church.

The life of the Christian is miraculous and supernatural in its very origin. How foolish the children of Israel were. They were not like other nations; they had been created a nation by the action of God himself. He had looked upon a man called Abraham and had called him out of his country and from among his people and had turned that man into a nation (Gen. 12:1). That nation had gone down to Egypt, and there it was in a hopeless condition of slavery and bondage. You cannot imagine a more dejected picture than that of the children of Israel in the first chapters of the book of Exodus—utter hopelessness and bondage and serfdom. You would think there would be no hope for such people, and yet God heard their cry, raised up a leader for them, and brought them out of Egypt by a succession of amazing miracles. Eventually he took them through the Red Sea and drowned their enemies behind them, bidding them to go forward upon their journey (Exodus 15). The whole thing was God's doing. The history of these children of Israel simply cannot be understood at all except in terms of God and his miraculous and almighty power. It is not ordinary history; it is not a human story. That is the message of the Bible. The whole story is miraculous from beginning to end. It is supernatural, and the pot of manna in the ark of the covenant reminded those people perpetually of that.

Do we not need to be reminded of that ourselves? Are we not constantly in danger of sinking to a lower level? Are Christians just ordinary men and women who are trying to be a little bit better than everybody else? Are Christians to be conceived of initially in terms of ordinary humanity? Are Christians just men and women with certain slight differences? The whole message of the Bible surely gives the lie to that. The Christian is a miracle; the Christian is someone absolutely separate, a new creation of God. Christians have not come into being as a result of their own activity and striving. It is God, the God who sent the manna, who gives life. The whole origin of the children of Israel is miraculous and supernatural, and the same thing is true of the Christian. The Christian is one who has been born again, one with whom God had dealt and into whom God has placed his own Spirit. A Christian is a "[partaker] of the divine nature" (2 Pet. 1:4). Christian people are not like other people. We are not just a little bit different or a little bit better; we are altogether different. We are God's people, a new creation, a people set apart for God's own pleasure, his "peculiar people" (1 Pet. 2:9).

Furthermore we start like that, and we continue in the same way. The children of Israel were not only unique in their origin and beginning—their whole life was meant to be different and unique. They were not sustained by any ordinary means. God kept his people alive and enabled them to continue upon their journey by giving them that amazing bread from heaven. This is a very essential part of Christian doctrine. If we are unique in our origin and in our beginning, is it not obvious that we must continue in a different and separate manner? Remember Paul's expostulation to the Galatians: "Having begun in the Spirit, are ye now made perfect by the flesh?" (Gal. 3:3). Those foolish Galatians were beginning to listen to the message of the Judaizers, and they were mistakenly beginning to think they ought to submit to circumcision. There is a consistency, a unity, about this life. It is supernatural; it is miraculous from beginning to end.

The church and individual Christians need to be reminded of this at this present hour. The church of God has always been a spiritual institution. She is not one institution among others in the world; she is not like anything else on earth. She is God's creation. She is something special; she is a purely spiritual being. Oh, how anxious she has so often been in her folly to become earthly, worldly; how often she has tried to sustain herself by such means and methods. But as with the children of Israel of old that has always led to trouble and disaster. She has tried to live by education and culture and philosophy. She has forgotten the prayer meeting, and the testimony meeting is gone. Men and women are no longer interested in such things, and the church has tried to live on human learning and wisdom.

This is not only true of the church in general. Alas, it is a temptation that besieges us as individual Christian people. We try to keep ourselves going in the Christian life, forgetting that we have been born supernaturally and that we must be fed and sustained in the same supernatural manner. God has provided the spiritual food we need. On what are we feeding? Are we feeding on the Word of God, on prayer? On what are we relying? Are we trying to make use of psychology or some type of learning or knowledge? These things are not altogether useless, but the soul can only be fed on the bread of God, the bread of heaven. Without the living Word, without prayer, without the things that God has given us, without drawing constantly from the wells of salvation, our souls cannot live as they should, and we cannot be healthy Christians. Oh, the tragedy when we forget the manna that God commanded to be put into the ark of the testimony.

Look at the Son of God himself. Look how he spent his life. Observe him rising a great while before dawn to pray to God. And yet you and I often in our folly go through an entire day with only casual prayers morning and evening. We need the manna. Without it our lives will languish, and we will lose this vital quality that should ever be the characteristic of the Christian man or woman.

I must also remind you of another aspect of the pot of manna. The Christian is entirely dependent upon God in every respect. Remember always his providential care for you. He provided for that recalcitrant people of old in spite of their murmurings and sin. You need never be in doubt about his providential care for his people. As Christian people today we are reminded of this in the New Testament. "The very hairs of your head are all numbered," said our Lord (Matt. 10:30). If only we believed that God is infinitely more concerned about our welfare than we are ourselves! His eyes are wandering to and fro in the earth seeking whom he may bless. That is the God in whom we believe. He has promised to look after us, to provide for us, and to supply our every need.

Let us remember God's infinite resources. There is no end to them; there is no limit to them. The people of Israel were traveling through the wilderness, and there was no natural food for them. So they said in effect, "Why did we ever come out of Egypt?" They wanted to go back to the garlics and the onions of Egypt. "Why have you brought us to this?" they asked Moses, and his reply was, "Don't you realize that you are being led by God and not by man? Tomorrow morning you will find a miracle staring you in the face." Oh, the infinite, endless resources of God. You might soon find yourself wandering through the wilderness; you might be in it now or might soon enter one. But never forget that the pot of manna is there to remind you that you have a God who loves you and will supply your every need. When you think you are about to die of hunger or thirst, the manna will be there, and the waters will gush out. He will never leave you or forsake you. He loves you with an everlasting love. Our utter dependence is upon him, and his providential care for us and his infinite resources will never fail us.

The second object in the ark of the covenant was Aaron's rod that budded. This is to be understood in terms of an Old Testament incident recorded in Numbers 16. At a certain point in the wanderings of the children of Israel, three men—Korah, Dathan, and Abiram—rebelled against the leadership of Moses and Aaron. They said in essence, "You men are taking too much upon yourselves. Aaron claims he alone is the high priest and that he alone can approach God. But are we not a holy people, and don't we have as much right as Aaron to offer incense and sacrifices to God?" So they rebelled, and after God punished them, there followed the incident of the rods that we read about in Numbers 17. Then God commanded that Aaron's rod that budded should be placed in the ark as a permanent reminder of the right way to approach God. As Christian people possessing miraculous life, the most important thing for us to know on our spiritual journey is how God is to be approached. That is where those people went wrong. Read Numbers 16–17 again and you will see that God established once and forever that he was to be approached in one way and in one way only.

Here again is a lesson that is so sadly needed by the church of God and so sadly needed by many of us at this present hour. I can put it under two headings. The first thing we are told is that God's way is the only way and that God has revealed his way. God is to be approached not according to man's idea but according to God's own idea. He gave detailed rules and regulations to Moses and gave him a pattern: "See . . . that thou make all things according to the pattern shewed thee in the mount" (Heb. 8:5). So it was to be, but these other men began to voice their questions. What a perfect picture this is of how God is to be approached. This answer is clearly presented in the Bible. "Well, we are not quite so sure," modern man says. Philosophy and human ideas have come in—human opinion over divine revelation. But the rod of Aaron is a permanent reminder that God has to be worshipped in God's way. The people who do not approach God in God's way will never find God.

What is that way? "I have appointed a priesthood," God said to that recalcitrant people, "and I am only to be approached through that priesthood. I called out the man Aaron, and I told him what to do. This alone is the way—a priesthood and a sacrifice." These tell us

that there is only one way to God—through the Lord Jesus Christ and
him crucified. There is no access to the throne of God except by means
of Christ's blood that was shed. Without an offering for sins God does
not receive us. It is no use telling me, "God is love." It is no use telling
me that you do not like the idea that a just and righteous God must
punish sin. Aaron's rod that budded reminds us that God said, "This
is my way, and it is the only way."

I defy any man on earth to get to know that his sins are forgiven, to
have peace of conscience and joy and happiness and an awareness of a
new life and a certain hope of heaven, without relying entirely upon the
fact that Jesus of Nazareth, the Son of God, bore that man's sins in his
own body on the tree and there made atonement before God. "Here is
my high priest," says God; "here is the only offering I am prepared to
accept. "This is the way, walk ye in it" (Isa. 30:21). "For other foundation can no man lay than that is laid, which is Jesus Christ" (1 Cor.
3:11). As you approach God in prayer do you always remind yourself
that your only right of access is that Christ has lived and died for you,
that your sins have been punished in his holy body, that he gave himself
for you and that he is now your High Priest, your advocate with the
Father? You need the blood from beginning to end. You not only start
with Calvary; you will always need it. Your only hope as you die in the
final agonies is that Christ has died for you and for your sins and has
reconciled you to God. "There is . . . one mediator between God and
men, the man Christ Jesus" (1 Tim. 2:5).

Finally, consider the tables of the covenant. We realize that our life
is supernatural and miraculous and wonderful. We realize that we have
only one way of access to this glorious God with whom we walk, and
we are reminded here of the life we are to live. That is the meaning of
the tables of the covenant. "Be ye holy," said God to the people, "for I
am holy" (1 Pet. 1:16). He gave the Ten Commandments in order that
his people might know how they were to live. The tables of the covenant, therefore, must be kept in the ark of the covenant because it is
essential that we should realize the kind of life we are to live. Someone
might object, "You are not going to preach holiness and sanctification,
you are not going to become narrow and list rules and regulations, are
you?" No, but if we are the people of God we must of necessity be a

holy people. There is no communion between light and darkness; you cannot mix right and wrong. "Can two walk together, except they be agreed?" (Amos 3:3). If I claim I am walking with God and am in fellowship with God, then I must be like God, and God is "of purer eyes than to behold evil" (Hab. 1:13).

If we would know the blessings of God, we must live this holy life. Paul says to Titus, "[God] gave himself for us, that he might . . . purify unto himself a peculiar people, zealous of good works'" (Titus 2:14). Why did the High Priest offer himself, why did the Son of God endure the contradiction of sinners against himself and endure the agony and the shame of the cross? Why did he do it all? Was it that you and I might continue to sin and have an easy forgiveness? No! Oh, the wonder and the glory of the high privilege made possible for us—to become a holy people, that we might become like himself, that we might live the life he lived, that we might be separated from sin and have the holy life of God within us, that evil might become abhorrent to us, that we might hate it as he hated it. He died that we might be a holy people.

So the tables of the covenant were laid in the ark of the covenant to remind us of God's will for us. This is the condition of blessing, and if we would be happy Christians, if we would experience the full glory of all that the New Testament has to offer, if we would, like the apostle Paul, be able to say, "To me to live is Christ, and to die is gain," if we want to be able to say on our deathbed that we want "to be with Christ; which is far better" (Phil. 1:21, 23)—if we desire all that, we must live the holy life that God has outlined for us and that he makes it possible for us to live by the gift of his Holy Spirit. "We are his workmanship, created in Christ Jesus unto good works, which God hath before ordained that we should walk in them" (Eph. 2:10). That is our position; that is what it means to be a Christian. A Christian is not just an ordinary man or woman but a little better. Christians are new creations of God, God's people held and sustained and provided for by him, called to a glorious destiny in fellowship with him, but in the meantime living a holy life worthy of our holy God.

Beloved people, let us rise to the true height of our high calling in Jesus Christ. Amen.

16

Avoiding the Judgment to Come

HEBREWS 11:7

By faith Noah, being warned of God of things not seen as yet, moved with fear, prepared an ark to the saving of his house; by the which he condemned the world, and became heir of the righteousness which is by faith.

But as many as received him, to them gave he power to become the sons of God, even to them that believe on his name: which were born, not of blood, nor of the will of the flesh, nor of the will of man, but of God. (John 1:12–13)

I bring those two statements together to show how the gallery of Old Testament saints in the eleventh chapter of the epistle to the Hebrews helps us understand and appropriate the glorious statement made in the prologue of John's Gospel. It is possible for us even in this world to become children of God. "As many as received him, to them gave he power [the right, the authority] to become the sons of God, even to them that believe on his name: born not of blood, nor of the will of the flesh, nor of the will of man, but of God" (John 1:12–13).

We are not only forgiven, not only reconciled, not only given access into the presence of God, but we become children of God, "partakers of the divine nature" (2 Pet. 1:4). Nothing is more important for Christian people to know for certain than that they are the children of God. The Christian is meant to know, he is meant to have assurance, he is meant to have certainty, and this is the only way to live a happy Christian life.

I am calling attention to this for a second reason. We can never truly function as Christian people unless we know that we are God's children, but we are saved in order that through us God may save others. The man who is uncertain about himself and his position before God cannot help anybody else. "Can the blind lead the blind?" as our Lord asked (Luke 6:39). From this practical and urgent standpoint nothing is more important than this question of assurance and certainty. "To them he gave the power to become the sons of God" (John 1:12). Have we done this? Are we functioning as God's children?

Having looked into the doctrine that is involved in all this, we now turn to the examples given in the eleventh chapter of the epistle to the Hebrews. The author of that epistle was writing to give his readers assurance, and he tells us that this is nothing new. This principle has always operated in God's people. They have all lived by faith, and faith is "the substance of the things hoped for" (Heb. 11:1); there is a certainty about it. He brings out example after example in order to illustrate this point. In other words, there is a common factor to all these people mentioned in Hebrews 11: they all walked by faith. In other words, they were all people who had certainty; they knew that they were the children of God, that Jesus Christ was "not ashamed," as he put it earlier, "to call them brethren" (Heb. 2:11).

Hebrews 11:2 says, "By [faith] the elders obtained a good report." Then the author tells us of the particular case of Abel: "By faith Abel offered unto God a more excellent sacrifice than Cain, by which he obtained witness that he was righteous, God testifying of his gifts" (Heb. 11:4). In other words, the secret of Abel was that God let him know that he was well-pleased with him. God gave him this certainty and assurance.

The same thing was true of Enoch. The important thing about Enoch was not that he went to be with God without seeing death, but that "By faith Enoch was translated that he should not see death;

and was not found, because God had translated him: for before his translation he had this testimony, that he pleased God" (Heb. 11:5). God had told him before he took him to be with himself that he was well-pleased with him. In other words, he was given assurance of his position and his salvation. He knew that "God . . . is a rewarder of them that diligently seek him" (Heb. 11:6).

The secret of these men was that they had a certainty of their relationship with God. That was how they were able to live in this evil world and triumph as they did. You and I are meant to know that we are the children of God. We are meant to appropriate the statement in John 1:12–13 and to be absolutely certain of it. We will now look at the case of Noah.

The great thing about this man was that he had this blessed assurance. He knew exactly what he was, where he stood, and what was going to happen to him. "By faith Noah, being warned of God of things not seen as yet, moved with fear, prepared an ark to the saving of his house; by the which he condemned the world, and became heir of the righteousness which is by faith" (Heb. 11:7). All these men illustrated justification by faith, the righteousness that is by faith. They all believed, they all appropriated, they all enjoyed assurance of this. "Being justified by faith, we have peace with God" (Rom. 5:1).

The life and walk of Noah is a particularly important and instructive case at this present hour. We find ourselves in a world that is amazingly like that of the world before the flood, and we are going to study a man who walked through it by faith. The world needs people like this man Noah. That is the greatest need of every country in the world.

His secret was that he enjoyed the assurance that he was a child of God. This is made plain in the sixth chapter of Genesis. Consider verse 8 in contrast to verse 7. "And the LORD said, I will destroy man whom I have created from the face of the earth; both man, and beast, and the creeping thing, and the fowls of the air; for it repenteth me that I have made them. But Noah found grace in the eyes of the LORD" (Gen. 6:5–7) He was in a special position. He "found grace." Note too Genesis 6:9: "Noah was a just man and perfect in his generations, and Noah walked with God."

Earlier in Genesis we read that "Enoch walked with God" (Gen.

5:22, 24). "Enoch walked with God," and "Noah walked with God." This is not merely an account of a righteous walk; that is given us in the preceding part of Genesis 6:9, where we are told that "Noah was a just man and perfect in his generations." But "Noah walked with God" means he was a companion of God. God deigned to give him the privilege of his companionship. When God walks with a man he is telling that man that he is well-pleased with him, that he loves him. He does not walk with everybody, but when he does walk with a man, that man can know beyond any doubt that he is a child of God. Noah was given intimations of God's nearness. God gave him manifestations of his glory.

God gave Noah instructions about building an ark in Genesis 6:14–16. Then God repeats what he had said in verse 13: "And, behold, I, even I, do bring a flood of waters upon the earth, to destroy all flesh, wherein is the breath of life, from under heaven; and every thing that is in the earth shall die. But with thee will I establish my covenant" (Gen. 6:17–18). This is the ultimate proof of that man's assurance. God, having warned him about the destruction that was coming, said in essence, "It is not going to apply to you; you are in a special position." So that man is no longer acting in the dark; he is acting on the basis of certain knowledge.

We find abundantly, then, in the case of Noah that here was a man to whom God himself gave assurance. It is always God who gives it. "The Spirit itself beareth witness with our spirit, that we are the children of God" (Rom. 8:16). This is the highest form of assurance. You can receive assurance from the Scriptures. You can say, "He that believeth on him is not condemned" (John 3:18). You can say, I am going to apply the tests of the Christian in 1 John—"We know that we have passed from death unto life, because we love the brethren" (1 John 3:14) and so on. But there is an assurance that goes beyond that: "The Spirit itself beareth witness with our spirit, that we are the children of God." The Spirit himself speaks to us as God spoke to Noah and told him, "I establish my covenant with you." The secret of Noah, as with all the others in Hebrews 11, was that he enjoyed this blessed assurance.

This is the kind of man the world needs. This is the kind of man we all ought to be. He lived a life of faith, a life of joy, a life of peace and rest of heart and conscience in the midst of the storm of wickedness that was raging around him. What made him the man he was? "Noah was a just man and perfect in his generations" (Gen. 6:9). He was "a just man." A better translation would be "a righteous man." That means he was a man who was concerned about the righteousness of God. This is "the righteousness which is by faith" (Heb. 11:7). That describes all the men mentioned in Hebrews 11. We will see it even more plainly when we come to Abraham, but it was true of all of them. The righteous man in the Bible is concerned about the righteousness of God; he is concerned about obeying our Lord's exhortation to "seek ye first the kingdom of God, and his righteousness; and all these things shall be added unto you" (Matt. 6:33). We have seen this in the case of Abel, we have seen it in the case of Enoch, and it was equally true of Noah.

Then we are told that Noah was "perfect in his generations" (Gen. 6:9). The word "perfect" does not mean he was sinless. There never has been anybody sinless in this world since Adam fell except our Lord. It means upright or genuine. There was no double-mindedness in him. He was a sincere man without impurity, without adulteration. He was all-out for God and the things of God.

"In his generations" should be translated "among his contemporaries" (Gen. 6:9). What do we know about his contemporaries? "God saw that the wickedness of man was great in the earth, and that every imagination of the thoughts of his heart was only evil continually" (Gen. 6:5). They were so bad that "it repented the LORD that he had made man on the earth, and it grieved him at his heart" (Gen. 6:6). It was one of the foulest generations the world has ever known, given over to sin and iniquity in all its horror. They departed from God; they were guilty of violence. "There were giants in the earth in those days" (Gen. 6:4). This really means on the earth were men guilty of violence and every abomination. The world was in a terrible state. But we are told that Noah was a just man and perfect among his contemporaries. Others were his physical contemporaries, but he stood out among them.

The next thing we read is that "Noah walked with God" (Gen. 6:9). This was his one great ambition, his supreme desire, the thing he sought above everything else. What mattered with him was that he should be enjoying companionship with God, that he should know that God was well-pleased with him. His desire was to carry out the commands of God. We are told in Genesis 4:26, "then began men to call upon the name of the LORD." That means that they began to indulge in public worship, and this man undoubtedly did that. All who walk with God will do that.

He separated himself from the world in which he lived and from his contemporaries. The condition of the world at that time is perfectly clear. It had become so deplorable that God decided to destroy it. But there is something else here that we might miss because of the difficulty in interpreting the statement "The sons of God saw the daughters of men that they were fair; and they took them wives of all which they chose" (Gen. 6:2).

Some have interpreted "the sons of God" as the angels, concluding that there was an admixture between angels and women, and the monstrosities born to them were called giants (Gen. 6:2). That seems to me to be expository nonsense. Rather what we have here is the division that has existed since the division between Abel and Cain. "The sons of God" were those who were like Abel. They were the descendants of Seth, the son born to Adam and Eve after the murder of Abel. This is the godly line. The sons of God were the people who lived for God. The Cainites were different. The human race had become divided into two groups—"sons of God" and Cainites; the godly and the ungodly. They had kept separate from each other.

But at the period of which we are reading now the distinctions were being blurred, and the difference between the godly and the ungodly was no longer apparent. There was an admixture, though they were never meant to mix. This is a great theme running right through the Bible. "Be ye not unequally yoked together with unbelievers" (2 Cor. 6:14). But that is precisely what they were doing. Instead of keeping themselves away from the Cainites and the worldliness and the sin and the evil, they were mixing up in it. Even the godly line had gone astray and were in a terrible condition of apostasy and evil. But we are told that Noah was not like that. This man held to the truth; he was not governed by the mind of the world, and he did not conform to it.

We are living in a foul age that is increasingly manifesting the

characteristics of the period prior to the flood. People are even querying whether there is such a thing as morality; it has become relative,
with every man deciding for himself. There is no truth, we are told; everything is speculation, and everything can be justified. We are living in
an age when the Christian church herself, through the mouth of some
of her spokesmen, is querying the very being of God and is attempting
to justify extramarital sex. Sons of God are too often no longer what
they were or what they are meant to be. We see this terrible admixture of Abel and Cain and the horror that follows. "God saw that the
wickedness of man was great in the earth, and that every imagination
of the thoughts of his heart was only evil continually" (Gen. 6:5). As
you read the newspaper do you not come to that conclusion? Men are
living like this, and they are gloating in it! But the man Noah stood
out; he did not conform to the world. He was not influenced by it. He
did not change his moral notions because everybody else was doing
so; he was not governed by the world, the flesh, and the Devil. He was
a just, righteous man, a man of God, a man who walked with God.
He preserved his integrity though he was surrounded by such evil and
license and sin. We are told that he "condemned the world" in his own
time (Heb. 11:7), and he is condemning our world as well. God grant
that we may take this to heart.

But what made him the man he was? What made Noah "a just
man" (Gen. 9:9), a perfect man among his contemporaries? "By faith
Noah . . . " (Heb. 11:7). What is faith? Faith simply means believing
God, banking everything upon what God has said. That was the secret
of Noah and of all the men in Hebrews 11. That is what made him the
man we have seen him to be.

He was the man he was because he believed what God revealed.
God had revealed truth in the garden of Eden. He had given an outline,
a preview of history. He had indicated the way of salvation that was
to come, which was to be believed by faith. And Noah believed it. He
did not just go on thoughtlessly and heedlessly; he did not just base
his position on the latest statement by one of the clever people in the
pre-flood period. Men ridiculed the notion of salvation by faith, and
they would advocate plunging into pleasure. But Noah did not listen;
instead he based his life on the revelation that God had given.

Specifically he believed the warning about the flood. "By faith Noah, being warned of God of things not seen as yet, moved with fear, prepared an ark . . . " (Heb. 11:7). Are you being influenced by the things that are being said at the present time? Are you feeling a little ashamed of yourself because people say that you are old-fashioned or a fundamentalist or something like that? Is it your ambition to be a modern man, questioning everything—the Bible, God, the miraculous, the atonement? If so you are very unlike Noah. Noah believed God when God warned him about the coming destruction.

In spite of all that was being said round and about him and the way people were living, Noah believed that the world had been made by God and that it was in God's hands still. He believed that man was not an animal but a creature made by God in the image of God. He believed that man was accountable to God. He not only believed that what was happening around him was wrong but that it was not going to go on forever. Of course many scoffed—Peter tells us that in his second epistle, the third chapter. This man was making an ark for a hundred and twenty years and was preaching about righteousness, and they ridiculed him. They said, "You say destruction is coming. Hah! Where is it? You have been saying that for many years now, and nothing has happened." That is the sort of position we are in today. People say, "The old preachers frightened people by preaching about God and about judgment, and people would tremble and become members of the church. But we know there is nothing to all that. You can deny God as much as you like, and you will still be blessed. The world will go on and on, and it will prosper."

Men in Noah's day ridiculed him. They said, "You say we are living a sinful life. If there is a God, why does he not stop us? He is doing nothing; either he does not want to or he cannot." That was the argument then, and people are saying the same thing today. We boast of our scientific advances and developments. There is nothing mighty man cannot do, we are told. We are confident in man's ability, and we no longer believe in a God who is going to judge the world in righteousness by the man he has appointed. But Noah believed God. He said in summary, "I do not understand the ways of God. I cannot tell you why he is delaying, but I know that he is still God and that he is seated on the throne of the universe and that he is going to judge us all in righteousness." He believed God in spite of all appearances to the contrary.

If you and I are to be like Noah, we have to believe God in the same way. Are you carried away by the modern knowledge and modern learning that ridicules the judgment of God? Do you say that God is not just and righteous, that God is only love? Do you say that you cannot believe in a God who has wrath against sin? Do you dismiss the apostle Paul when he says, "The wrath of God is revealed from heaven against all ungodliness and unrighteousness of men, who hold the truth in unrighteousness" (Rom. 1:18)? Do you say you no longer believe in a God of justice and of righteousness who is going to judge the whole world? If you answer affirmatively, you do not belong to Noah and his company. Can you not see the judgment of God already abroad in the earth? Can you not see that the things that are horrifying us day after day are a manifestation of the righteous judgment of God? Consider the first chapter of the epistle to the Romans, from verse 18 to the end of the chapter. "God gave them over to a reprobate mind" (Rom 1:28). "God gave them up unto vile affections: for even their women did change the natural use into that which is against nature: and likewise also the . . . men with men working that which is unseemly" (Rom. 1:26–27). All the horror of Romans 1:18 to the end is what we are witnessing today, and according to the apostle it is part of the wrath of God upon sin. It is a warning. God is allowing modern-day man to see what he makes of life when he forgets God. The Lord is letting the clever man who does not believe in God, who does not believe in salvation, the man who says he can make a perfect world for himself, see what he makes of his world when he puts himself in God's place.

I believe he is speaking equally to the Christian church. The Christian church in the nineteenth century began to question the authority of the Bible, the fact of judgment, the existence of hell. People have believed the church, and the consequences of this are now evident. You cannot have morality without godliness, try as you will. It is impossible. The world has never done it.

Noah believed God about the flood, and then we are told that he was "moved with fear." What a wonderful statement that is. "Noah, being warned of God of things not seen as yet, moved with fear . . . "

(Heb. 11:7). This does not mean a craven fear. "Perfect love casteth out fear" (1 John 4:18). But there is a right kind of fear. What does the statement in Hebrews mean? Noah was given a realization, vaguely and dimly, of the greatness of the glory and the holiness and the purity of God. The trouble with us is that we do not fear God. "There is no fear of God before his eyes," says the psalmist (Ps. 36:1). God is so pure that he cannot even look upon sin. That is the thing that was revealed to Noah. God came near to Noah and said in essence, "I am sorry that I have created man. Look how evil he has become!" Noah saw something of the holiness and the glory of God, and he trembled in the presence of the holy God. Every man in the Bible who has ever had a glimpse of the holiness of God has trembled. Isaiah was given a glimpse of God and said, "Woe unto me! . . . I am a man of unclean lips, and I dwell in the midst of a people of unclean lips" (Isa. 6:5). Noah feared God! He was a godly man because he was moved with fear.

"But," you say, "I believe the gospel. I am saved." Paul says to you, "Work out your own salvation with fear and trembling" (Phil. 2:12). "Fear and trembling"? At what? At the enormity of sin, at the evil that is still left in you. You are saved, yes, but are you perfect? Think of the evil in your heart, your thoughts, your imaginations, your lusts, your desires. If you not afraid, you should be.

Noah was given a glimpse of the terrible nature of the judgment that was coming to the people of that day, and he trembled. That was what the apostle Paul meant when he said that when he went to Corinth he went "in weakness, and in fear, and in much trembling" (1 Cor. 2:3); he had a heart that trembled at the approach of sin. We are told about the early Christians in Acts 9:31, "Then had the churches rest . . . and walking in the fear of the Lord, and in the comfort of the Holy Ghost, were multiplied." "Walking in the fear of the Lord." That is Christianity. Or listen to Paul again: "Knowing therefore the terror of the Lord, we persuade men" (2 Cor. 5:11). The apostle knew that God is the righteous Judge and that he will have to stand before him and give an account of the deeds done in the body; he knew that we all will. John tells us that he was given a vision of Jesus Christ, and "His eyes were as a flame of fire. . . . And when I saw him, I fell at his feet as dead" (Rev. 1:14, 17). Why? Because of the glory, the majesty, the holiness, the brightness of our Savior and Lord. Have we seen this? It is not surprising that the world is as it is when the church is lighthearted and superficial and back-slapping and confident and assured in a false and carnal sense. We must know something of the fear of the Lord and the horror of the fate that is awaiting those who are in sin.

That leads me to the last thing we are told here, which is that he "prepared an ark to the saving of his house; by the which he condemned the world" (Heb. 11:7). Noah was "a preacher of righteousness" (2 Pet. 2:5). We too must be preachers of righteousness. I do not say we must become moral prigs; I say we must become preachers of righteousness. I am not advocating what you get in the newspapers and from so many of the politicians. They are not preachers of righteousness. They do not believe in it. They have never seen it; they have no conception of it. They are concerned about a superficial respectability. We too must be preachers of righteousness. We must tell others about God and his holiness and his justice and his truth; we must tell them that his judgment of the whole world is coming. They will laugh at you, they will ridicule you, they will call you a fool. Let them say what they like. The Bible proclaims that there will be an ultimate judgment day. We must tell others what is going to happen as the result of their sin and that there is only one way to escape from it, and that is to believe in and to submit to God's way of salvation, to fly to Christ. We must tell them that, even as they are, vile as they are, if they believe and turn to him, they can be forgiven. They can be washed, they can be cleansed, they can be sanctified, they can be justified in the name of the Lord Jesus and by the Spirit of our God.

Noah walked that holy walk of his in the midst of the abomination that was all around him, and because he was that sort of man God loved him and was well-pleased with him. "Noah found grace in the eyes of the Lord" (Gen. 6:8). God said to him in essence, "You are going to be spared. I am going to make a covenant with you; you belong to me." Whatever people might have said to him, Noah did not care. He knew God, and he knew that he was a child of God, so on he went. He condemned the world for its blindness and its folly and its unbelief. But his example gives us glorious encouragement.

God's Word was verified in its every detail—in the flood, in the deliverance of Noah and his family, in everything. In this evil age and hour may we be like Noah and walk with God, be concerned about righteousness, and be sincere. May we seek God and submit to his will and his way and his teaching. As we do so we will not only condemn the world in which we are living, we will be given the blessed assurance that we are well-pleasing in God's sight, will have no fear of the judgment that is to come, and can "rest in the LORD, and wait patiently for him" (Ps. 37:7). Amen.

17

If God Be for Us . . .

HEBREWS 11:8

By faith Abraham, when he was called to go out into a place
which he should after receive for an inheritance, obeyed; and
he went out, not knowing whither he went.

The greatest problem confronting us all is the problem of how to face
life and all its attendant circumstances, especially the problem of an
unknown future. In the last analysis that is the great business of life
and how to face all that happens to us.

The Bible is a book about life. It teaches us how to face everything
that comes to meet us in this world. The Bible goes even further and
makes the claim that it alone can teach us how to do this. There is
nothing quite so foolish and ridiculous as the notion held by many
people today that the Bible is remote from life, that it really has nothing to tell us in a practical manner, and that it is not relevant any
longer because it is such an old book. They feel it may be a very beautiful book, they may like it as literature, they may think it presents
certain beautiful thoughts and ideas, but they feel it has no practical
bearing upon life. They say, "If you are concerned about facing hard,
practical realities, do not spend your time reading the Bible. Read
modern novelists and philosophers and theorists; read newspapers."

Such people fondly and foolishly imagine they are prepared for the battles of life.

That point of view is utterly ridiculous, for no book is more practical and more relevant to today than the Bible itself, on the condition, of course, that we allow it to speak to us, that we allow it to give its own message to us and in its own way. The Bible gives us teaching, and at the same time it gives us history, and both of these are important and valuable. It is not only teaching. If it were, some might say, "That is all right in theory, but how does it work out in practice?" The Bible answers that immediately by giving us history and by showing us how it works out in practice. The Bible is not mere theory; it is not just an academic discussion. In the Bible we meet men and women like ourselves who lived in this same world and who applied this teaching.

That is in particular the theme of the eleventh chapter of the epistle to the Hebrews. Here the author puts a number of men before us. He says in effect, "Here are men who have lived in this particular way. They are the great heroes who stand out in the history of the Jews, the Hebrew people." At the same time he explains the secret of their successful lives. Why did he write this chapter and give us this kind of gallery of saints, these great heroes of the faith? He did so because he was writing to a number of people who had run into trouble and difficulties in their daily living. These Hebrew Christians were a depressed and a discouraged people, and they were beginning to wonder whether they had not made a mistake in becoming Christians at all. They had endured many troubles and trials, they had been persecuted, and they had been robbed of their goods and of their homes, as he tells us in the previous chapter.

As a result of all this, some of them were beginning to say, "We have believed this message, but is it true or is it just some sort of fairy tale? We are practical men, and we want to know what results it produces. Is this Christianity really God's way with men? We know the old story, the ancient history. The people had a land, they had goods and possessions and animals and so on, but we seem to have nothing. Is this Christianity compatible with the teaching of the Old Testament?"

That is the matter that the writer of this epistle takes up at this point, and he says in summary, "The trouble with you people is that you are not aware of the central and fundamental principle of the Christian life, and that is the principle of faith. God has always dealt with his people through this principle. There is nothing new, in that sense, in Christianity. There is no essential difference between God's dealings in the Old Testament and his dealings in the New Testament. God has always dealt with people in terms of this faith principle." Having laid down that proposition in the first verse ("Now faith is the substance of things hoped for, the evidence of things not seen," Heb. 11:1), he then proceeds to illustrate it by taking up these great Old Testament characters one after another and saying, "Look at them. What was their secret?" and the answer always is, "It was their faith." These men became the men they were because they lived on this principle of faith, and that is the secret of successful living in a world such as this.

As a particular example, consider the case of Abraham because he is a crucial person in these matters. Abraham is the father of the faithful. We are all, even as Christians, the children of Abraham because we are the children of faith. He was absolutely basic to the whole position of the Jews because he was a man out of whom the whole nation had evolved. So the writer takes up this striking case of Abraham and gives him more space and attention than any one of the other characters he mentions.

What was the first great event in his life? "By faith Abraham, when he was called to go out into a place which he should after receive for an inheritance, obeyed; and he went out, not knowing whither he went" (11:8). This is a reference to the call of Abraham. He had been born and brought up in a district known as Ur of the Chaldees. It was a pagan society, and he was living like everybody else. Suddenly he received a call from God to go from there. God said he was going to give him a great inheritance. He did not tell him where it was, but just told him to move out in faith along with his wife and his possessions.

He was called to break with his past and go into an absolutely unknown future, relying simply on the word of God and nothing more. God said, "I have a place for you," but he did not say where it was or how Abraham would get there. The astounding thing we are told about Abraham is that he obeyed—"He went out, not knowing whither he went"—and this was the great secret of the life of Abraham. He was known as "the Friend of God" (James 2:23). He stands out as perhaps the greatest man in the whole Old Testament, a man who mastered life, a great hero. How did Abraham live such a triumphant life? What was his secret? Hebrews 11:8 gives us the secret of life, the key to facing an unknown future. This is the way Abraham lived, and all the others in that chapter lived in the same way.

What, then, are the principles of this life? The first is that Abraham was not at all concerned to know the future. "He went out, not knowing whither he went" (Heb. 11:8). He was not told where he was going; he was given absolutely nothing in his hands as it were. He only had God's promise, God's command to him. But in spite of being utterly uncertain as to what was going to meet him, Abraham obeyed and went out.

I remember a book I once read, and I have never forgotten its very first sentence. I did not agree with the philosophy of the book, but the first sentence contained the principle we are considering. It said, "It is not life that matters, it is the courage that you bring to it." The principle is this: it is not life that matters, nor the things that happen to us in life—it is the way in which we face them. Once we grasp that, we are no longer concerned about the things that will happen. "He went out, not knowing whither he went" (11:8) and not caring what was going to happen.

This is important because many people—actually everyone in the whole world—do not know anything about this principle. Most people think of life and the future in terms of what they will get, what is going to happen to them, what will take place. That is the basis on which most people operate. The things I possess, the things that happen to me—that is their whole process of thinking, and it is the antithesis of what guided Abraham. The moment you start with that idea, you develop an inordinate desire to know exactly what will happen to you, and you want to peer into the future. People are interested in prophecies, forecasts, foretelling, what is going to take place.

But again it is not life that matters, it is the courage that you bring to it, it is the way in which you face it. The moment you put your emphasis upon life itself or upon the things you possess or the things that happen to you, you are already in a wrong position, and you will be feverishly anxious to know what is coming. That false attitude leads to impatience. Abraham did nothing of the sort. "He went out, not knowing whither he went" (11:8).

Is not life an extraordinary thing? When we are young we are all impatient to get to the future; time seems to be so slow, so lethargic. We are not thinking about living at this moment but about what is going to happen, future happiness. Everything depends upon what might or might not come to us, and the whole time we are stretching forward with overanxiety. Then we get to a stage in which we get tired of all that and feel that we have been just chasing illusions, and we begin to sink into a kind of cynicism. Finally we reach a stage in which we find time galloping, and everything comes and goes so quickly that we are just trying to hold on to the present because the future will be here too soon.

All that is the result of not understanding life; it is because we attach such significance to where we are going, who we are going to meet, what we are going to possess. But Abraham "went out, not knowing whither he went" (11:8), not caring about it. That was his secret. Wherever he was and whatever was happening to him, he was not concerned about those things; he was concerned about something else. Because the world has never discovered this principle of Abraham and his way of living, it is a victim of false hopes, unnecessary anxieties, and disappointments. The moment we fail to grasp this principle, we are candidates for anxiety, the disease more prominent than all others at the present time. The increasing medical problem today is not so much physical, organic diseases but tension, stress, overanxiety about what is going to happen.

The world has become an uncertain place full of dread possibilities, but there should be no anxiety or stress or strain. We are the reverse of Abraham, who was not a bit concerned about his future. We want to know exactly what is going to happen and how we can prepare for it, and immediately we are tense. We are preparing and fearing, we are filled with foreboding, and our whole life is in a sense already ruined. But the Bible from beginning to end teaches us this other principle; it says this is the great fallacy. The important thing in life is not to know what is going to happen, nor to speculate about it, but to learn how to live in such a way that it does not matter what happens.

I know of nothing that is such an utter contradiction of biblical teaching as the way in which so many in the Christian church think that it is their business to try to forecast the future or to prepare people for it by trying to prevent certain things from happening. That is not the business of the Bible at all. The Bible is not concerned about the future in that sense. It is concerned to teach us how to live, how to understand life in such a manner that we are ready for anything. It is not my business to speculate about the future; it is not my business to give advice to statesmen as to what they ought to do to reduce tensions or whatever. That is not Christianity.

The biblical message is the most profound message in the world. It is a message that can put you right whatever may happen to you. Thank God for that! "[Abraham] went out, not knowing whither he went" (11:8), but he went happily, he went in a spirit of rejoicing. What enabled him to do so? Was it a kind of philosophical calm that he had developed, a stoicism, a spirit of resignation? Was he just a very wise man who said to himself, "I can anticipate all sorts of possibilities and eventualities, and I can make myself really sick with fear and anxiety, but what a fool I would be. That does not determine anything; all my thinking is not going to affect the future." That is good reasoning, in a sense that is the right thing to do, but that is not Christianity, and that is not how Abraham did it. Of course it is a foolish thing to waste your energy speculating about mere possibilities. But the Christian way is not merely negative resignation; it is not a kind of philosophic detachment and calm or a fatalism that says, "Whatever will come will come, and all the worrying in the world will not affect it." That is quite true, but that is not Christianity.

So what is Christianity? "[Abraham] went out, not knowing whither he went." Why? Because he went "by faith," because he had faith in God. An old writer put this in a most wonderful way: "He went out, not knowing whither he went, but he knew with whom he went." That was the secret of Abraham. He was not concerned to know where he was going; he was only concerned about going with God! This is the great principle of living by faith in God!

It does not matter where you are if God is with you. You might be crossing a mountain, you might be in the depths of a valley, you might be struggling in a bog, you might be walking along a smooth road, it does not matter. Is God with you? That is what matters. Abraham went out cheerfully because he knew with whom he went; he knew that God was with him.

As you face life with all its possibilities this is the only thing that matters, and if this is right it does not matter at all what happens to you. Just think for a moment of the character of the fellowship that Abraham had with God and that it is possible for all of us to enjoy if we go to him in the name of the Lord Jesus Christ. Christianity is not just holding on to a number of principles or ideas—it is walking with God. That is what Abraham did; he was "the Friend of God" (James 2:23). We read that "Enoch walked with God" (Gen. 5:22). What a privilege it is to enjoy companionship and fellowship with the Creator of the universe, the Lord God Almighty! It does not matter very much where you are if he is with you. Oh, the privilege of knowing something about the love of God, realizing the almightiness of his power. Can you think of anything greater than knowing that such a God, such a being is interested in you and that he is concerned about you, that he went and spoke to Abraham and he also comes and speaks to you, that though he has made everything out of nothing and plays with the constellations just as a child plays with marbles, nevertheless he knows you personally and has a great concern for you and for your well-being? Does it matter what is going to happen as long as you know that such a One is with you and is walking with you? And not only that, he has a great plan and purpose for us, and his purposes with respect to us are always good. That is what he has told us about himself.

It is the companionship of God that matters. Abraham knew God, he believed him, he trusted him because he knew him. He knew something about the character of God—God had revealed it to him. Abraham said in essence, "You do not need to tell me where I am going. All I want to know is, are you going with me?" God answered, "I am. I am going to lead you. But I am asking you to leave everything and come with me." So Abraham went. As long as God was with him, nothing else mattered. Not knowing whither he went, being with God was enough. We can say of a man who knows God, "Having nothing, and yet possessing all things" (2 Cor. 6:10). "Blessed are the meek: for they shall inherit the earth" (Matt. 5:5).

Consider also the nature of the promise that God makes to us. "By faith Abraham, when he was called to go out into a place which he should after receive for an inheritance, obeyed; and he went out, not knowing whither he went" (Heb. 11:8). God said to him in effect, "Abraham, I have a place for you, an inheritance, so come with me." No details were given as to what would happen between the starting point and arrival at the inheritance. God's promise is absolutely fundamental to the Christian life. What matters is not what will happen to me this year; what matters is where we are going to spend eternity. The destination matters, not the journey.

God told Abraham in Ur of the Chaldees, "I want to take you"— where? " . . . to an inheritance." He told Abraham nothing about what would happen before he got there, and it did not matter; the inheritance was what mattered. "Are you saying," somebody might ask, "that this world doesn't count?" Not at all, but I am saying that this world is like a preparatory school. We are "strangers and pilgrims on the earth" (Heb. 11:13). An inheritance is coming, or as the writer said earlier in this great epistle, "For it became him, for whom are all things, and by whom are all things, in bringing many sons unto glory, to make the captain of their salvation perfect through sufferings" (Heb. 2:10).

" . . . in bringing many sons unto glory" (Heb. 2:10)—that is the inheritance. Many things might happen, or they might not happen, but all who know Jesus Christ are headed for the "glory" that is coming! God has told me he will bring me there, and that is what matters. When you and I stand on the shore that lies beyond time in glory everlasting, this world will seem trivial to us. All the comings and goings, all the interviews and conferences, all the headlines will be unworthy of even momentary consideration. How small and how petty they will all appear to be! It is the glory that matters, the inheritance! Being with God and sharing all that he has prepared for us—that is what matters. Abraham had been told about that, and therefore he went out, without knowing where he was going.

We have the certainty that God is with us; we have the certainty of the glory to which he is bringing us. But what happens in the meantime?

We do not know what is going to happen, but of this we can be certain: God will never change. Whatever may happen in the future God will still be God. There will be many changes in our circumstances, many things will come and go, and we will wonder what is going to happen, but God is "the Father of lights, with whom is no variableness, neither shadow of turning" (James 1:17). We are all very changeable; we cannot rely on one another or trust one another. But God will never change. Time writes no wrinkle on the brow of the eternal. He is the everlasting God. He and his blessed Son are "the same yesterday, and to day, and for ever" (Heb. 13:8).

> His love in time past
> Forbids me to think
> He will leave me at last
> In trouble to sink.

> John Newton, "Be Gone, Unbelief; My Savior Is Near"

Of course he will not! God will not and cannot change. He is the immutable, eternal, everlasting God! He said, "I Am that I Am" (Ex. 3:14). He is eternally "I Am." What a wonderful thought!

We also know that his promises are sure because of his character, because of his holiness, his justice, his righteousness, his unchangeableness, his eternality. We know that every promise God has ever made will never be changed; it is always sure. He tells us at the beginning of our journey with him, "I will never leave thee, nor forsake thee" (Heb. 13:5). Never! And when God says that, you can be sure of it. He assures us, "In the sunshine I will be with you; in the storm I will be with you. Radiant health, sickness, accident, death—it does not matter. 'I will never leave thee, nor forsake thee' (Heb. 13:5)." Wherever you are, whatever is happening to you, he will be with you. The God of love, the God who has numbered the very hairs of your head, the God who has a great and glorious purpose for you will never leave you or forsake you. Nothing that can happen to us matters because he is with us.

> I fear no foe at hand, with Thee at hand to bless;
> Ills have no weight, and tears no bitterness.

> Henry Lyte, "Abide with Me"

My name from the palms of His hands
Eternity will not erase;
Impressed on His heart it remains,
In marks of indelible grace.
Things future, nor things that are now,
Nor all things, below or above,
Can make Him His purpose forego,
Or sever my soul from His love.

> Augustus Toplady, "A Debtor to Mercy Alone"

God is unchanging, and his promises are ever sure.

Another comforting thought is this: Nothing that meets us can ever be more powerful than God. We do not make enough of the power of God. We think so much in terms of the power of bombs and of men, but it is the power of God that matters. Because he is omnipotent, nothing that comes our way can ever be too great for him. The apostle Paul said: "For I am persuaded, that neither death, nor life, nor angels, nor principalities, nor powers, nor things present, nor things to come, nor height, nor depth, nor any other creature shall be able to separate us from the love of God, which is in Christ Jesus our Lord" (Rom. 8:38–39).

Some might say, "I believe in the love of God, but I might have an illness, I might lose my health, my dear ones might die! What happens then?" Nothing will be able to separate us from the love of God that is in Christ Jesus our Lord.

A sovereign protector I have,
Unseen, yet forever at hand,
Unchangeably faithful to save,
Almighty to rule and command.
He smiles, and my comforts abound;
His grace as the dew shall descend;
And walls of salvation surround
The soul He delights to defend.

> Augustus Toplady, "A Sovereign Protector I Have"

You can be absolutely certain that whatever comes to meet you, it will never be more powerful than God, and it will never separate you from his power.

This might be a year of terrible adversity for some of us; everything might go against us. But it does not matter if God is with us because "all things work together for good to them that love God, to them who are the called according to his purpose" (Rom. 8:28). "*All* things work together for good to them that love God." Surely not troubles, not trials, not tribulations? Yes! "Therefore," says Paul, "being justified by faith, we have peace with God through our Lord Jesus Christ: by whom also we have access by faith into this grace wherein we stand, and rejoice in hope of the glory of God. And not only so, but we glory in tribulations also: knowing that tribulation worketh patience; and patience, experience; and experience, hope" (Rom. 5:1–4). If Christian people maintain this relationship with God, no matter what happens to them, even trials and tribulations, they can rejoice; these things will send them into the arms of the beloved, and they will know him as they have never known him before.

Sometimes we have to experience adversity before we really get to know God. We have to experience some terrible need before we know the Father's heart. We can look back at our life and say, "All things work together for good. I thank him for everything. It has brought me nearer to him." The apostle Paul says, "If God be for us, who can be against us?" (Rom. 8:31). Or listen to the way the author puts it in Hebrews 13:6: "So that we may boldly say, The Lord is my helper, and I shall not fear what man shall do unto me." Having looked at the character of God and at anything that might happen, we can confidently say, "The Lord is my helper" (Heb. 13:6). That was Abraham's secret. He went out, not knowing whither he went, but he knew with whom he went.

We must be obedient, as Abraham was. "By faith Abraham, when he was called to go out into a place which he should after receive for an inheritance, obeyed" (11:8). He left his home, he left his ancestors, he left everything; he went out with his wife and possessions. He obeyed. If we want to know this kind of life of faith, triumph, and joy, a life that is not concerned to know what the future holds because we are with God, then we must observe the conditions God gives us—we must obey.

This means we must believe God's Word. We must believe that Christ is the Son of God and that he died for us. No matter how much we have sinned or how dark our life has been, we believe on the Lord Jesus Christ and we are safe. Accept the offer of free pardon and forgiveness in Christ Jesus. Separate yourself from the sinful world in which you live. Give your life to God. Live to please him, submit to his leading and his guidance, submit to being led by the Holy Spirit. "For as many as are led by the Spirit of God, they are the sons of God" (Rom. 8:14). Leave yourself and your every concern entirely in the hands of God. Say to him:

> My times are in Thy hand;
> My God, I wish them there;
> My life, my friends, my soul I leave
> Entirely to Thy care.
>
> William F. Lloyd, "My Times Are in Thy Hand"

Abraham believed God and acted upon his belief. He put himself and his every concern unreservedly into the hands of God. Do that, and it will not matter what trials might come. "If God be for us, who can be against us?" (Rom. 8:31). Let us walk with God and be concerned about nothing except knowing him and walking step-by-step with him. Amen.

18

The Two Views

These all died in faith, not having received the promises, but having seen them afar off, and were persuaded of them, and embraced them, and confessed that they were strangers and pilgrims on the earth.

The writer goes on in the next verse to say, "For they that say such things declare plainly that they seek a country" (Heb. 11:14).

This chapter of Hebrews is a collection of brief cameos of heroes of the faith. The author was anxious to encourage and comfort and stimulate Hebrew Christians who were suffering a great deal, were being persecuted, and were experiencing a difficult time.

Here, then, we are provided with a pattern that we are meant to follow. The Bible is both teaching and history. There is great value in the history because it shows us the teaching applied and put into practice and reminds us that we are not left merely with theory. The view of life we are to consider together in the name of Christ has been put to the test and has been tried. The particular value of Hebrews 11 is that it tells us of mighty, extraordinary people who have experienced this life.

It is generally agreed that the men and women in this chapter stand out in history as those who are worthy of our admiration. They are beyond any question some of the noblest characters the world has ever known, men and women who lived life as it ought to be lived. That is why they stand out in history. They are people who were not defeated by life; they were triumphant, and they are in this gallery of heroes for that particular reason.

That is why we are exhorted to consider them and to learn certain lessons from them. Here were men and women who were living in exactly the same world as countless thousands of others. Why does the whole world know the names Abel, Abraham, Noah, Moses, along with others listed in this chapter? Though they lived in exactly the same world as everybody else, though they were heirs to the same flesh and to the same weaknesses and problems as we are, these people lived their lives in a different way. They stand out like great mountain peaks because though they were in exactly the same situation as everybody else, they reacted to it in an utterly different manner. What made them different from others? What enabled them to be so successful in their life in this world, whereas the vast majority of people failed and that is why we know nothing about them?

Someone might be temped to suggest it is a matter of temperament. Perhaps these people had an especially optimistic, sanguine, hopeful outlook on life, and that was what kept them going. Life is hard and difficult, and many people become pessimistic and hopeless and cynical about it. Were these people particularly resilient in their very nature, refusing to be carried helplessly down the stream?

The answer to that is perfectly obvious. Read the account of these people as it is given here and the accounts given at greater length in the pages of the Old Testament and you will see at a glance that these people differ tremendously from one another. Take men like Moses and Abraham—I pick these two at random for the purpose of illustration. These two men are essentially different temperamentally and psychologically. Or take some of the others—David, Barak, Jephthah, Gideon, and others—and you will find the same thing. So that is not the explanation.

"Well then," someone might say, "perhaps they were so successful in life because they did not have to face the difficulties and the trials that so many others have to face." People are often prone to try to discredit the Christian claim by saying, "Many of you Christian people have been brought up in glass houses. You have been shielded. If you had suffered as I have, if you had the problems that I have . . . " Many who are outside of Christ say that life has dealt so harshly with them that they have been crushed and cannot possibly accept the Christian view and teaching.

Again just read the stories of these people and you will find that these men and women were subjected to grievous trials. This chapter was written to comfort Hebrew Christians who were having a hard time. The writer says in essence, "Look at these heroes of the faith. Consider what they had to endure, look at the troubles they had to face, look at the conflicts they had to wage, and you will find that they rose triumphant over them all." What was the secret of these people?

What does the future hold for us? We do not know what is awaiting us. Life is full of uncertainties. I am not only speaking nationally and internationally and in a political and economic sense. I am also speaking of all the intimate personal relationships of life. We do not know what lies ahead of us, but we do know that life is difficult, arduous, and trying, and it tests our stamina severely.

In spite of all the things that assailed them and tried them, these people in Hebrews 11 went on gloriously and triumphantly. They never gave up. "These all died in faith, not having received the promises" (11:13). This means they died full of the hopefulness that is born of faith. Though they did not receive the promise, they did not die in dejection and despair. They did not say at the end, "We have held on to this hope, but nothing has materialized, and I wonder whether we have made a mistake." Not at all! They died triumphantly and confidently. They had strong faith right to the end, even through death itself—uncrushed, rising above and over all, more than conquerors.

What was their secret? The first thing we can say about these people, having read their story, is that unlike the vast majority of people, they did not accept the philosophy of the world around them with respect to life and its meaning and purpose. That is the point that this author makes, not only in this particular chapter, but also in the whole epistle. Take Noah, for instance, who "being warned of God of things not seen as yet, moved with fear, prepared an ark to the saving of his house; by the which he condemned the world, and became heir of the righteousness which is by faith" (Heb. 11:7). Here was a man living in the same world as everybody else, but he did not hold the same views as most of his fellow countrymen. They held one view, but Noah, "being warned of God," accepted another and began to live by it.

Abraham did exactly the same thing. That is why though he was born among pagans, "he went out, not knowing whither he went" (Heb. 11:8). He was willing to leave security for uncertainty.

Look at a man like Moses. He was brought up as the son of Pharaoh's daughter, with great prospects lying ahead of him, but he turned his back upon them all and identified himself with slaves. Then a few years later he was living as a shepherd—a degrading occupation in those times. Think of it—a man who had been brought up in the lap of luxury in a palace reduced to that. Why? He did not hold the same view of life as those around him.

The people of Hebrews 11 are unique in that sense. They had a different outlook and philosophy, and the same thing is true in the world today. The world, in the last analysis, consists of two groups of people: those who view life in the Christian way and those who do not.

Someone might say, "You surely do not mean to tell us that all people who are not Christian ultimately believe the same philosophies." That is exactly what I am saying. The world is divided into political parties, but they all fundamentally take the same view. It is a materialistic view, not a spiritual one. There are only two views of life in this world—the Christian view and the non-Christian view—and the characteristic of those who walk by faith and are Christians is that they do not believe or espouse that other view.

What is the non-Christian philosophy and view of life? The great characteristic of that view is that in the vast majority of cases it refuses to think at all. Is not the mere refusal to think one of the greatest problems of our age? I believe that men and women are being driven into this position by the pressure of events around and about them. The argument that the average person puts forward is, "What is the use of thinking? Look at all the world powers, look at the uncertainty of life in the world—what is the value of thinking? Let us eat, drink, and be merry."

Furthermore, those who do think only think in terms of life in this present world and within the bounds of time. If you have discussions with them about these things, you find that their thoughts are confined within the bounds of the existence of the body. And when you begin to ask about the body after death they say, "We are concerned only about life in this world." This was the philosophy of the men of the world who did not believe in faith in the time of Abel, Noah, Abraham, Moses, and all these others in Hebrews 11. They lived for the day, for the hour, for their generation, for their own particular conception of life on earth, and that is always the main characteristic of their outlook. In other words, it is the outlook that is concerned about enjoying life in this world; that is their chief end and object in life.

Does what I am saying put you into that position yourself? A man's or woman's philosophy is that which they see finally in themselves. They think about life and say, "I am in this world. How can I get maximum enjoyment out of this life?" Of course this may take many different forms. You see it in the mania for pleasure—drinking, dancing, gambling. People are all out to enjoy themselves, to get what they can out of life, to have a good time while they are on earth.

Others spend their time in libraries and in reading. They are concerned about the arts, music, and philosophy. Surely, you say, their fundamental philosophy is not the same as those who are in the dance hall. But ultimately it is precisely the same.

In some shape or form all these people are pulling down the blinds of their houses. They say, "There is trouble in this world, but we do not want to see it. It will come into our house soon enough. So we will pull down the blinds and enter into all the enjoyment we can and refuse to think of those other things that are disconcerting." According to our Lord Jesus Christ, that was exactly the outlook and mentality of the people before the flood. He said, "As the days of Noah were . . . they were eating and drinking, marrying and giving in marriage . . . until the flood came, and took them all away" (Matt. 24:37–39). Is that not a perfect description of mankind today? What is truly amazing is that men and women can be content with that outlook and philosophy in view of the things that are happening in the world. Is it not amazing that they do not stop to ask, "What lies ahead of us? What happens when one dies?" They want their thoughts confined to this life and world and to enjoyment in it.

So the first characteristic of the people who are recorded in Hebrews 11 is that they did not accept that philosophy. Most of their contemporaries held that view, exactly as men and women do today, but these people said, "That is not good enough; that is not right." They espoused a different philosophy of life. This can be summed up in the words of our text: "These all died in faith, not having received the promises, but having seen them afar off, and were persuaded of them, and embraced them, and confessed that they were strangers and pilgrims on the earth. For they that say such things declare plainly that they seek a country" (Heb. 11:13–14). Instead of accepting the other philosophy, they believed the message of God. God revealed himself to these people in ancient times, and he has revealed himself more fully to us in Jesus Christ. These people believed that message and acted upon it.

The first thing they believed was the message concerning the person and character of God. Many say they believe in God, but it is a vague belief; to all practical intents and purposes, they do not believe in God at all. As the psalmist put it, "The fool hath said in his heart, There is no God" (Ps. 14:1). God does not enter into their thoughts. But here were people who started with the fundamental postulate that God is and that he is the maker of this world and life. They believed that he is a holy and righteous God and that all of us in this life and world will answer to him.

The second thing that characterized their outlook was their view of man. They did not regard man as the others did, more or less as an animal whose chief function in this world is to eat and drink. They believed that God has placed within men and women a soul and spirit. What does the Bible mean by that? These people believed God when he told them that in spite of sin and all the havoc that has been wrought by sin, God determined to save the world and deliver it from the bondage of Satan, and he began to give promises to them, all of which are fulfilled in the Lord Jesus Christ. God said at the very beginning that the seed of the woman would bruise the serpent's head (Gen. 3:15). He later called out Abraham and gave him certain promises, telling

210 The Two Views

him that out of him would ultimately come the Messiah, the Deliverer (Gen. 12:3), and he went on repeating that promise throughout the Old Testament dispensation.

The secret of these people was that they believed that. They said, "God has provided a way of escape." He said to them, "Live life as I am telling you, and I will deliver you and will pardon you, and in the fullness of time I will send my Son. He will make atonement for sin, and I will pardon men and women, and they will ultimately be perfect." These people believed that; they accepted it and acted upon it. That is the characteristic of these people; that was the philosophy they espoused. You see how different it is from the other.

Furthermore these people of faith gave proofs of the genuineness of their faith. As the author of Hebrews puts it in verse 14, they "declare[d] plainly" (Heb. 11:14) that these things were to them not just theory; they believed them to be factual. They showed this by living in a way that corresponded to what they claimed to believe. Abraham said that he believed God, and he, therefore, left his country and went out, "not knowing whither he went" (Heb. 11:18). Noah believed God, and though everybody laughed and mocked him, he said in essence, "God has told me that he is going to destroy this world," so he began to build an ark. It took him a hundred and twenty years to finish it, but he did what he said he believed. Every one of these people declared that they were strangers and pilgrims on the earth. They obeyed God and did exactly what he told them, especially in their outlook upon this present world.

The Christian life is altogether different from the life of the average man and woman in this world. It is a special life, a unique life. The New Testament puts it like this: "Come out from among them, and be ye separate" (2 Cor. 6:17). We know what the life of the world is like—all the immorality, the drunkenness, the gambling, the thieving and robbery, and all the consequent problems—living for this life alone, living only for the material, living only for pleasure in some form. The men and women who believe the view of life given in the Bible come out of all that, but their belief is valueless unless they give proof of their faith. If people really believe the gospel, they regard the worldly life as dangerous to their souls, and they say, "I am afraid of it, so I therefore separate myself from it and live out the life of God." Letting their faith show is essential to true believers.

I will go even further and say that these people showed the genuineness of their belief by holding on to it at all costs. They were persecuted, their lives were threatened, but that did not matter; they were ready to sacrifice everything rather than sacrifice their faith. Consider what Moses had to come to; see what Abraham and all these other people had to give up. That is the characteristic of these men and women; they so believed the truth that when they had either to give up or lose this truth that meant everything to them, at all costs, even at the cost of life itself, they held on to it. And, thank God, Christian people in the world are still doing the same thing. There were men in the Christian church in Germany who would not give in to Hitler and his party. They stood firm; they faced the concentration camps and death, but they never denied that Jesus Christ is Lord.

The last thing that always characterizes the people of faith in Hebrews is that they sought the blessing of God with a diligence and zeal that never flagged. They put into practice what the sixth verse tells us: "But without faith it is impossible to please him: for he that cometh to God must believe that he is, and that he is a rewarder of them that diligently seek him" (Heb. 11:6).

They believed in him, they knew that he mattered above everything else, and they diligently sought him. That was the characteristic of these people. They triumphed in life and over life; they triumphed in death and over death.

The world today is exactly the same as the world in the time of Noah and of Abraham and of Moses. There is no difference at all in its outlook and philosophy. What is your view of life? How are you facing it? What is your idea concerning it? There is the worldly view, and there is the gospel of Jesus Christ that tells us we have an immortal soul, and we have to meet God someday. We have all sinned against him; we can never make ourselves fit to meet that holy God. But in his infinite kindness and compassion, God sent his only begotten Son into this world to redeem us. Christ has borne our sins and died for us, and in him God pardons and forgives us. There is a new kind of life that will take us to be with him, to share eternity and glory with him.

Which of these two views do we hold? Which is the life we are living? These people, says the author of Hebrews, "declare plainly that they seek a country" (Heb. 11:14). They not only lived that kind of life, they were looking for something else. Is it obvious to everyone who knows us that we are different from the world? Is it evident in our conduct that our life is based on an entirely different view from that of the man of the world who does not believe in God and is not interested in the Lord Jesus Christ? That is the test.

The way to triumph in life and in death is to live for God. It is to believe on the Lord Jesus Christ and to submit ourselves to him, to allow him to control and govern us, to be concerned, above everything else, about knowing him, pleasing him, following him. If that is our position, then we can say, not only on the basis of this chapter of Hebrews, but on the basis of the testimony of the saints throughout the ages, that whatever life may have in store for us, we will be more than conquerors, we will triumph, we will prevail.

If you believe these things, prove it, declare it to yourselves, declare it to God, declare it to your loved ones, declare it to those who are around and about you. That is the characteristic of these people of God whose lives stand out so gloriously in the history of the human race. God grant that we all may be found in their company. Amen.

19

Unashamed of Their God

HEBREWS 11:16

Wherefore God is not ashamed to be called their God: for
he hath prepared for them a city.

This text is parallel to Hebrews 2:11: "For both he that sanctifieth and
they who are sanctified are all of one: for which cause he is not ashamed
to call them brethren." We must take these two verses together.

We are looking at these passages in order to consider together how
we can live godly lives in this troubled world that is so full of problems
and perplexities. The gospel, the message of the Bible, is not some mere
academic subject that people can study or not as they wish. The whole
object of the Christian message is to teach people how to live, especially
how to meet life with all its attendant circumstances, and to do so as
"more than conquerors" (Rom. 8:37).

How are we reacting to present difficult circumstances? The whole
argument of the Bible is that people who are Christians should be in an
entirely different position from those who are not. So we ask ourselves
the question, is this true of us? Are we reacting to the present scene in
a manner that marks us out as being the people of God? The epistle
to the Hebrews was written to people who were in terrible trouble for
many reasons. They were being called upon to endure persecution and

trials, and the faith of some of them was beginning to waver. So that Bible book has a message that is vital and up-to-date for all of us who claim to be Christians at this present time.

This epistle answers the questions about how one can live in a triumphant manner in this world in spite of everything that may be set against us. One part of the answer is our relationship to the Lord Jesus Christ—"for which cause he is not ashamed to call them brethren" (Heb. 2:11). The Christian message, clearly, is primarily about this relationship, and the first thing that is necessary is that we become Christians. The Bible offers no comfort whatsoever to people who are not Christians. It has only warnings for them. But the Bible offers much comfort to Christians.

So we have seen that the basis of all our comfort and all our hope and all our strength is that Jesus Christ is not ashamed to call us his brothers and sisters. However weak and unworthy we may be, however sinful, however failing, the blessed Son of God has come down and has taken upon himself our own nature. He has taken on flesh and blood in order that he might be one with us and stand with us and represent us and die for us, that he might satisfy the law and the holiness of God and reconcile us to God and be with us as our leader and our guide.

The Lord Jesus Christ came into this world and did all he did in order to bring us to God. That statement is liable to misunderstanding, but it is essential. We must not stop even at the Lord Jesus Christ himself. He is the Mediator; he is not the end. Many people pray to our Lord, but they never pray to the Father, they never talk about the Father. That is unscriptural. We go through Jesus Christ to the Father. So we move from the statement that he is not ashamed to call us brethren to the statement in Hebrews 11:16 that God is not ashamed to be called our God. This demands our consideration.

This matter is presented in chapter 11 in terms of the history of men and women like ourselves who have actually lived in this world. That brings it home to us and reminds us that we are not dealing with something theoretical. What matters in Christianity is not what you and I feel when we are in church; it is what we are like when we are everywhere else. What we receive in church is of no ultimate value to us unless it transforms what we are everywhere else. So we are told about these people as they were in the midst of life—troubled, perplexed, surrounded by all sorts of difficulties. They lived in this selfsame world in which we live, and yet they triumphed.

The author of this epistle adduces this evidence at this point because he is concerned to show that all he has been arguing really does work. He says in summary, "You may wonder whether all this is true. It sounds wonderful, it is great to read all this, but does it actually work?" His answer is that it had even worked under the old dispensation. Those people were not in the position that we are in; they had not received the promises we have. But not having received them and seeing them afar off, they, on the strength of that alone, were enabled to be more than conquerors; they did triumph. So he gives us a list of these men one after another, reminding us of all that they had to suffer and endure and how in spite of it all they rose up triumphant, heroes of the faith, the greatest men the world has ever known.

So the question that arises for us is this: How did they achieve this? In other words, how can one be an Abel, an Enoch, a Noah, an Abraham, a Moses, a David, and all the rest mentioned in Hebrews 11? Go back to your Old Testament, read the stories of these men, and you will see that they were not characters in fairy tales. They lived in this world just as you and I are living in it, and this old world has always been the same. It is very bad today, but it has always been bad. Indeed these men had to endure some of the most terrible agonies and sufferings that men have ever faced, and yet in spite of it all they lived and died gloriously.

What was their secret? Everybody is ready to answer that it was their faith. Yes, they were men of faith, but we must be careful here. If we conclude that the sole secret of these men was their remarkable faith, we have hold of a truth, but it is only half of a truth, and in fact the half that is of lesser importance. If we stop at admiring these men and their wonderful faith and the courage that came out of that faith, then we have missed the most important thing of all.

I must emphasize this because some people tend to work up a kind of faith in themselves; their great endeavor is to become men and women of great faith. In one sense that is good, but in another sense it can be extremely dangerous, because faith is only an instrument, only a channel. In a sense faith merely links us to the One who does everything. Faith must never be regarded as an end in and of itself. The important thing about faith is that it is faith in God, that it leads to God, that it leads to a relationship with God. We must concentrate not on faith but on the God who deals with men and women through faith. That distinction is crucial. The great thing about these people, therefore, was not their faith—it was their relationship with God. "Wherefore God is not ashamed to be called their God" (11:16). It was their relationship with God that made them what they were.

These statements in Hebrews are the greatest statements that can ever be said about anybody. Jesus Christ is not ashamed to call them brethren (Heb. 2:11); "God is not ashamed to be called their God" (11:16). Position, greatness, possessions do not ultimately matter. What matters is knowing God. Do we know something of what this means? Can we honestly say that the greatest thing we know about ourselves, the greatest thing that can ever be true about us, is that God is our God? These people could, and that was the secret of their victorious life. Can we apply this to ourselves? If we know this for certain, all will be well with us, and nothing can defeat us.

However, this statement "Wherefore God is not ashamed to be called their God" (11:16) is not true of all men and women. Many believe in what is called the universal fatherhood of God. But that view is not true. It is dangerous to believe that we can go to God whenever we like and get whatever we want. We see a great division in the human race throughout the Bible. We must be clear about this.

There is a sense in which God is the God of all men and women in that he created them all and has given life and being to all. He is over all, and in his providence he deals kindly with all. Our Lord himself, in his Sermon on the Mount, found in the fifth chapter of Matthew's Gospel, says that God "maketh his sun to rise on the evil and on the good, and sendeth rain on the just and the unjust" (Matt. 5:45). He is the God of all people and of the entire universe in that he has made it and controls it and deals with it. We are all recipients in that way of the goodness of God. But there is a special sense in which the statement we are considering is true. "Wherefore God is not ashamed to be called their God" applies only to certain people. The author of Hebrews is not describing mankind universally; he is describing a particular section of it.

This is, I suppose, the most basic distinction that can ever be drawn. While we are all the creatures of God, these particular blessings and promises are applicable only to certain people—"they . . . their God . . . them." Our Lord himself told Jews who were persecuting him and trying to trap him, "Ye are of your father the devil, and the lusts of your father ye will do" (John 8:44). "If God were your Father," he said, "ye would love me" (John 8:42). There is the distinction. We must not take this text in Hebrews 11 universally, though people tend to do that. In times of trouble people rush to God in prayer; though they have not prayed for years they imagine that now everything will be all right. But that is not true! There are conditions here. These words apply to certain people only.

Listen to the apostle Peter putting the same truth very plainly. Writing to Christian people he says, "Which in time past were not a people, but are now the people of God" (1 Pet. 2:10). He says there was a time when God had certainly nothing to do with us; it was not true of us to say then that he was not ashamed to call himself our God. We "were not a people"; we were not "the people of God." But as a result of what has happened to us we "are a chosen generation, a royal priesthood, an holy nation, a peculiar people; that ye should shew forth the praises of him who hath called you out of darkness into his marvellous light; which in time past were not a people, but are now the people of God: which had not obtained mercy, but now have obtained mercy" (1 Pet. 2:9–10). "Wherefore God is not ashamed to be called *their* God" (Heb. 11:16)—not all people, but people of whom this alone is true.

What does this relationship mean exactly? What is its value to us? How did it enable these great heroes of the faith to live and die as they did? Here is the most glorious comfort and consolation we can ever know in this world. We have a wonderful exposition of this very truth in 2 Corinthians 6:14–18 where the apostle Paul calls the Corinthian Christians to "be not unequally yoked together with unbelievers. . . . And what agreement hath the temple of God with idols? for ye are the temple of the living God; as God hath said, I will dwell in them, and walk in them; and I will be their God, and they shall be my people.

Wherefore come out from among them, and be ye separate, saith the Lord, and touch not the unclean thing; and I will receive you. And will be a Father unto you, and ye shall be my sons and daughters, saith the Lord Almighty."

That is a parallel statement to the one we are looking at, a fuller exposition of it, and I am going to interpret the Hebrews text in the light of the teaching in 2 Corinthians. God is in a special relationship with these people. He is over all, and he will be the Judge of all, and he deals kindly with all in his providence, but with these people there is something much bigger, much richer, much deeper, something that is only true of them. What is it? All the terms imply that God enters into a covenant relationship with these people. God binds himself to these people. He does not bind himself to everybody. He does not bind himself to the godless, nor does he enter into a covenant relationship with them. He does not make any agreement with them. He does not give them any special promises. But with these particular people he does. He tells them in essence, "I will be to them a God, and they shall be to me a people. I will be to them a Father, and they shall be my sons and my daughters."

In other words—and this is the most astounding thing anywhere in the Bible—God identifies himself with these people; he puts himself among them. He assures them in essence, "I will dwell among them and live in them." He gives them his name. The Almighty, everlasting God, the Creator of the ends of the earth, binds himself and his great and glorious name with these people. Let me give you an example of this. We read in the third chapter of the Book of Exodus about the call of Moses to his great work of leading the children of Israel out of Egypt and its bondage and into the land of Canaan. God begins to address Moses, but notice how he does it. He eventually speaks of himself as the great Jehovah, "I AM." "If I go and speak to them" says Moses, "they will say to me, 'Who is this God you are representing?'" God says, "Say, 'I AM THAT I AM, Jehovah.'"

But God had said something else to Moses before that. When he first spoke to Moses, Moses was fearful and trembling. He had spent forty years as a shepherd, as if he was a nonentity. When God came and spoke to him, he said to him, "I am the God of Abraham." He did not just say, "I am God." He tied himself to Abraham; he involved his name with that of Abraham. He, as it were, went into partnership with Abraham; he shared the life of Abraham. "I am . . . the God of Abraham, the God of Isaac, and the God of Jacob" (Ex. 3:6). He was "not ashamed to be called their God." He does not put his name with the name of every man, but he does so with Abraham and with Isaac and with Jacob. He bound himself to them in a personal covenant relationship. God was not ashamed of Abraham. He said, "This is my friend," and Abraham was called "the Friend of God" (James 2:23).

Or consider the man called Enoch. We are told that he "walked with God" (Gen. 5:22, 24). God was not ashamed, as it were, to be seen walking with him. There are some people you would not like to be seen with; you would not dream of going for a walk with them. But God was not ashamed to be called the God of Enoch. God came down, as it were, and walked with him. That is what is meant by the statement "wherefore God is not ashamed to be called their God" (Heb. 11:16). He has entered into a special relationship with them.

God is not the father of all; some are the children of the Devil. But God is not ashamed to be called the God of those who follow him. We will look at this first from God's standpoint and then from ours. Regarding God's side God has said, "I will dwell in them, and walk in them" (2 Cor. 6:16). In a sense, this is much the same thing as the Lord Jesus Christ himself tells us in the fourteenth chapter of the Gospel according to John, where he makes some of the most amazing statements we can ever read. He says there, "He that loveth me shall be loved of my Father, and I will love him, and will manifest myself to him." Then note this: "If a man love me, he will keep my words: and my Father will love him, and we will come unto him, and make our abode with him" (John 14:21, 23). "I will dwell in them, and walk in them" (2 Cor. 6:16). This is part of what it means when we are told that God is not ashamed to be called our God. He enters into us and into our lives; he takes up his abode in us. His name is upon us; he is dwelling in us; we become the temple of the living God. That is taught in many places in the Scriptures.

Those words convey the special interest that God takes in us. The apostle Peter writes, "Ye are a chosen generation, a royal priesthood, an holy nation, a peculiar [special] people" (1 Pet. 2:9). We are God's particular possession. God owns everything, but he owns his people in a special way, He takes a special interest in us. He is involved in our lives in a way that he was not before and that he is not in the case of others. As a Father he takes an interest in us that is the particular interest of a father in his children. A father may be interested in the children next door and other children down the street, and he may do many kindnesses to them. But that is not the relationship between father and child. That is very special, and that is God's relationship to us—always watching over us, always with us, always caring for us. He is no longer a God far off, but a God who is very near.

God is in heaven, "dwelling in the light which no man can approach unto" (1 Tim. 6:16). But if we know God through Jesus Christ, God is in us; he is dwelling in us; he is walking with us. "Ye who sometimes were far off are made nigh by the blood of Christ," as Paul puts it in Ephesians 2:13. God has brought us into this intimate relationship. And that includes—and at this moment and in the days ahead of us this may be the most precious thing we can ever know—God's giving revelations and intimations of himself to his people that he does not give to anybody else. He dwells in us, which means that he manifests himself to us. It is one thing to believe in God and to believe things about God, but if this intimate personal relationship is ours, then God has given us an absolute certainty that he is our God and that he is not ashamed to be called our God. Romans 8:16 tells us, "The Spirit . . . beareth witness with our spirit, that we are the children of God." He is not ashamed to be called our God, and he lets us know that. These people in Hebrews 11 knew it. That was the secret of their glorious and victorious lives. He gives us intimations of his love; he lets us know that he is interested in us; he lets us know that we are his children and that all these promises are applicable to us.

Think of all his promises and pledges to us. The apostle Peter says we have all things "that pertain unto life and godliness . . . whereby are given unto us exceeding great and precious promises" (2 Pet. 1:3–4). He only gives those promises and provisions to his special people. The world knows nothing about these things, but you and I ought to know something about them. Here is one of those "exceeding great and precious promises": "God is able to make all grace abound toward you; that ye, always having all sufficiency in all things, may abound to every good work" (2 Cor. 9:8). What a tremendous promise! God is able to make all grace "*abound*" toward you! When you are lying flat on your back, knocked down by circumstances and by the cruelty of life and all that hell lets loose, remember that God, the God of all grace, the God to whom there is no limit, is able to make all grace abound toward you.

Then listen to the apostle Paul writing to the Philippians. He is in prison, he may be put to death at any moment at the whim of Nero, but he says, "Not that I speak in respect of want: for I have learned, in whatsoever state I am, therewith to be content. I know both how to be abased, and I know how to abound. . . . I can do all things through Christ which strengtheneth me" (Phil. 4:11–13). The Philippians had kindly sent him a gift, and he said in essence, "I am grateful to you, but I am happy to tell you that I do not need it at the moment, though I am a prisoner." And he adds, "You need not worry about yourselves in the future." Why? "My God shall supply all your need according to his riches in glory by Christ Jesus (Phil. 4:19). Notice that he says, "My God." Can you appropriate the God of the whole universe to yourself and say "My God"? You have a right to do so because he has told you that he is not ashamed to be called your God.

When you know things like this to be true, you are not afraid of the future, and you are not worried as to what will happen to you. If you are fearful, it is because you do not know these things; you do not know that God is not ashamed to be called your God, that he has bound himself to you in this way, and that all these things that he has promised are true for you. Our Lord, because you are in a relationship with him, says, "the very hairs of your head are all numbered" (Matt. 10:30). Nothing can happen to you apart from him. Your relationship with him is one of grace and of fatherhood, and the "very hairs of your head are all numbered" (Matt. 10:30). God knows all about you, he has a personal interest in you. He has put his name on you, and nothing can happen to you without his knowing it. He promises, "I will never leave thee, nor forsake thee" (Heb. 13:5). That is what God says to you because he is not ashamed to be called your God.

We see another glorious statement of this in Isaiah 46:3–4, one of the greatest of all. Here God is addressing his ancient people in spite of all their unworthiness. "Hearken unto me, O house of Jacob, and all the remnant of the house of Israel, which are borne by me from the belly, which are carried from the womb: And even to your old age I am he; and even to hoar hairs will I carry you: I have made, and I will bear; even I will carry, and will deliver you." God had bound himself to those people, and he was not going to leave them. "When thou passest through the waters, I will be with thee" (Isa. 43:2).

Note too the gracious statement "I will receive you" (2 Cor. 6:17). It is wonderful to look at the Father in all his greatness and all his power and all his glory and all his precious promises, but when you and I are in trouble and feel small and frail and weak, nothing is more comforting than the statement that he is always ready to receive us. God is our Father, and though he sustains the whole universe, he is ready to listen to our tapping at his door.

What does God's not being ashamed to call us his mean from our side? It means endless confidence. It means that we know we are not left to ourselves. It means we know that we are always being carried and looked after. Often we do not understand what is happening to us, but we know that God does and that he is our God. We know that "he giveth his beloved sleep" (Ps. 127:2) and that "he that keepeth Israel shall neither slumber nor sleep" (Ps. 121:4). Day and night he is always on duty for us, guarding us, watching over us. This also means that we have access to him at all times and in all places, whatever the circumstances and conditions. Is that the first thing that comes to your mind? As one hymn puts it, "When all things seem against us, to drive us to despair, we know one gate is open, one ear will hear our prayer" (Oswald Allen, "Today Thy Mercy Calls Us"). Do we say that instinctively? As children of God, we should. Wherever we are, we always have access to him. "The name of the LORD is a strong tower: the righteous runneth into it, and is safe" (Prov. 18:10).

God promises, "I will be their God . . . and will be a Father unto you, and ye shall be my sons and daughters, saith the Lord Almighty" (2 Cor. 6:16, 18). The God who is not ashamed to be called our God is "the Lord Almighty." Therefore we can say with the apostle Paul, "For I am persuaded, that neither death, nor life, nor angels, nor principalities, nor powers, nor things present, nor things to come, nor height, nor depth, nor any other creature, shall be able to separate us from the love of God, which is in Christ Jesus our Lord" (Rom. 8:38–39). Hebrews 13:6 says, "We may boldly say, The Lord is my helper, and I will not fear what man shall do unto me."

"Wherefore God is not ashamed to be called their God: for he hath prepared for them a city" (11:16). As proof that he is not ashamed to be called our God, he has prepared a city for us. What is this? It is the world to come that God is preparing for us. This is the great hope of the Christian, "new heavens and a new earth, wherein dwelleth righteousness" (2 Pet. 3:13), being prepared for us.

How can we know that we will get there? The writer has given us absolute proof in the sixth chapter of this great epistle to the Hebrews: "Which hope we have as an anchor of the soul, both sure and stedfast, and which entereth into that within the veil; whither the forerunner is for us entered, even Jesus, made an high priest for ever after the order of Melchisedec" (Heb. 6:19–20). How do we know that God is preparing a place for us? The Resurrection! The Ascension! A forerunner has gone ahead of us. Christ, who said at the end of his earthly life, "Let not your heart be troubled: ye believe in God, believe also in me. In my Father's house are many mansions," is preparing a place for us. "If it were not so, I would have told you. I go to prepare a place for you. And if I go and prepare a place for you, I will come again, and receive you unto myself; that where I am, there ye may be also" (John 14:1–3). "Wherefore God is not ashamed to be called their God: for he hath prepared for them a city" (Heb. 11:16). The city of God is for us.

Of whom is all this true? "*Wherefore* God is not ashamed to be called their God" (11:16). This statement is made in the light of something that has already been said. Who are these people of whom alone this is true? How can we know whether we are among them? Certain tests are given here. The passage we are looking at is a summary. The author of Hebrews has been talking about certain heroes of the faith, and he has come to Abraham, and then he says, "These all died in faith" (Heb. 11:13). These were all people who had submitted themselves utterly to God. Abel obeyed God; Cain did not. Noah believed God and acted on his word when everybody else was against God.

"By faith Abraham, when he was called to go out into a place which he should after receive for an inheritance, obeyed; and he went out, not knowing whither he went" (Heb. 11:8). These people submitted themselves absolutely to God and his word and his commandments. God spoke to them, and they believed him. They accepted his message and acted upon it. That is the characteristic of these people; that is what makes a man or woman a Christian—they believe the gospel, they believe its condemnation of a life of sin, they believe that Christ is the Son of God and that he died for them and that believing in him is the only way of salvation.

These people believed the word of God, and they gave proof that they believed it. What was the proof? We are told they were seeking "a better country" (11:16), they were looking "for a city which hath foundations" (Heb. 10:10). These people saw the real character of life in this world as it is. They didn't say, "Isn't life wonderful? Isn't this world glorious?" They said, "It is an evil world full of sin and shame and woe; it is a wicked world." Not only that, they left it and turned their backs upon it. As Abraham came out of Ur of the Chaldees and went out not knowing whither he went, so these people no longer lived for this life or for this world though they were in it. They turned their backs upon it and sought a better country. Notice the terms that the writer uses: "These all died in faith, not having received the promises, but having seen them afar off, and were persuaded of them, and embraced them" (Heb. 11:13). That is it!

We too are men and women who have seen what this world is, and we no longer want it; we no longer live for it. We are looking for a city that has foundations. We are looking for the city of God. We are looking for that better land. Our eye is upon the glory that is coming. They "confessed that they were strangers and pilgrims on the earth" (Heb. 11:13). We must do the same. We cannot be Christians and worldlings at the same time. Because they were not ashamed of God, God was not ashamed to be called their God. May the same be true of us. Amen.